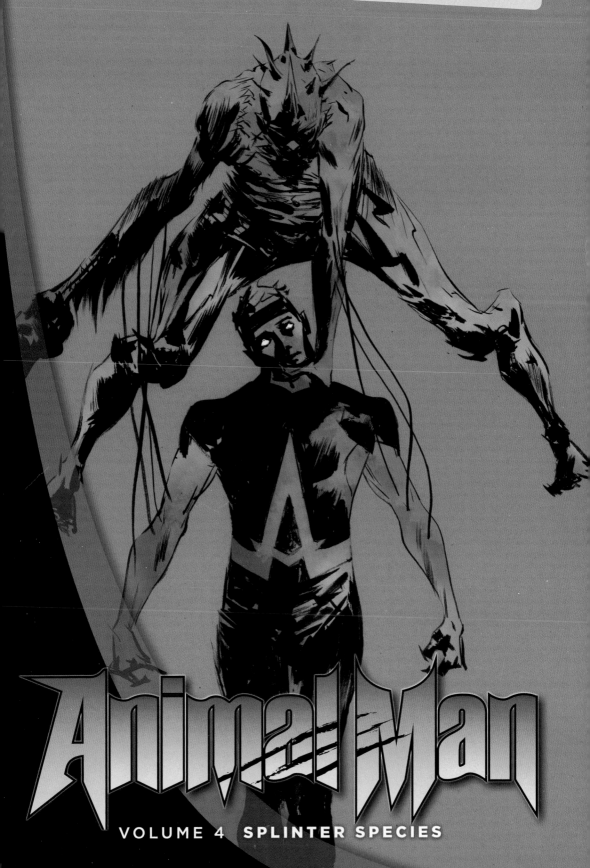

Animal Man

VOLUME 4 SPLINTER SPECIES

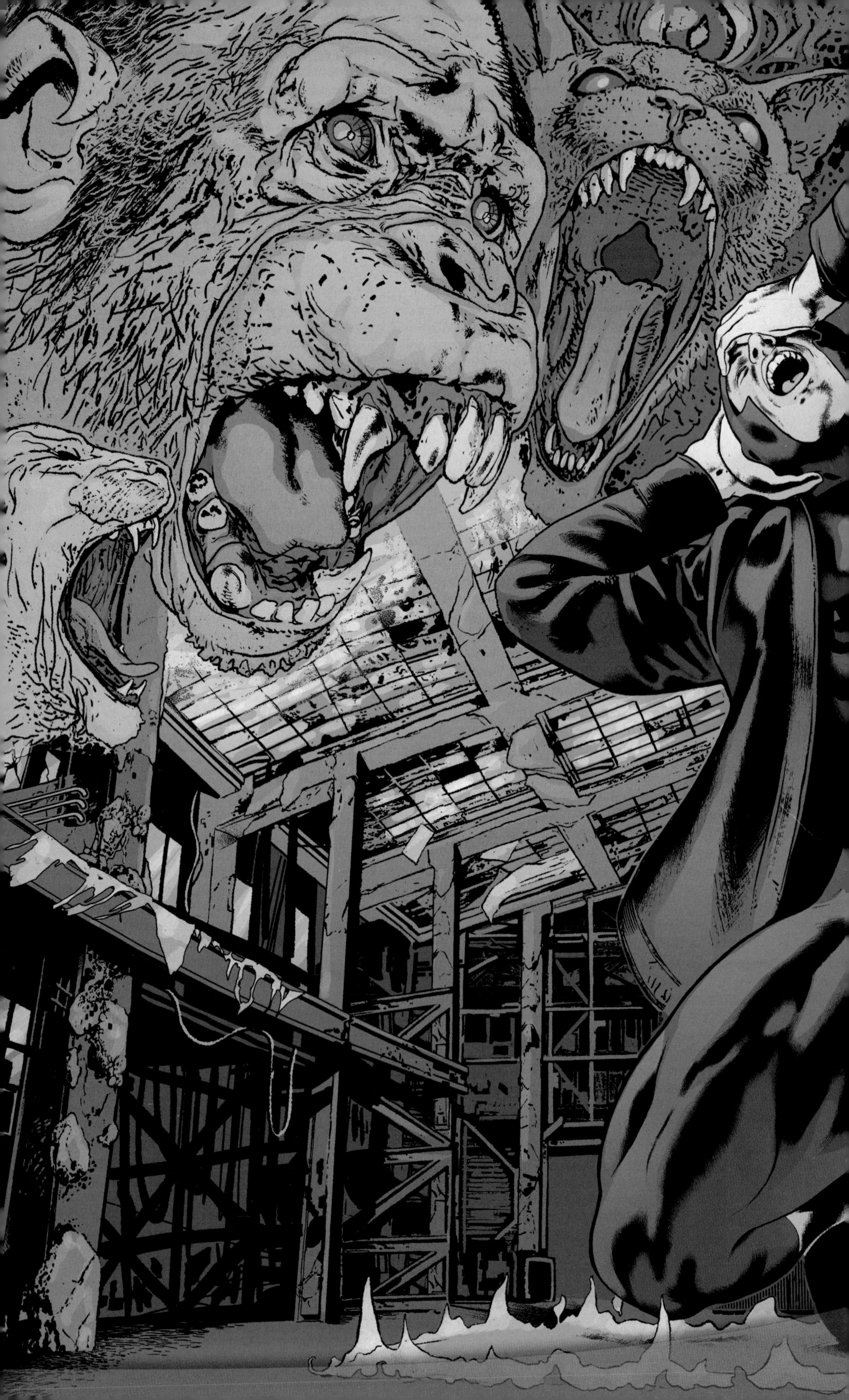

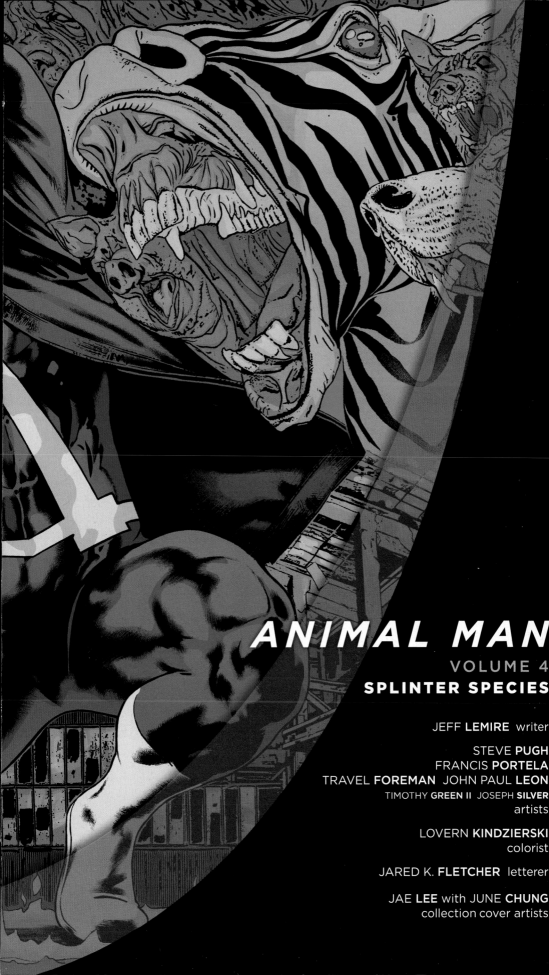

ANIMAL MAN
VOLUME 4
SPLINTER SPECIES

JEFF **LEMIRE** writer

STEVE **PUGH**
FRANCIS **PORTELA**
TRAVEL **FOREMAN** JOHN PAUL **LEON**
TIMOTHY **GREEN II** JOSEPH **SILVER**
artists

LOVERN **KINDZIERSKI**
colorist

JARED K. **FLETCHER** letterer

JAE **LEE** with JUNE **CHUNG**
collection cover artists

JOEY CAVALIERI Editor – Original Series
KYLE ANDRUKIEWICZ KATE STEWART Assistant Editors – Original Series
ROBIN WILDMAN Editor ROBBIN BROSTERMAN Design Director – Books

BOB HARRAS Senior VP – Editor-in-Chief, DC Comics

DIANE NELSON President DAN DIDIO and JIM LEE Co-Publishers
GEOFF JOHNS Chief Creative Officer JOHN ROOD Executive VP – Sales, Marketing & Business Development
AMY GENKINS Senior VP – Business & Legal Affairs NAIRI GARDINER Senior VP – Finance
JEFF BOISON VP – Publishing Planning MARK CHIARELLO VP – Art Direction & Design
JOHN CUNNINGHAM VP – Marketing TERRI CUNNINGHAM VP – Editorial Administration
ALISON GILL Senior VP – Manufacturing & Operations HANK KANALZ Senior VP – Vertigo & Integrated Publishing
JAY KOGAN VP – Business & Legal Affairs, Publishing JACK MAHAN VP – Business Affairs, Talent
NICK NAPOLITANO VP – Manufacturing Administration SUE POHJA VP – Book Sales
COURTNEY SIMMONS Senior VP – Publicity BOB WAYNE Senior VP – Sales

ANIMAL MAN VOLUME 4: SPLINTER SPECIES

DC Comics, 1700 Broadway, New York, NY 10019
A Warner Bros. Entertainment Company.
Printed by RR Donnelley, Salem, VA, USA. 1/31/14. First Printing.
ISBN: 978-1-4012-4644-0

Library of Congress Cataloging-in-Publication Data

Lemire, Jeff, illustrator.
Animal Man. Volume 4, Splinter Species / Jeff Lemire ; [illustrated by] Steve Pugh.
pages cm. — (The New 52!)
ISBN 978-1-4012-4644-0 (paperback)
1. Graphic novels. I. Pugh, Steve, illustrator. II. Title. III. Title: Splinter Species.
PN6728.A58L49 2014
741.5'973—dc23
2013045549

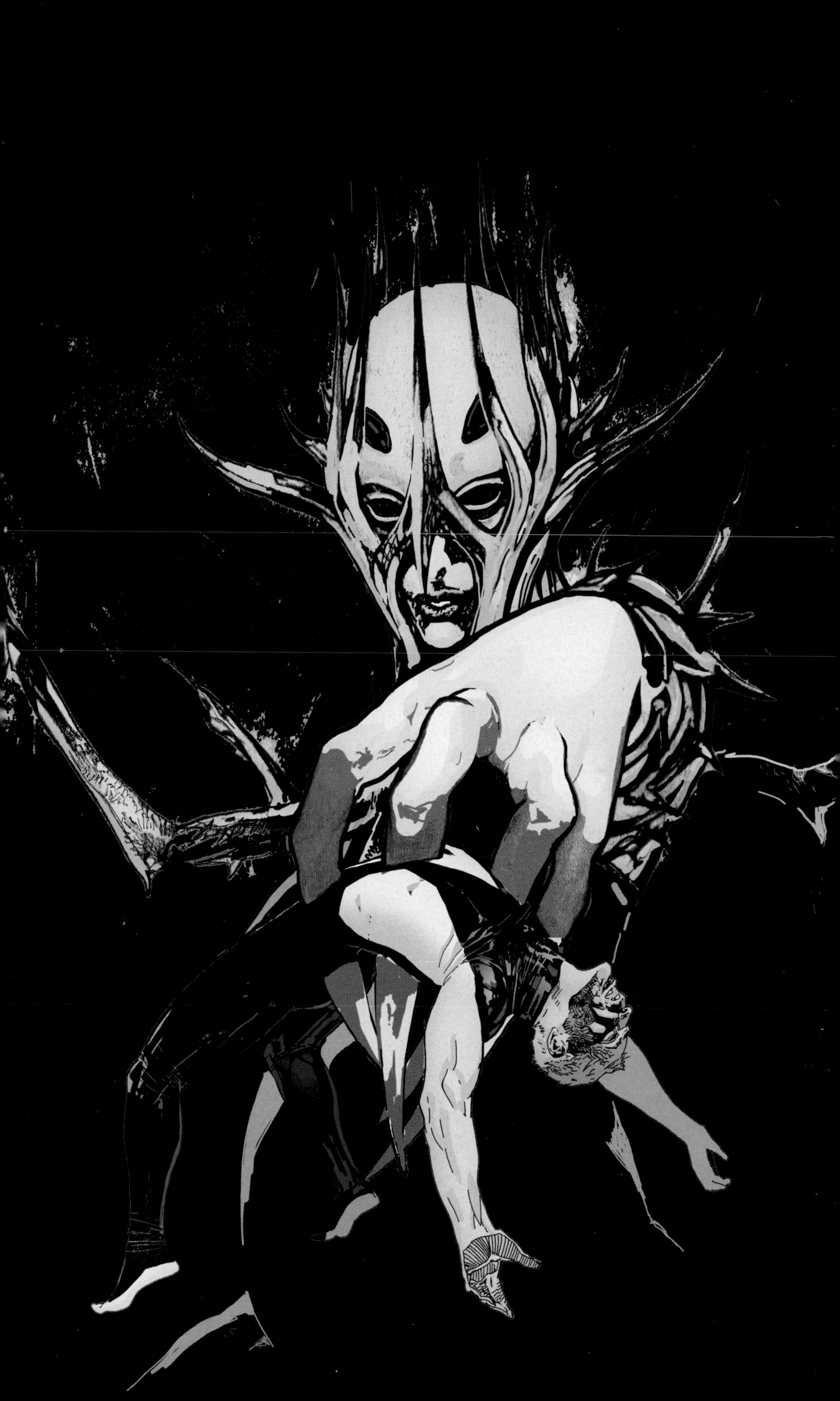

JEFF LEMIRE
writer

TRAVEL FOREMAN
artist

TRAVEL FOREMAN with LOVERN KINDZIERSKI
cover artists

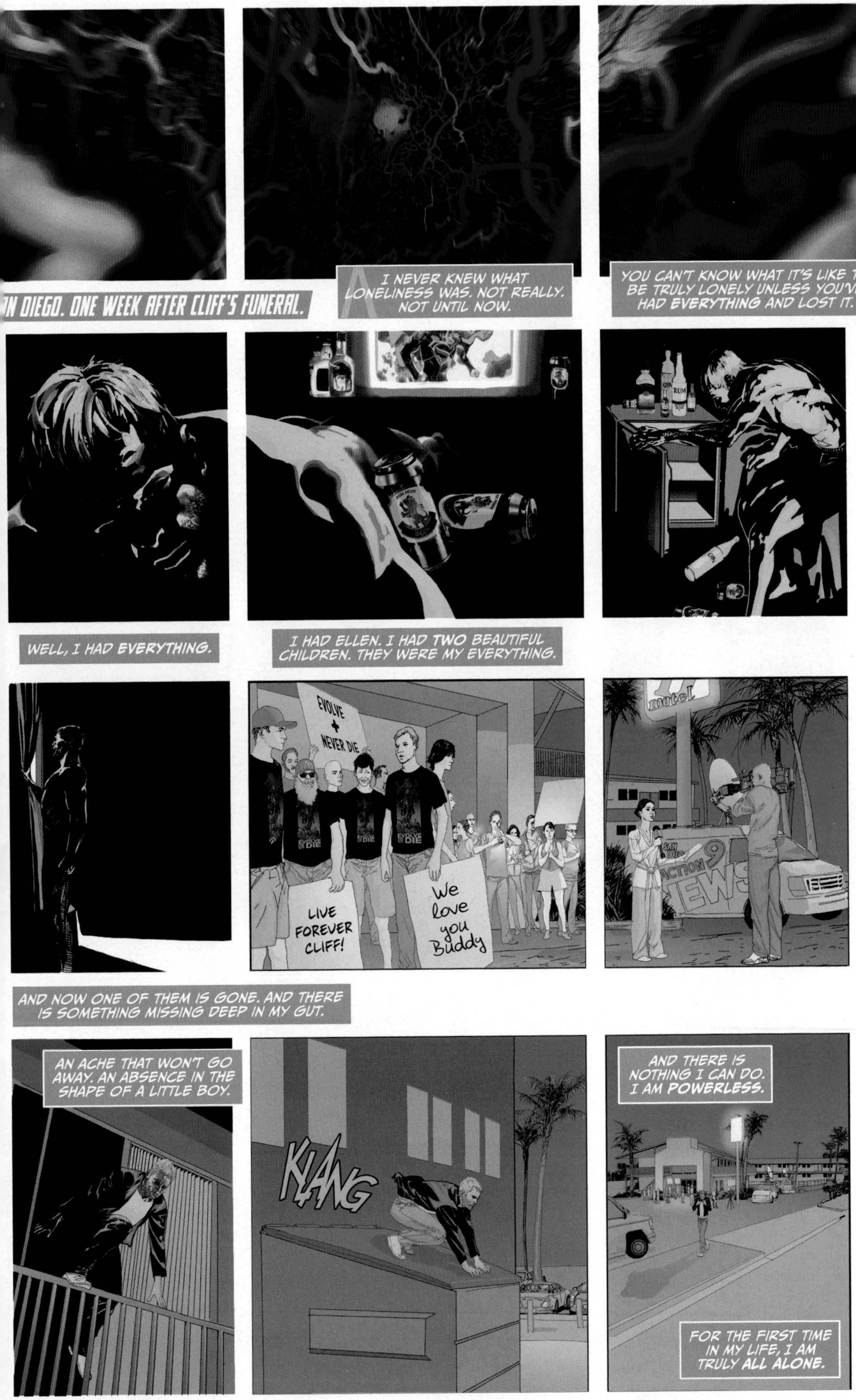

N DIEGO. ONE WEEK AFTER CLIFF'S FUNERAL.
I NEVER KNEW WHAT LONELINESS WAS. NOT REALLY. NOT UNTIL NOW.
YOU CAN'T KNOW WHAT IT'S LIKE TO BE TRULY LONELY UNLESS YOU'VE HAD EVERYTHING AND LOST IT.
RUM
WELL, I HAD EVERYTHING.
I HAD ELLEN. I HAD TWO BEAUTIFUL CHILDREN. THEY WERE MY EVERYTHING.
EVOLVE + NEVER DIE
EVOLVE OR DIE
LIVE FOREVER CLIFF!
We love you Buddy
motel
SAN DIEGO ACTION 9 NEWS
AND NOW ONE OF THEM IS GONE. AND THERE IS SOMETHING MISSING DEEP IN MY GUT.
AN ACHE THAT WON'T GO AWAY. AN ABSENCE IN THE SHAPE OF A LITTLE BOY.
KLANG
AND THERE IS NOTHING I CAN DO. I AM POWERLESS.
FOR THE FIRST TIME IN MY LIFE, I AM TRULY ALL ALONE.

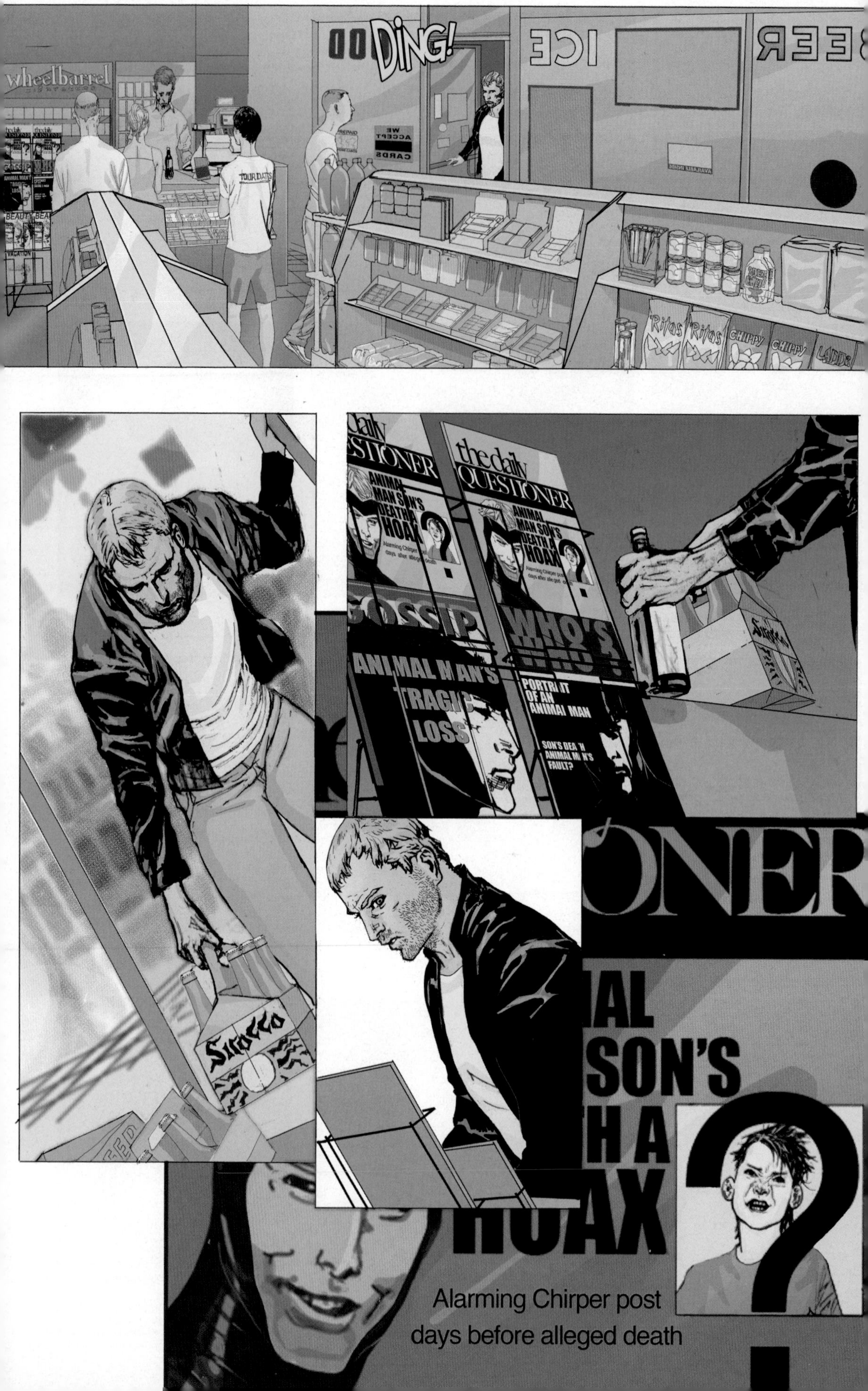
DING!
ICE
wheelbarrel
TOUR DATES
Ritos
Ritos
CHIPPY
CHIPPY
ANIMAL MAN'S
BEAUTY
VACATION
the daily QUESTIONER
ANIMAL MAN SON'S DEATH A HOAX
Alarming Chirper post days after alleged death
GOSSIP
ANIMAL MAN'S TRAGIC LOSS
WHO'S WHO
PORTRAIT OF AN ANIMAL MAN
SON'S DEATH ANIMAL MAN'S FAULT?
Sirocco
ONER
AL
SON'S
TH A
HOAX
Alarming Chirper post
days before alleged death

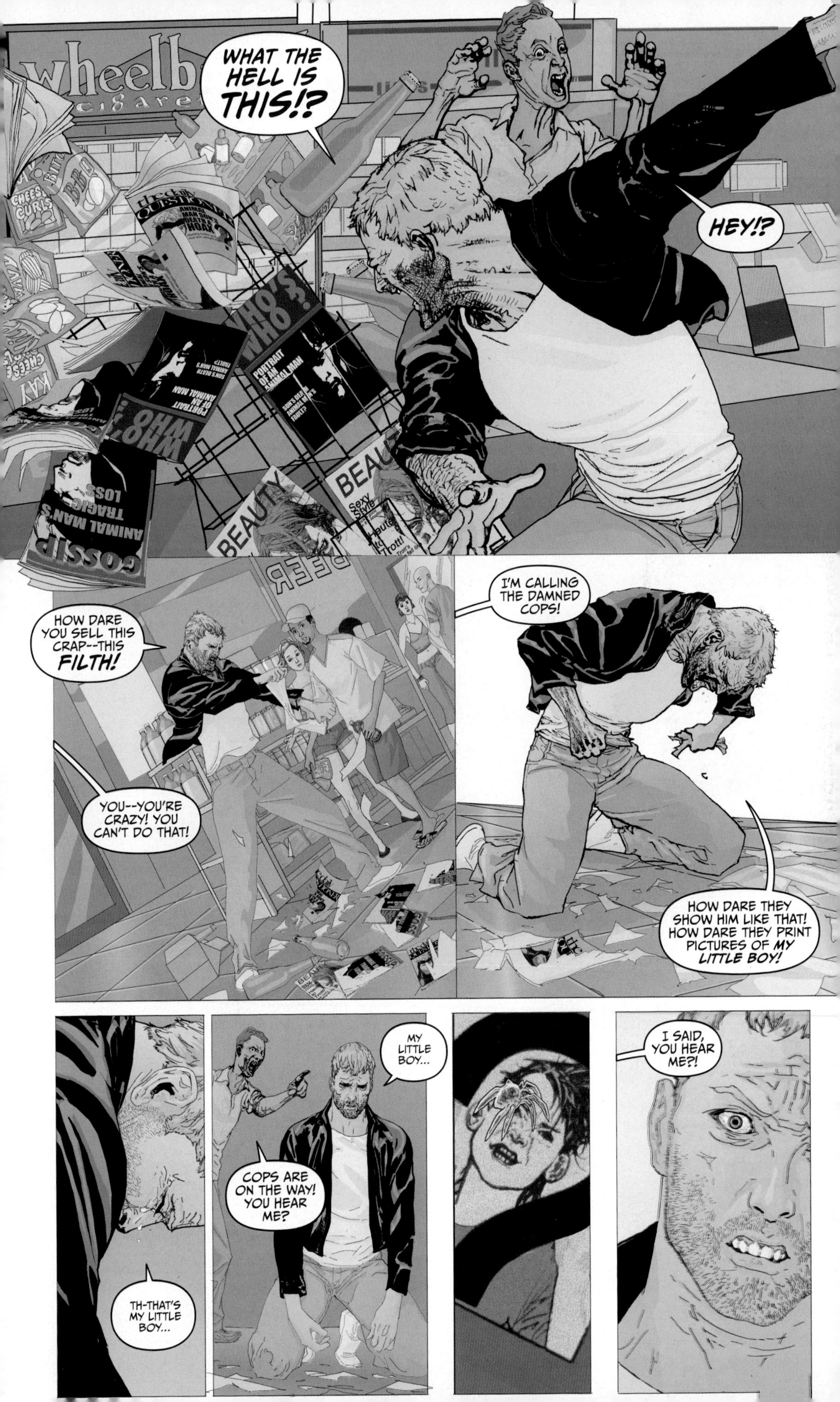

WHAT THE HELL IS THIS!?
HEY!?
HOW DARE YOU SELL THIS CRAP--THIS FILTH!
YOU--YOU'RE CRAZY! YOU CAN'T DO THAT!
I'M CALLING THE DAMNED COPS!
HOW DARE THEY SHOW HIM LIKE THAT! HOW DARE THEY PRINT PICTURES OF MY LITTLE BOY!
TH-THAT'S MY LITTLE BOY...
MY LITTLE BOY...
COPS ARE ON THE WAY! YOU HEAR ME?
I SAID, YOU HEAR ME?!

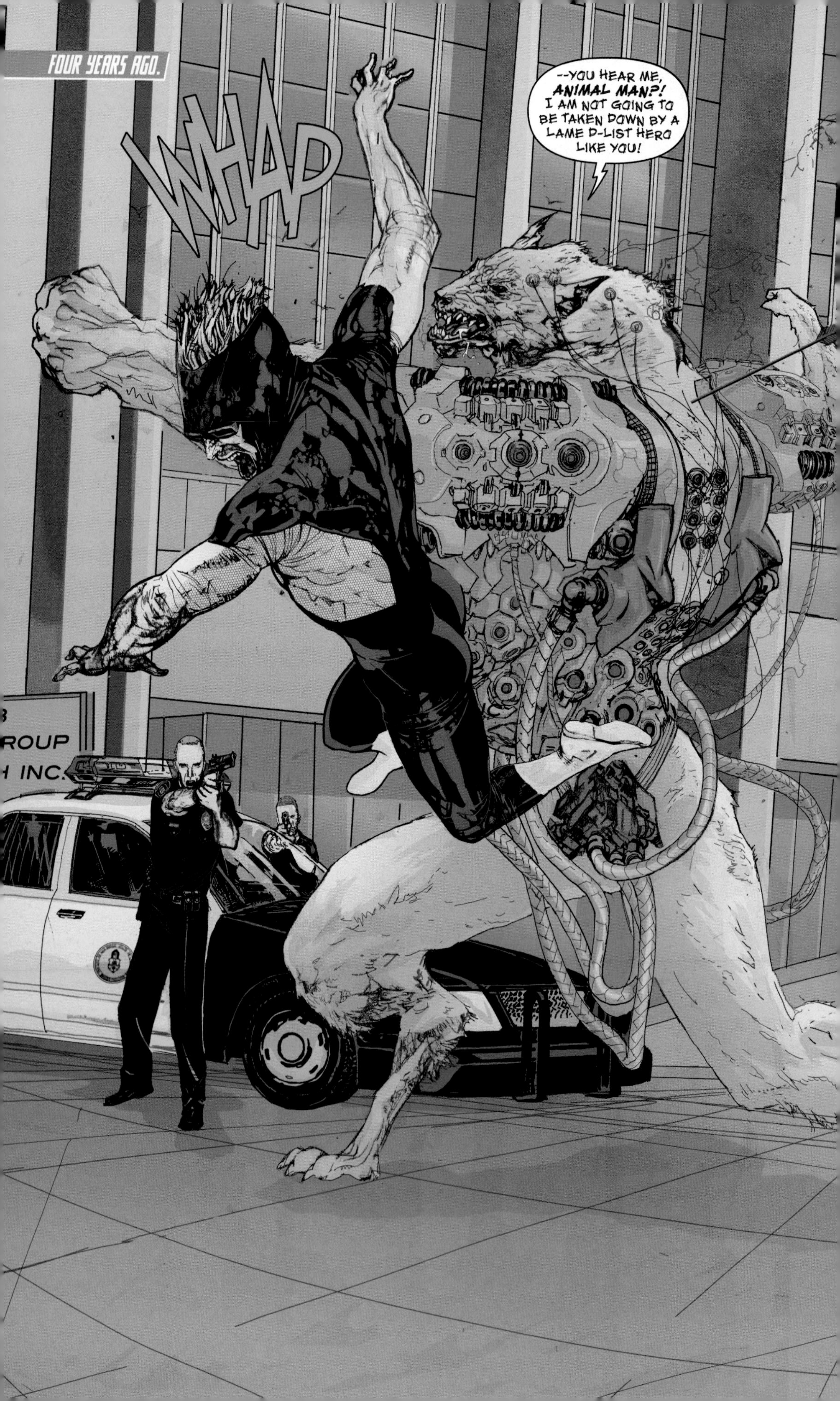
FOUR YEARS AGO.
WHAP
--YOU HEAR ME, ANIMAL MAN?! I AM NOT GOING TO BE TAKEN DOWN BY A LAME D-LIST HERO LIKE YOU!
ROUP
H INC.

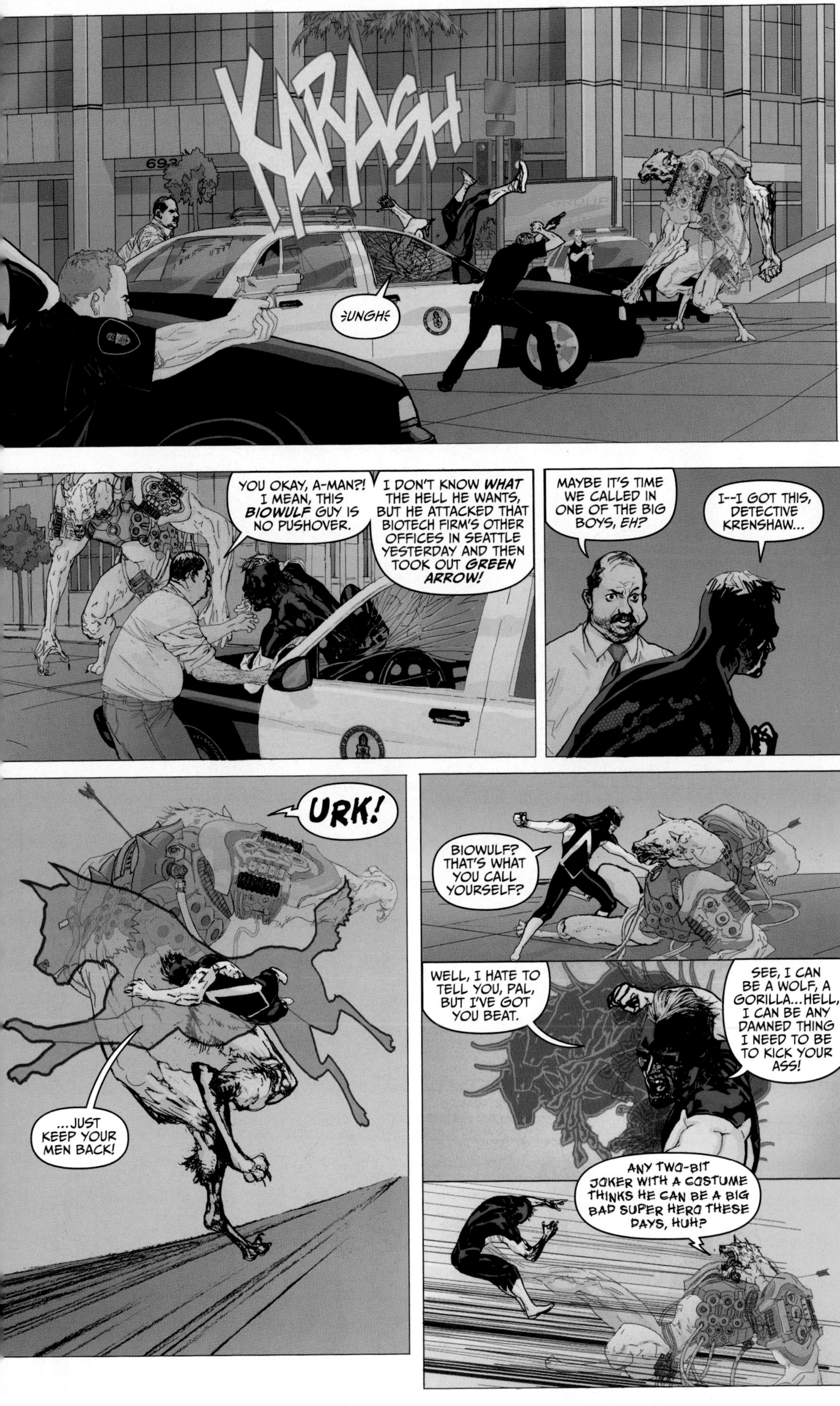
KRRASH
UNGH
YOU OKAY, A-MAN?! I MEAN, THIS BIOWULF GUY IS NO PUSHOVER.
I DON'T KNOW WHAT THE HELL HE WANTS, BUT HE ATTACKED THAT BIOTECH FIRM'S OTHER OFFICES IN SEATTLE YESTERDAY AND THEN TOOK OUT GREEN ARROW!
MAYBE IT'S TIME WE CALLED IN ONE OF THE BIG BOYS, EH?
I--I GOT THIS, DETECTIVE KRENSHAW...
URK!
...JUST KEEP YOUR MEN BACK!
BIOWULF? THAT'S WHAT YOU CALL YOURSELF?
WELL, I HATE TO TELL YOU, PAL, BUT I'VE GOT YOU BEAT.
SEE, I CAN BE A WOLF, A GORILLA...HELL, I CAN BE ANY DAMNED THING I NEED TO BE TO KICK YOUR ASS!
ANY TWO-BIT JOKER WITH A COSTUME THINKS HE CAN BE A BIG BAD SUPER HERO THESE DAYS, HUH?

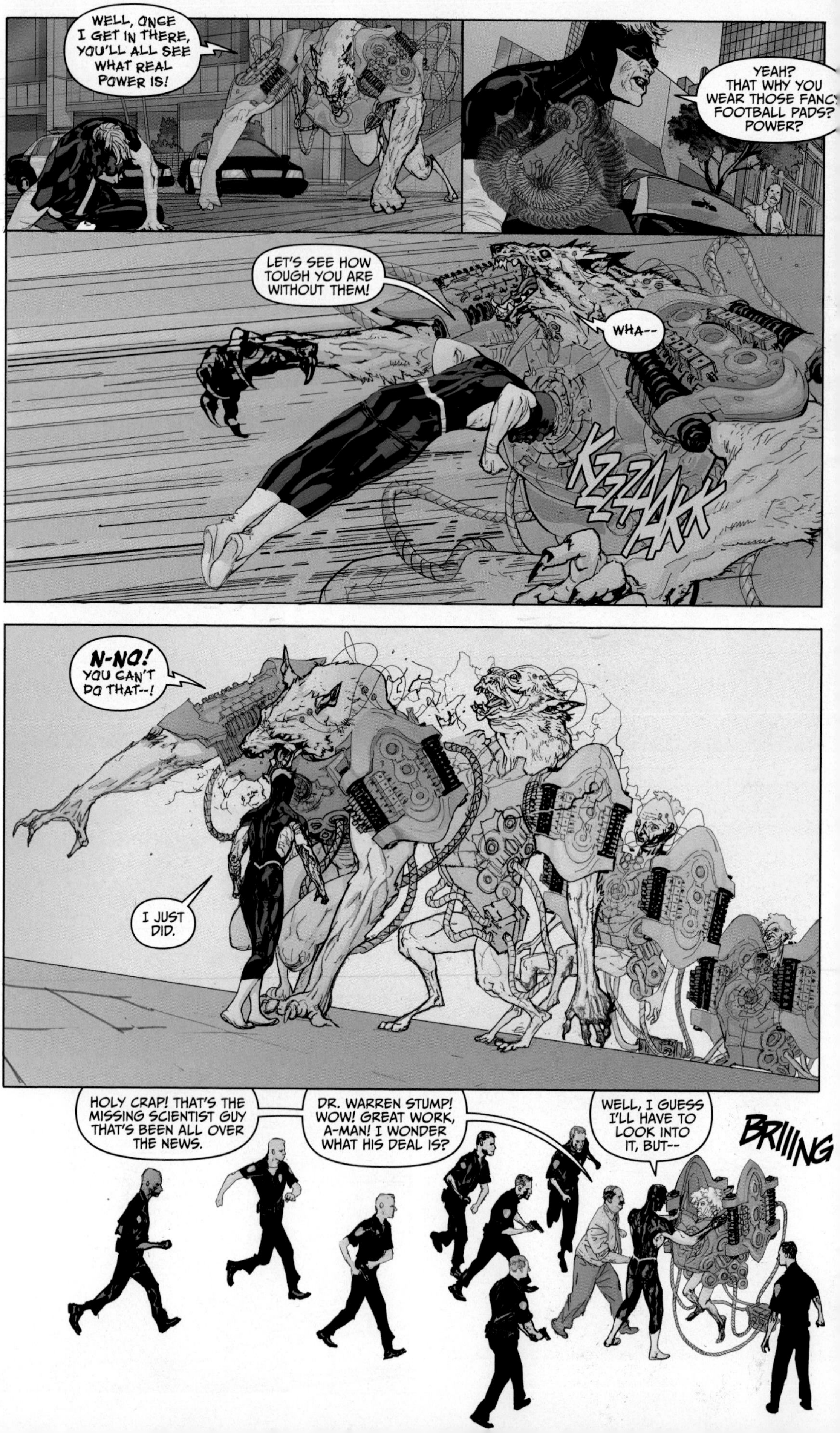
WELL, ONCE I GET IN THERE, YOU'LL ALL SEE WHAT REAL POWER IS!
YEAH? THAT WHY YOU WEAR THOSE FANCY FOOTBALL PADS? POWER?
LET'S SEE HOW TOUGH YOU ARE WITHOUT THEM!
WHA--
KZZZAKK
N-NO! YOU CAN'T DO THAT--!
I JUST DID.
HOLY CRAP! THAT'S THE MISSING SCIENTIST GUY THAT'S BEEN ALL OVER THE NEWS.
DR. WARREN STUMP! WOW! GREAT WORK, A-MAN! I WONDER WHAT HIS DEAL IS?
WELL, I GUESS I'LL HAVE TO LOOK INTO IT, BUT--
BRIIING

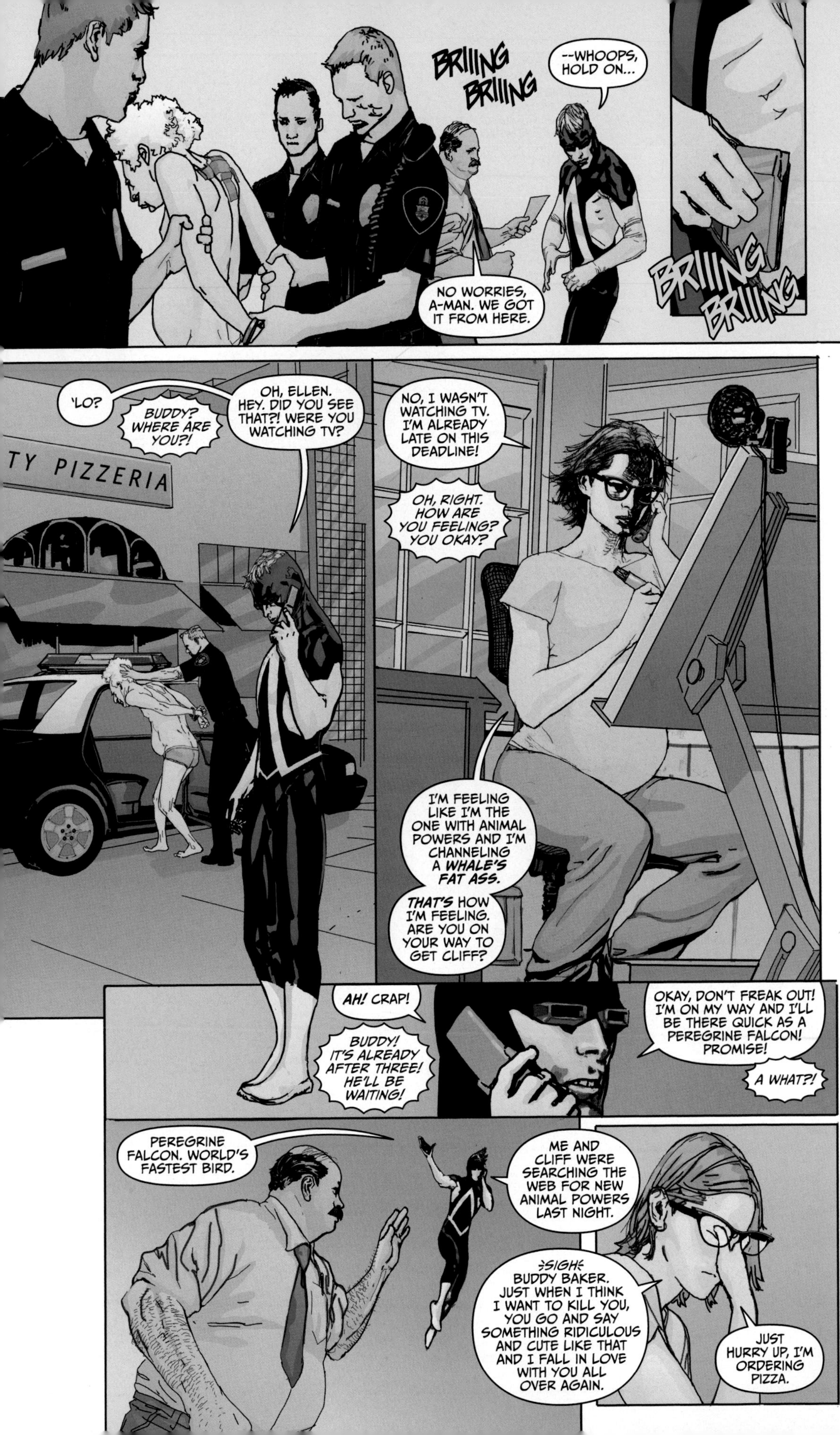
BRIIING BRIIING
--WHOOPS, HOLD ON...
NO WORRIES, A-MAN. WE GOT IT FROM HERE.
BRIIING BRIIING
'LO?
BUDDY? WHERE ARE YOU?!
OH, ELLEN. HEY. DID YOU SEE THAT?! WERE YOU WATCHING TV?
TY PIZZERIA
NO, I WASN'T WATCHING TV. I'M ALREADY LATE ON THIS DEADLINE!
OH, RIGHT. HOW ARE YOU FEELING? YOU OKAY?
I'M FEELING LIKE I'M THE ONE WITH ANIMAL POWERS AND I'M CHANNELING A WHALE'S FAT ASS.
THAT'S HOW I'M FEELING. ARE YOU ON YOUR WAY TO GET CLIFF?
AH! CRAP!
BUDDY! IT'S ALREADY AFTER THREE! HE'LL BE WAITING!
OKAY, DON'T FREAK OUT! I'M ON MY WAY AND I'LL BE THERE QUICK AS A PEREGRINE FALCON! PROMISE!
A WHAT?!
PEREGRINE FALCON. WORLD'S FASTEST BIRD.
ME AND CLIFF WERE SEARCHING THE WEB FOR NEW ANIMAL POWERS LAST NIGHT.
SIGH BUDDY BAKER. JUST WHEN I THINK I WANT TO KILL YOU, YOU GO AND SAY SOMETHING RIDICULOUS AND CUTE LIKE THAT AND I FALL IN LOVE WITH YOU ALL OVER AGAIN.
JUST HURRY UP, I'M ORDERING PIZZA.

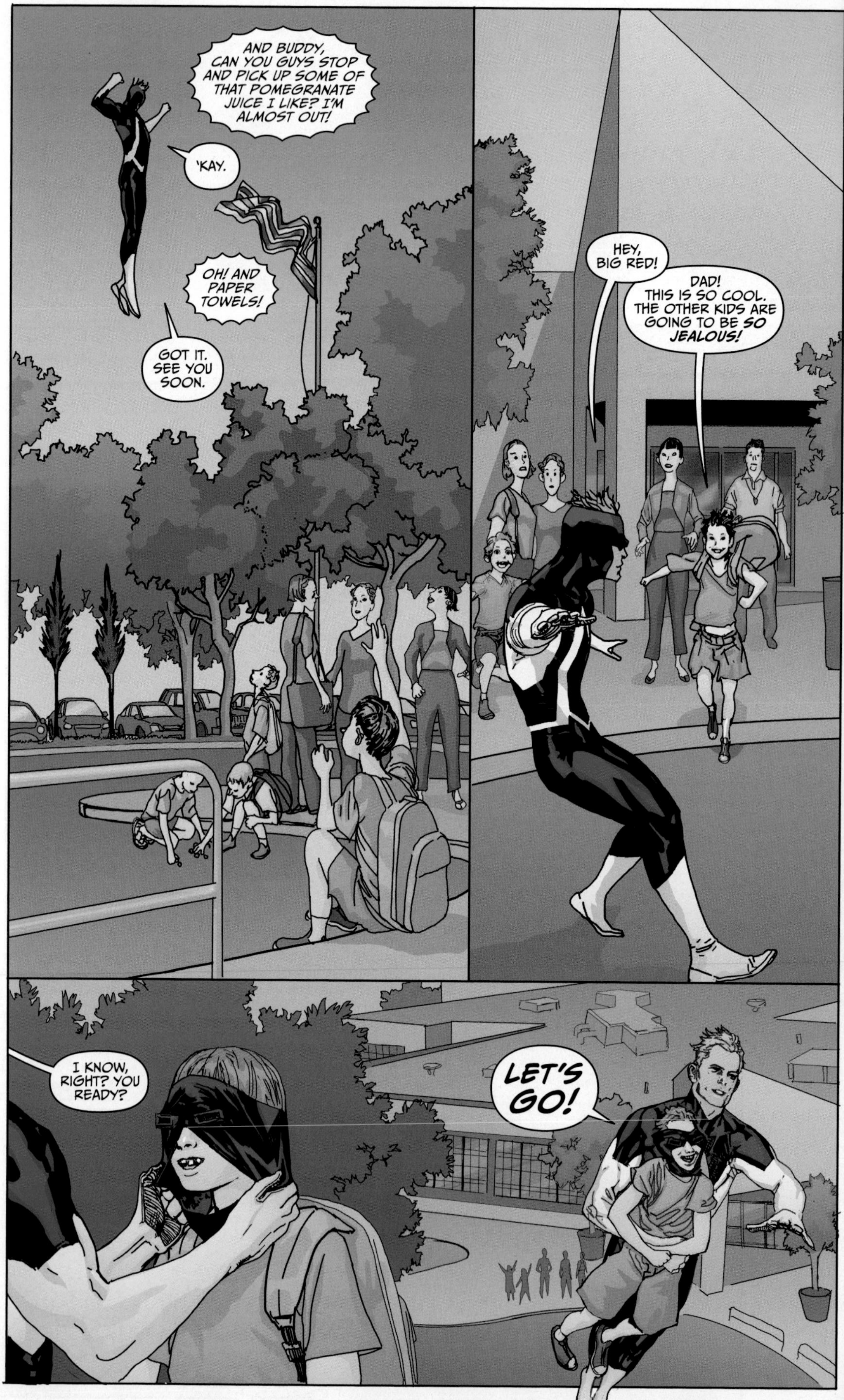
AND BUDDY, CAN YOU GUYS STOP AND PICK UP SOME OF THAT POMEGRANATE JUICE I LIKE? I'M ALMOST OUT!
'KAY.
OH! AND PAPER TOWELS!
GOT IT. SEE YOU SOON.
HEY, BIG RED!
DAD! THIS IS SO COOL. THE OTHER KIDS ARE GOING TO BE SO JEALOUS!
I KNOW, RIGHT? YOU READY?
LET'S GO!

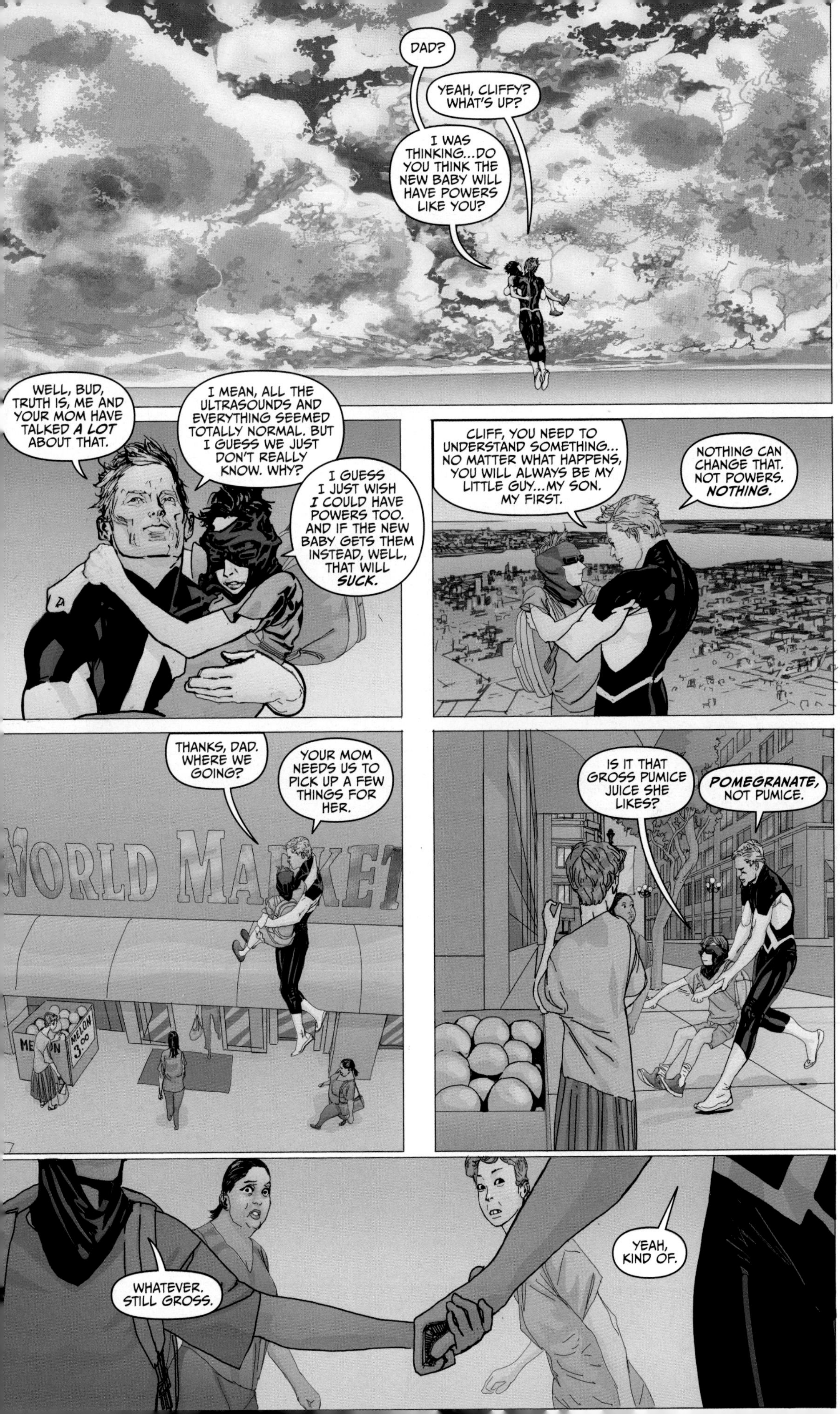
DAD?
YEAH, CLIFFY? WHAT'S UP?
I WAS THINKING...DO YOU THINK THE NEW BABY WILL HAVE POWERS LIKE YOU?
WELL, BUD, TRUTH IS, ME AND YOUR MOM HAVE TALKED *A LOT* ABOUT THAT.
I MEAN, ALL THE ULTRASOUNDS AND EVERYTHING SEEMED TOTALLY NORMAL. BUT I GUESS WE JUST DON'T REALLY KNOW. WHY?
I GUESS I JUST WISH *I* COULD HAVE POWERS TOO. AND IF THE NEW BABY GETS THEM INSTEAD, WELL, THAT WILL ***SUCK.***
CLIFF, YOU NEED TO UNDERSTAND SOMETHING... NO MATTER WHAT HAPPENS, YOU WILL ALWAYS BE MY LITTLE GUY...MY SON. MY FIRST.
NOTHING CAN CHANGE THAT. NOT POWERS. ***NOTHING.***
THANKS, DAD. WHERE WE GOING?
YOUR MOM NEEDS US TO PICK UP A FEW THINGS FOR HER.
WORLD MARKET
MELON 3.00
IS IT THAT GROSS PUMICE JUICE SHE LIKES?
POMEGRANATE, NOT PUMICE.
WHATEVER. STILL GROSS.
YEAH, KIND OF.

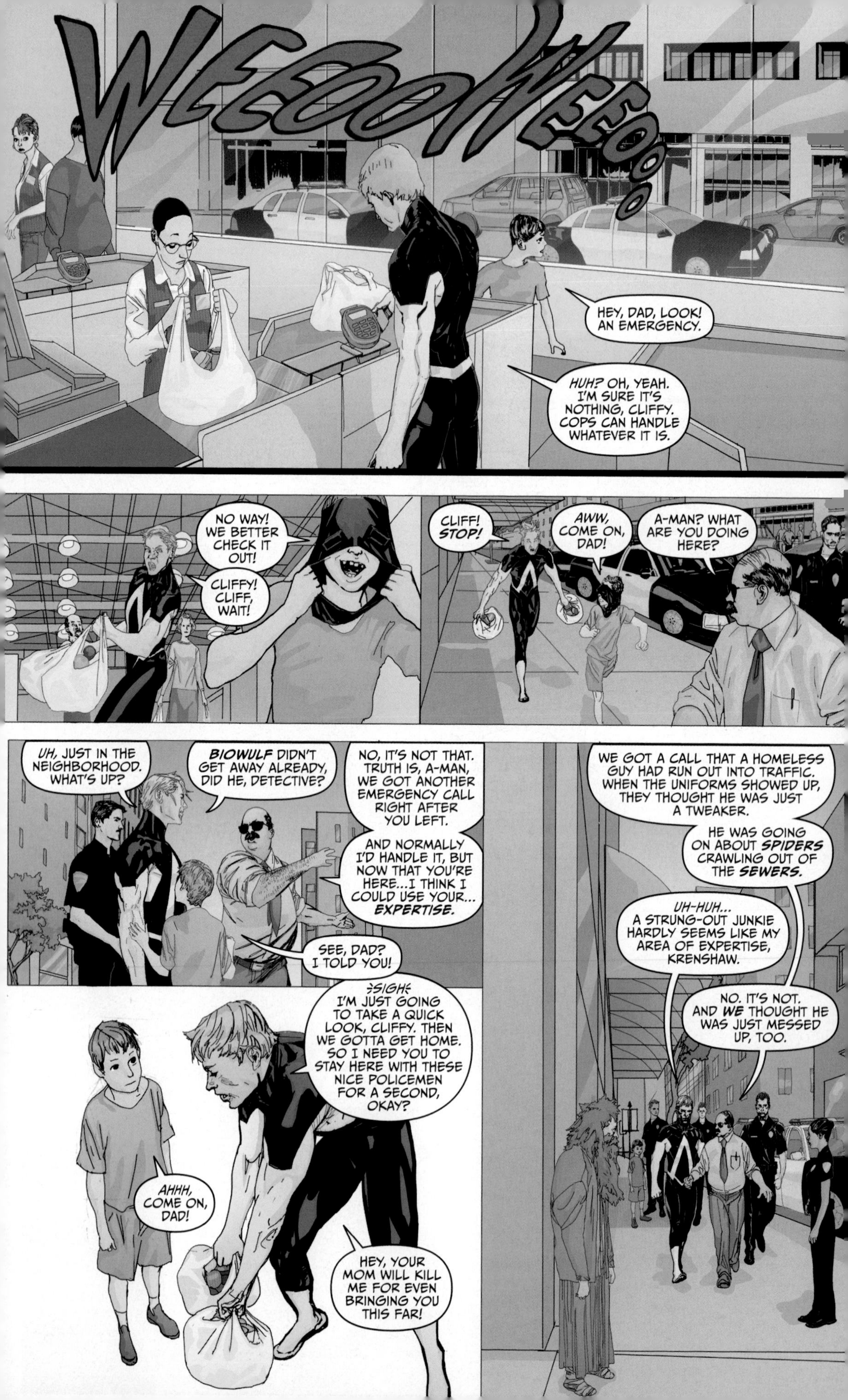
WEEOOWEEOOO
HEY, DAD, LOOK! AN EMERGENCY.
HUH? OH, YEAH. I'M SURE IT'S NOTHING, CLIFFY. COPS CAN HANDLE WHATEVER IT IS.
NO WAY! WE BETTER CHECK IT OUT!
CLIFFY! CLIFF, WAIT!
CLIFF! STOP!
AWW, COME ON, DAD!
A-MAN? WHAT ARE YOU DOING HERE?
UH, JUST IN THE NEIGHBORHOOD. WHAT'S UP?
BIOWULF DIDN'T GET AWAY ALREADY, DID HE, DETECTIVE?
NO, IT'S NOT THAT. TRUTH IS, A-MAN, WE GOT ANOTHER EMERGENCY CALL RIGHT AFTER YOU LEFT.
AND NORMALLY I'D HANDLE IT, BUT NOW THAT YOU'RE HERE...I THINK I COULD USE YOUR... EXPERTISE.
SEE, DAD? I TOLD YOU!
SIGH
I'M JUST GOING TO TAKE A QUICK LOOK, CLIFFY. THEN WE GOTTA GET HOME. SO I NEED YOU TO STAY HERE WITH THESE NICE POLICEMEN FOR A SECOND, OKAY?
AHHH, COME ON, DAD!
HEY, YOUR MOM WILL KILL ME FOR EVEN BRINGING YOU THIS FAR!
WE GOT A CALL THAT A HOMELESS GUY HAD RUN OUT INTO TRAFFIC. WHEN THE UNIFORMS SHOWED UP, THEY THOUGHT HE WAS JUST A TWEAKER.
HE WAS GOING ON ABOUT SPIDERS CRAWLING OUT OF THE SEWERS.
UH-HUH... A STRUNG-OUT JUNKIE HARDLY SEEMS LIKE MY AREA OF EXPERTISE, KRENSHAW.
NO. IT'S NOT. AND WE THOUGHT HE WAS JUST MESSED UP, TOO.

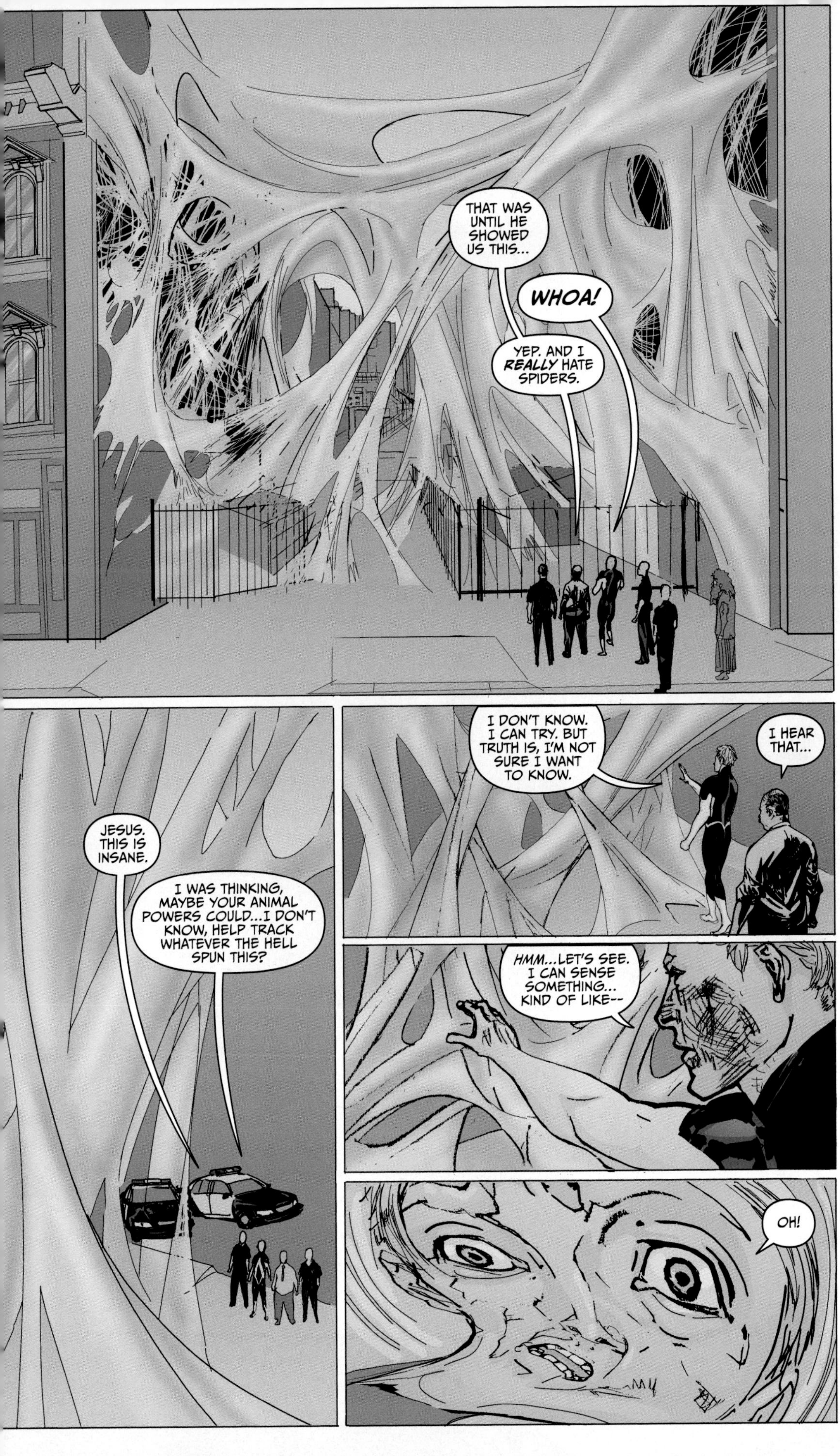
THAT WAS UNTIL HE SHOWED US THIS...
WHOA!
YEP. AND I REALLY HATE SPIDERS.
JESUS. THIS IS INSANE.
I WAS THINKING, MAYBE YOUR ANIMAL POWERS COULD...I DON'T KNOW, HELP TRACK WHATEVER THE HELL SPUN THIS?
I DON'T KNOW. I CAN TRY. BUT TRUTH IS, I'M NOT SURE I WANT TO KNOW.
I HEAR THAT...
HMM...LET'S SEE. I CAN SENSE SOMETHING... KIND OF LIKE--
OH!

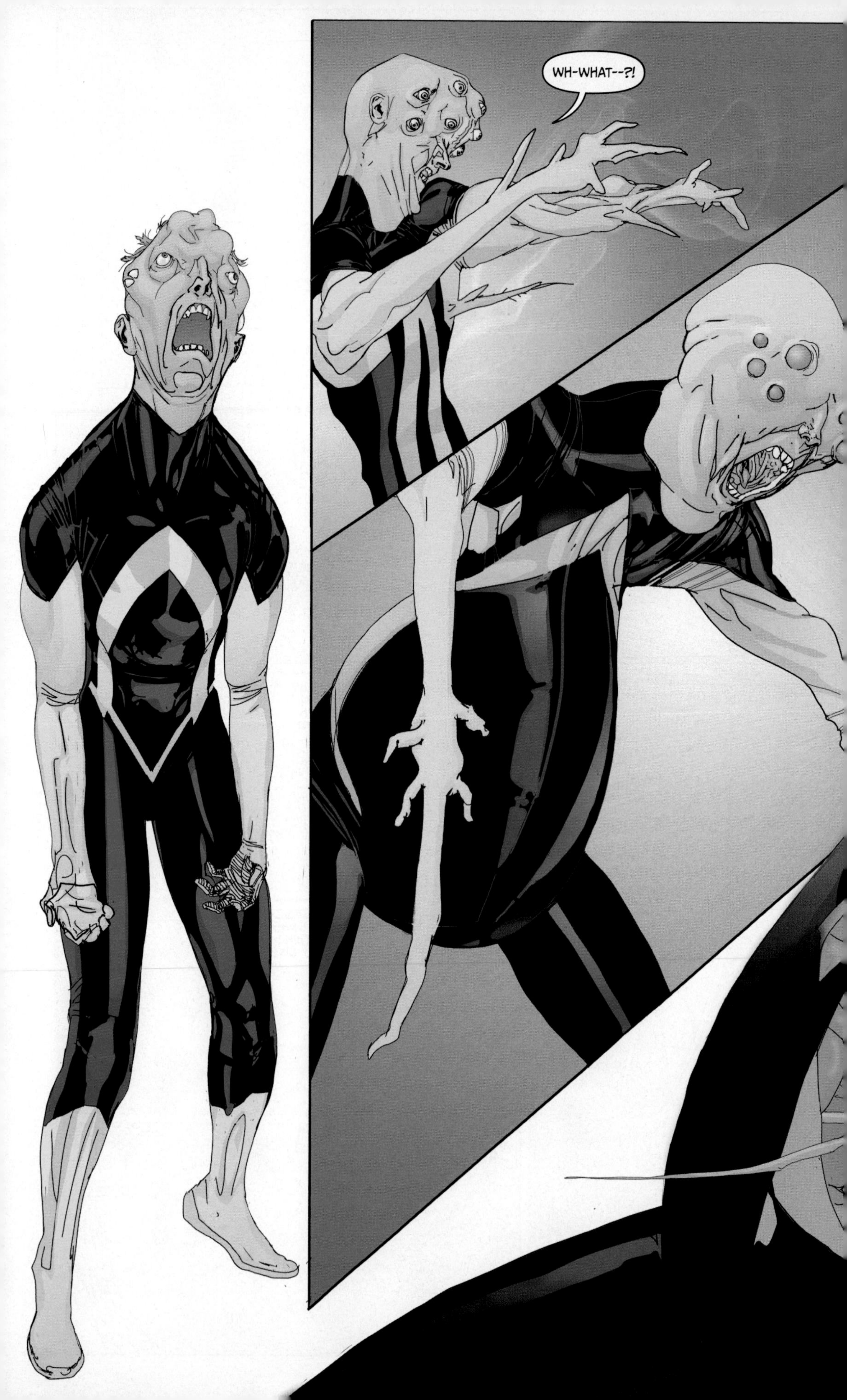
WH-WHAT--?!

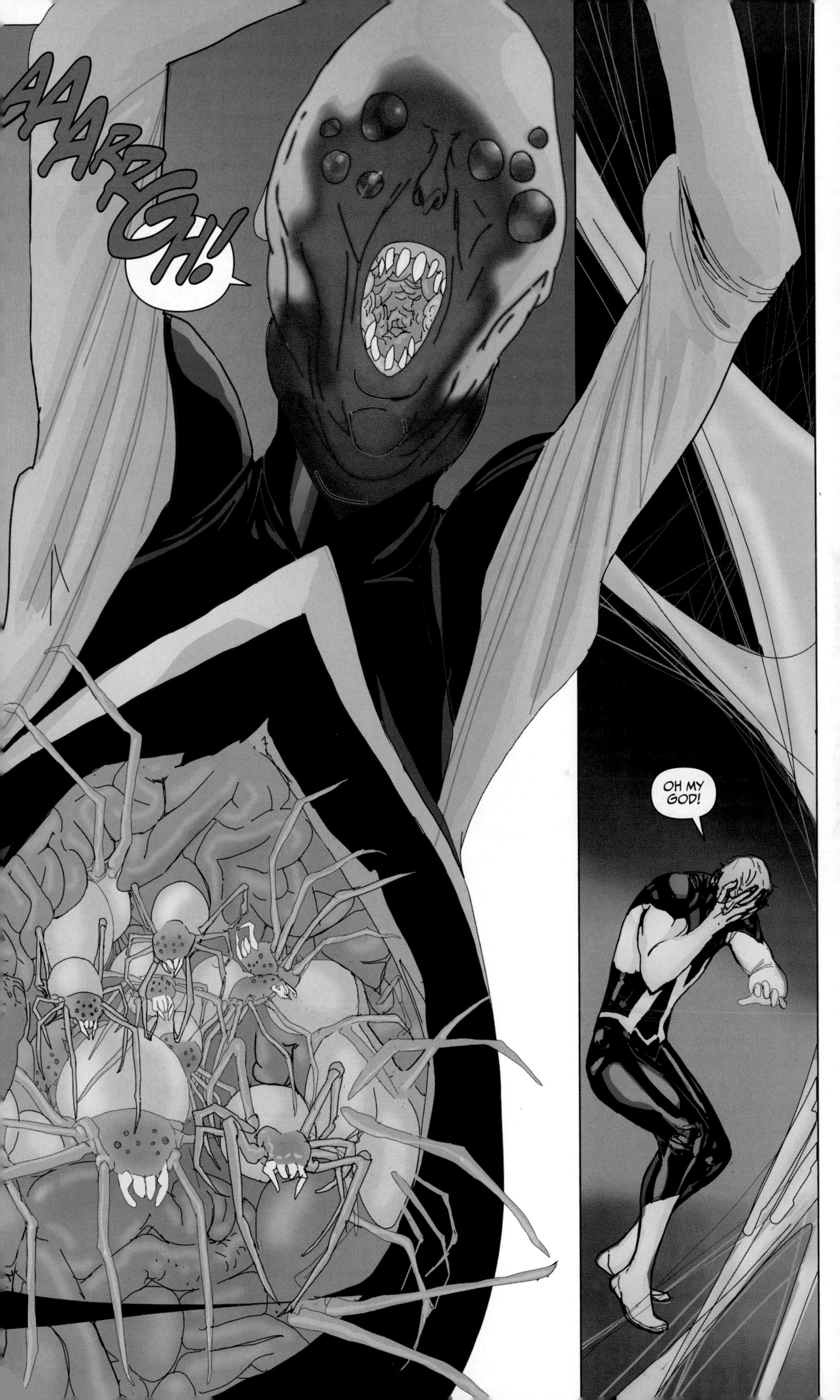
AAARRGH!
OH MY GOD!

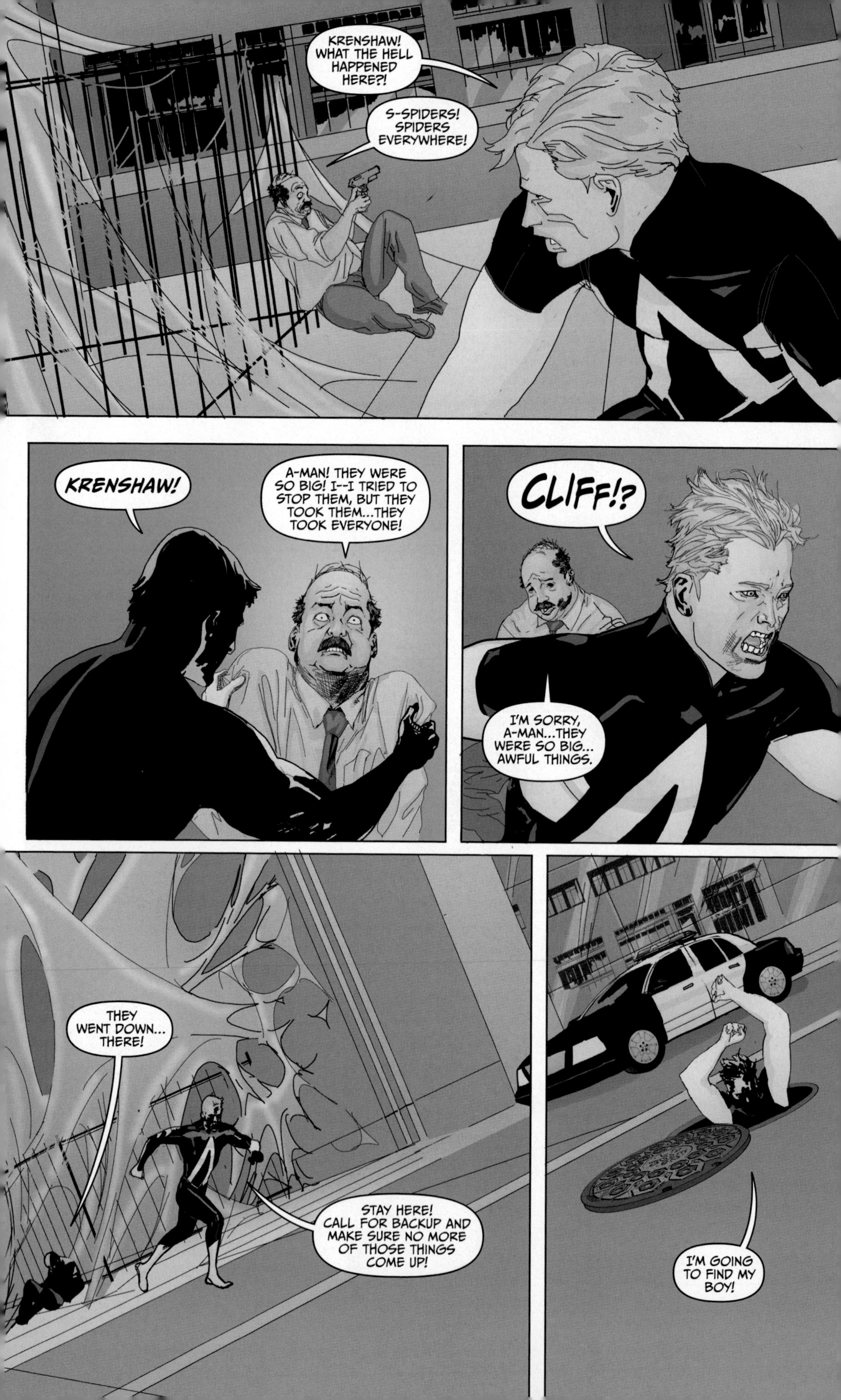
KRENSHAW! WHAT THE HELL HAPPENED HERE?!
S-SPIDERS! SPIDERS EVERYWHERE!
KRENSHAW!
A-MAN! THEY WERE SO BIG! I--I TRIED TO STOP THEM, BUT THEY TOOK THEM...THEY TOOK EVERYONE!
CLIFF!?
I'M SORRY, A-MAN...THEY WERE SO BIG... AWFUL THINGS.
THEY WENT DOWN... THERE!
STAY HERE! CALL FOR BACKUP AND MAKE SURE NO MORE OF THOSE THINGS COME UP!
I'M GOING TO FIND MY BOY!

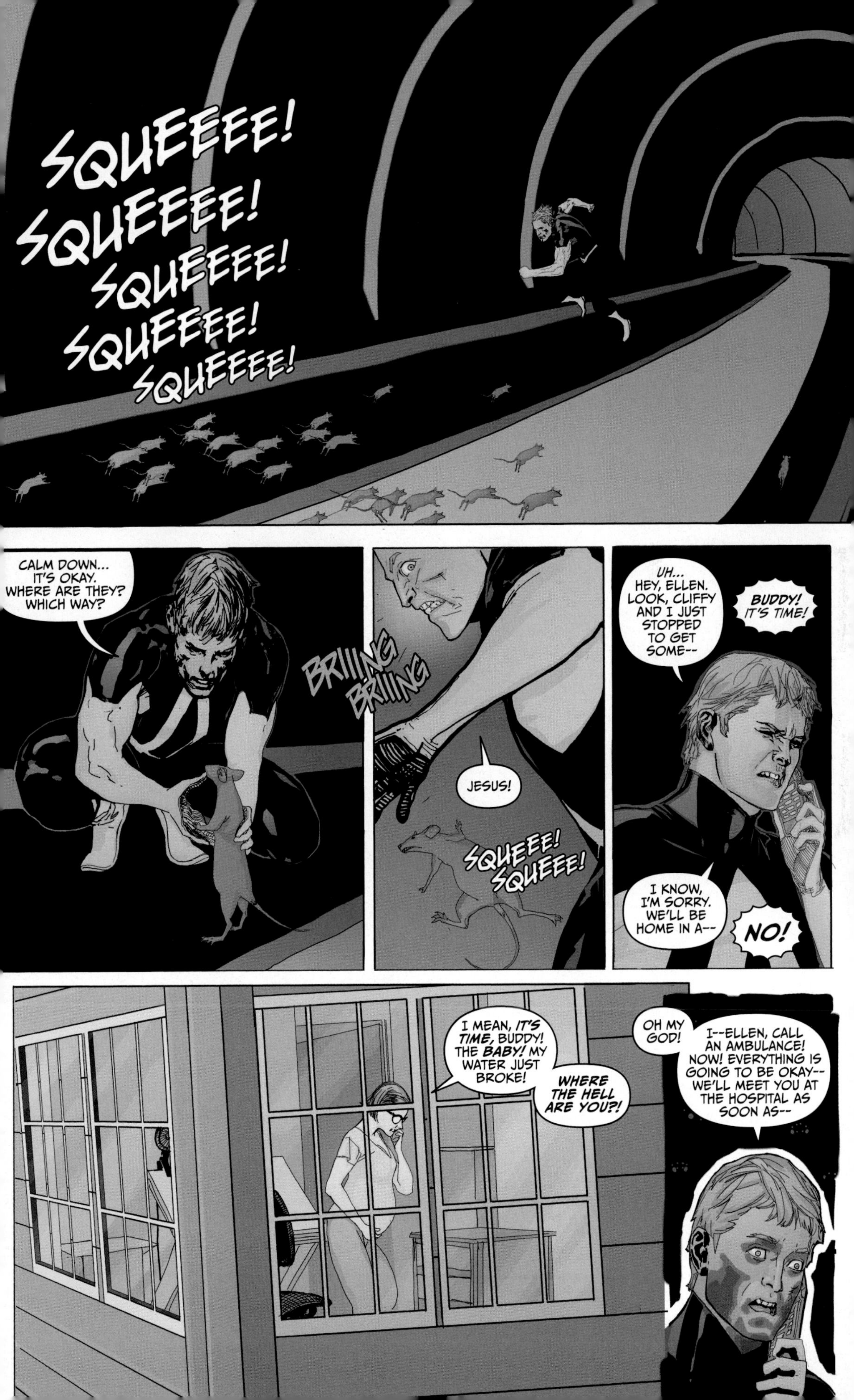
SQUEEEE!
SQUEEEE!
SQUEEEE!
SQUEEEE!
SQUEEEE!
CALM DOWN... IT'S OKAY. WHERE ARE THEY? WHICH WAY?
BRIIING BRIIING
JESUS!
SQUEEE! SQUEEE!
UH... HEY, ELLEN. LOOK, CLIFFY AND I JUST STOPPED TO GET SOME--
BUDDY! IT'S TIME!
I KNOW, I'M SORRY. WE'LL BE HOME IN A--
NO!
I MEAN, IT'S TIME, BUDDY! THE BABY! MY WATER JUST BROKE!
WHERE THE HELL ARE YOU?!
OH MY GOD!
I--ELLEN, CALL AN AMBULANCE! NOW! EVERYTHING IS GOING TO BE OKAY-- WE'LL MEET YOU AT THE HOSPITAL AS SOON AS--

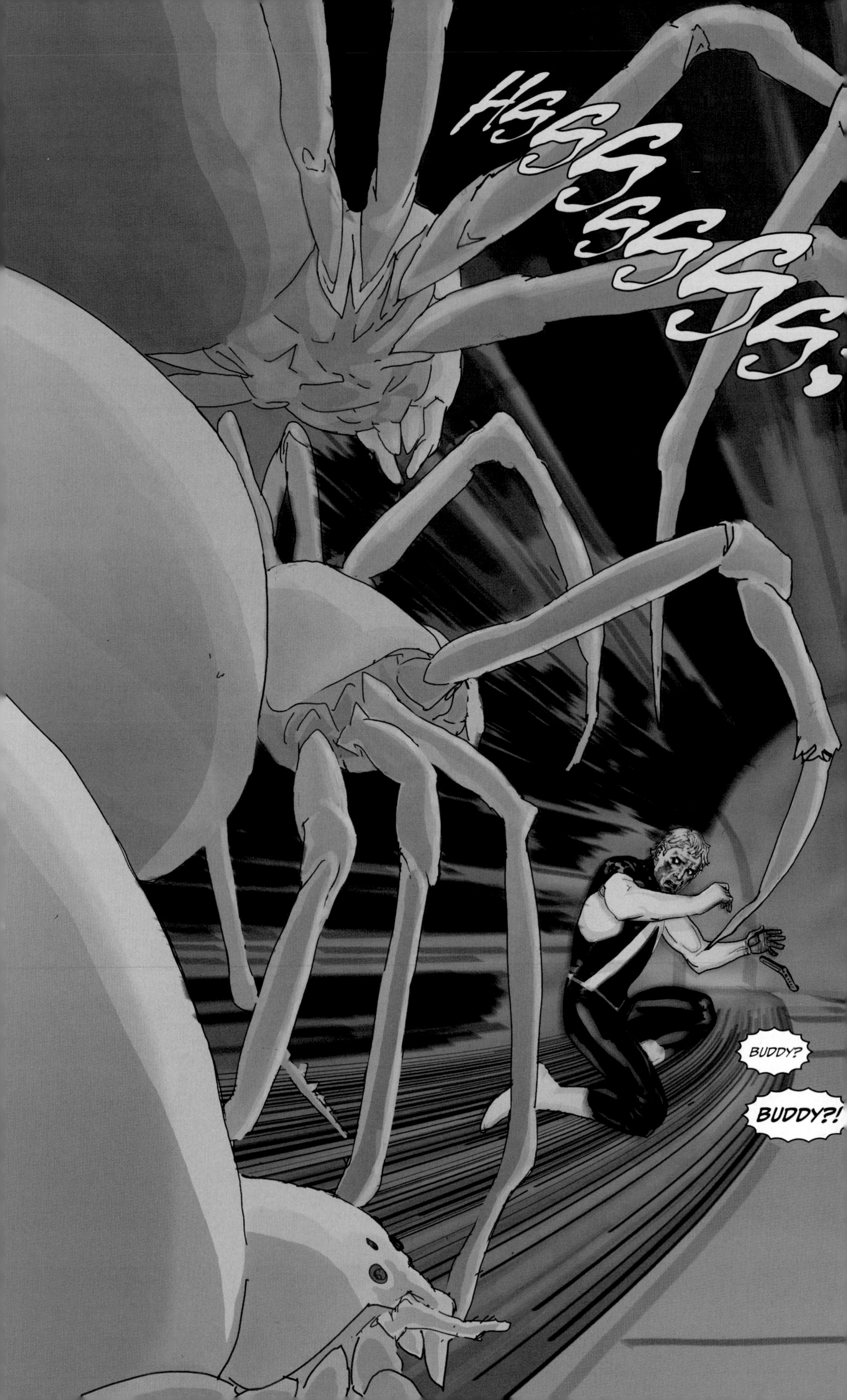
HSSSSSSS!
BUDDY?
BUDDY?!

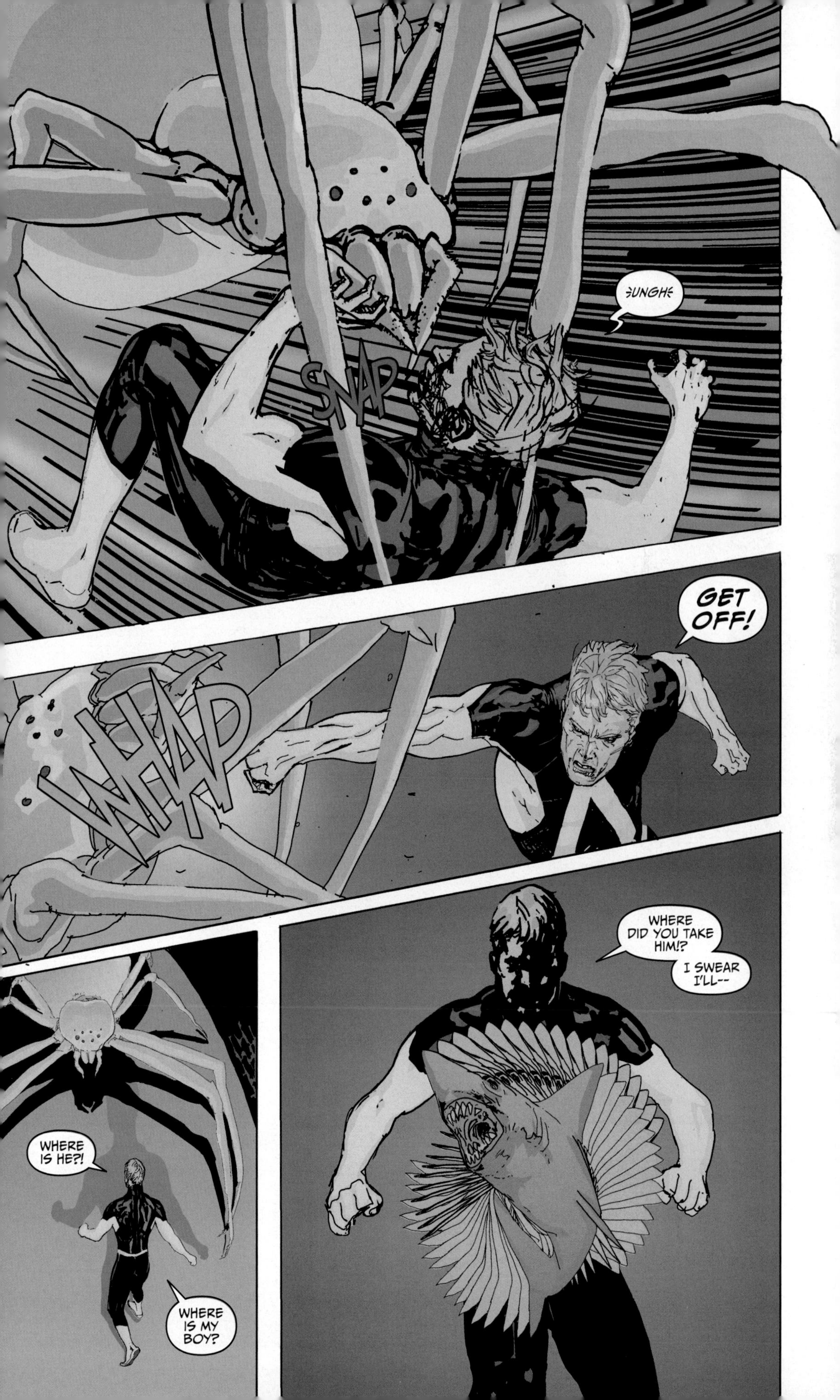
UNGH
SNAP
GET OFF!
WHAP
WHERE IS HE?!
WHERE IS MY BOY?
WHERE DID YOU TAKE HIM!?
I SWEAR I'LL--

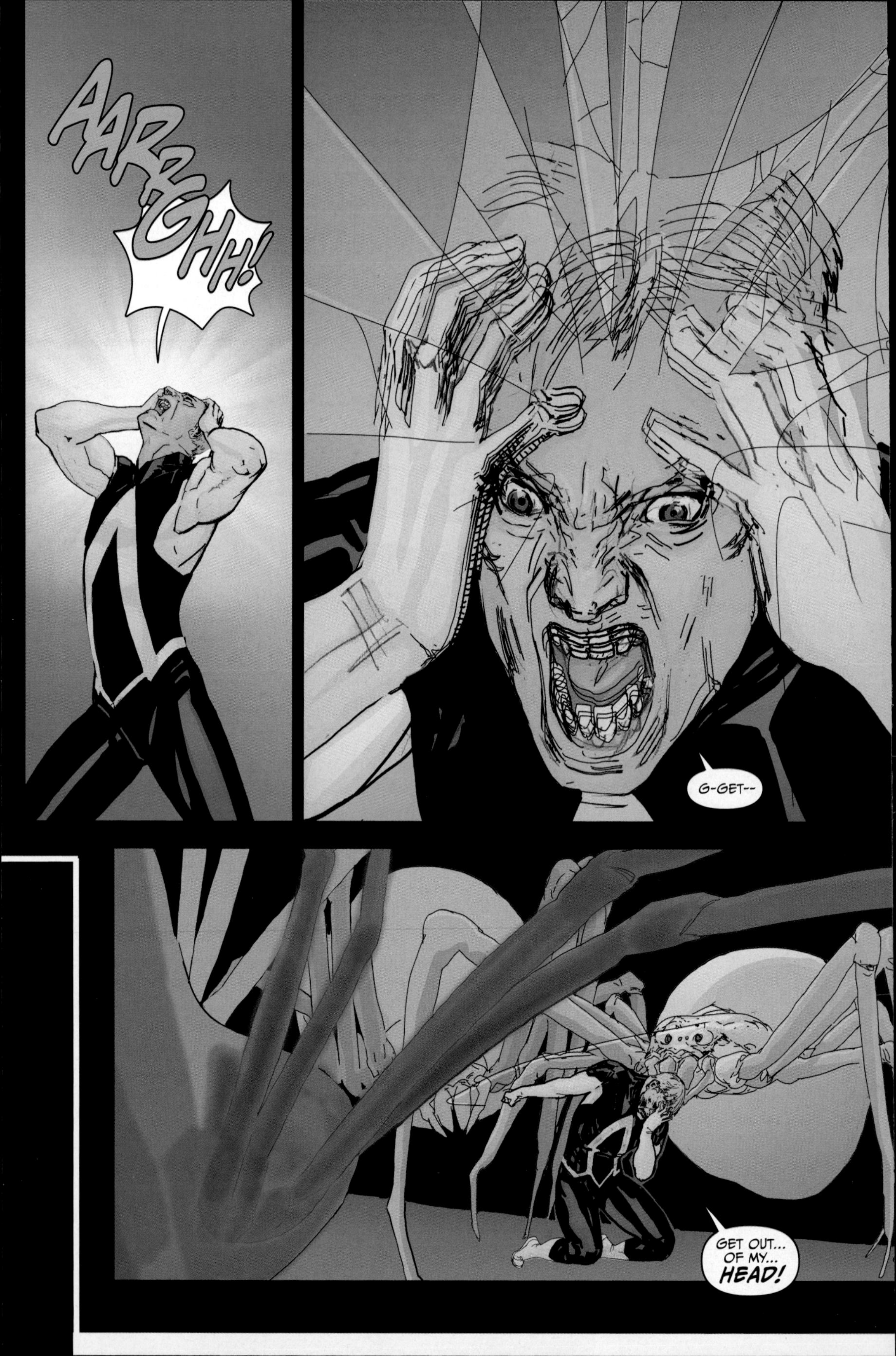
AARRGHH!
G-GET--
GET OUT... OF MY... HEAD!

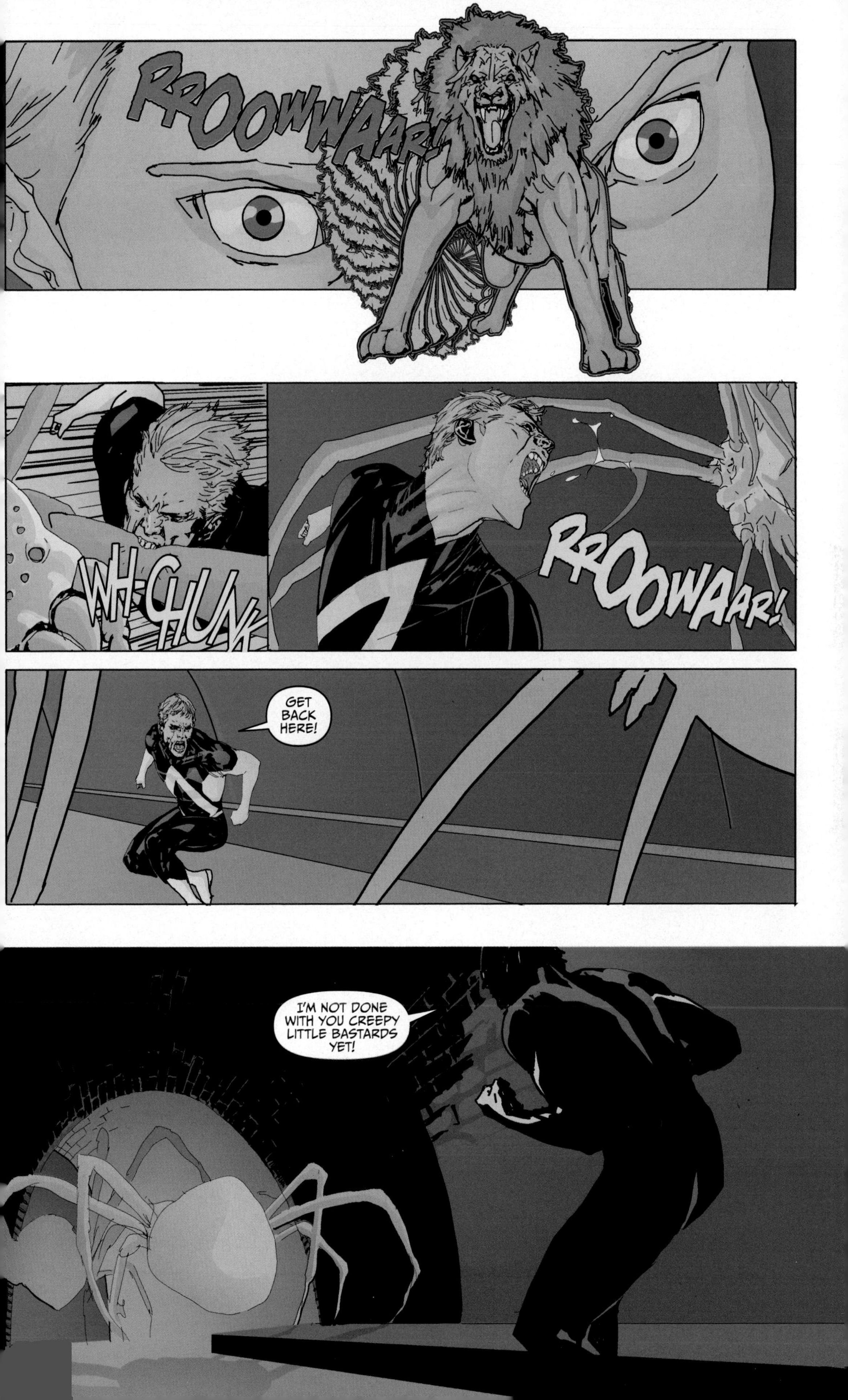
RROOWWAAR!
WH-CHUNK
RROOWAAR!
GET BACK HERE!
I'M NOT DONE WITH YOU CREEPY LITTLE BASTARDS YET!

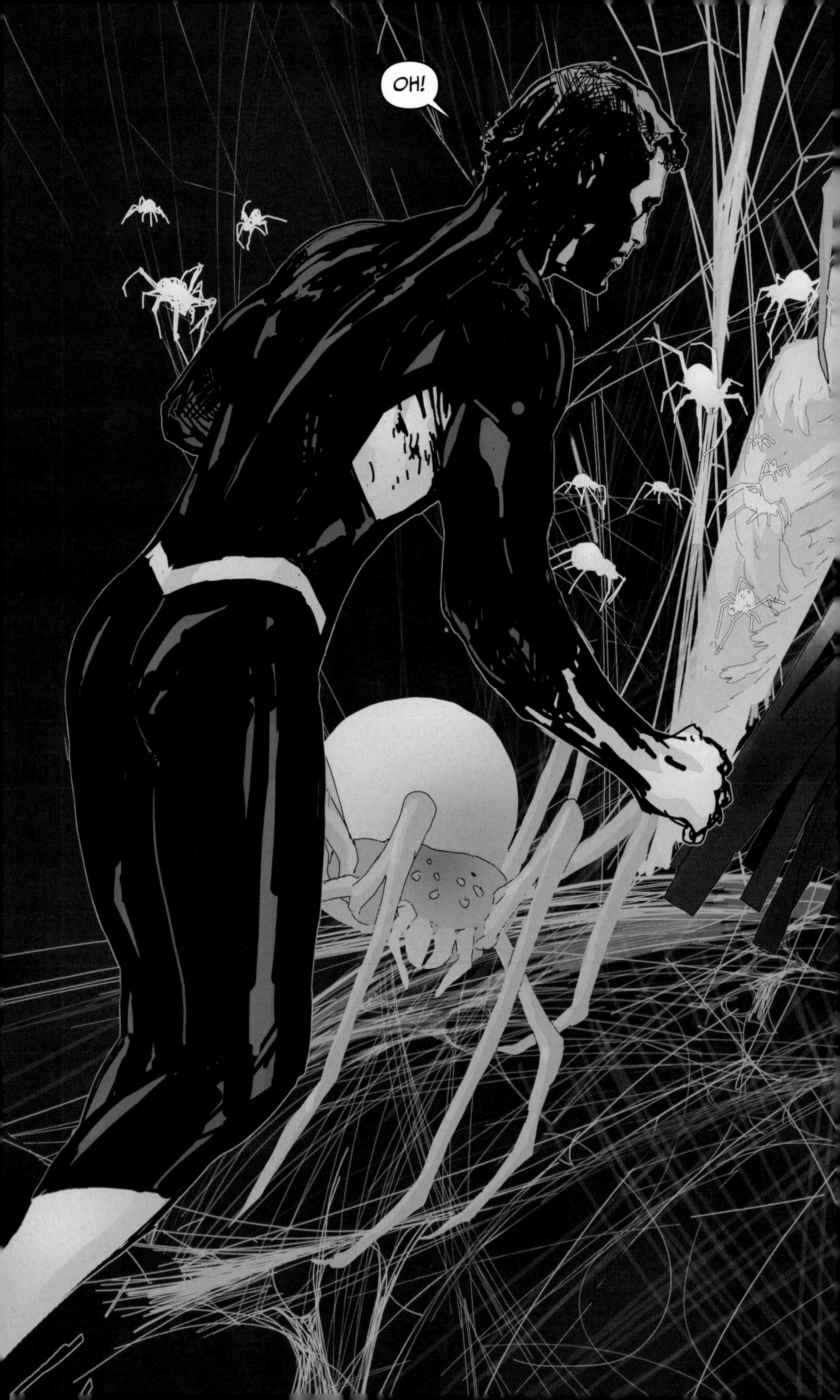
OH!

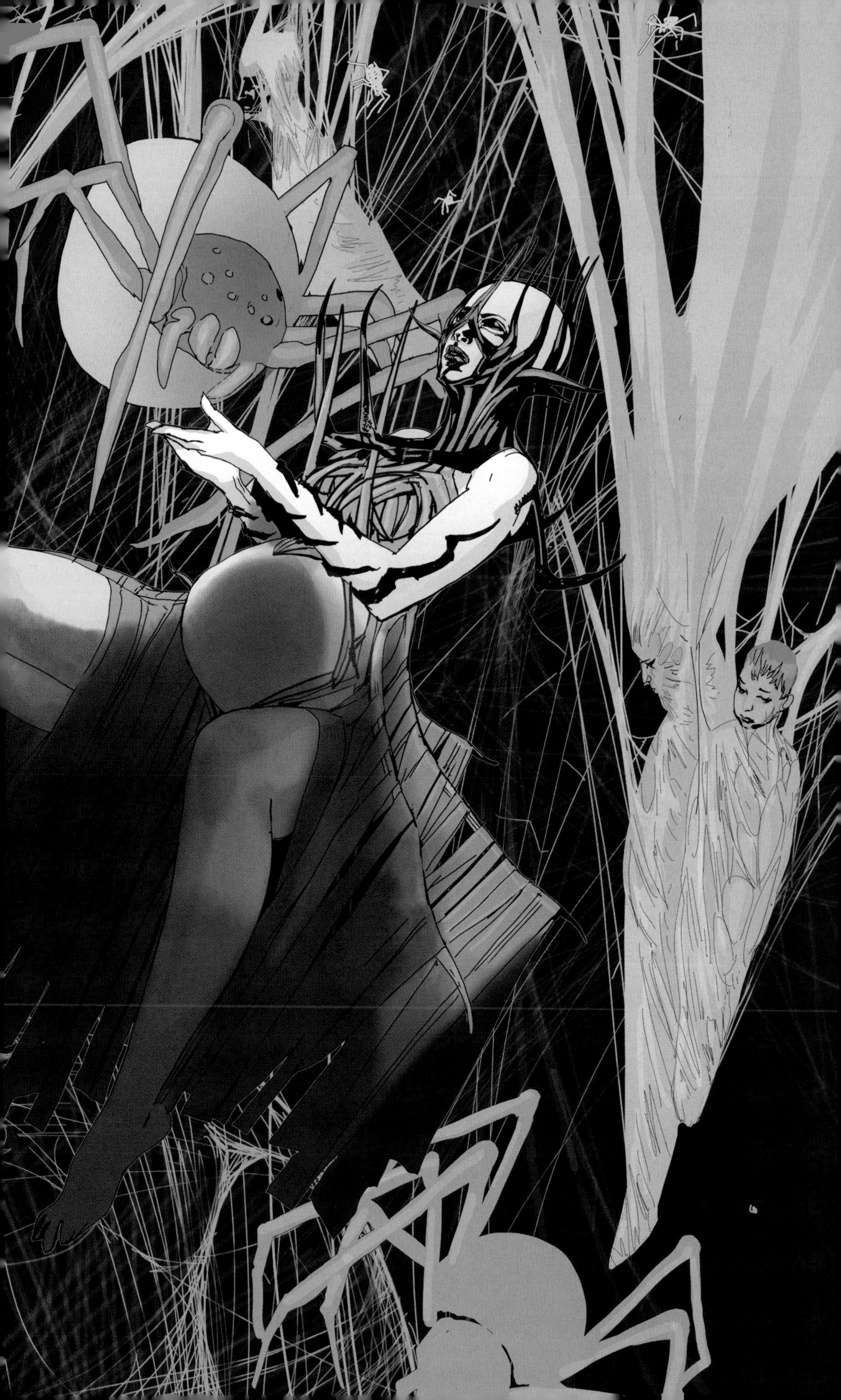

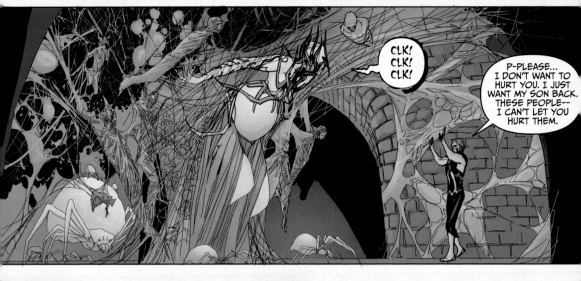

CLK!
CLK!
CLK!

P-PLEASE...
I DON'T WANT TO
HURT YOU. I JUST
WANT MY SON BACK.
THESE PEOPLE--
I CAN'T LET YOU
HURT THEM.

CLK?

DO YOU
UNDERSTAND?
I DON'T WANT TO
FIGHT YOU.

I'M JUST
GOING TO GET
MY BOY. AND THE[N]
WE CAN TALK ABO[UT]
THESE OTHER
PEOPLE...
OKAY?

HSSSS
SSS!

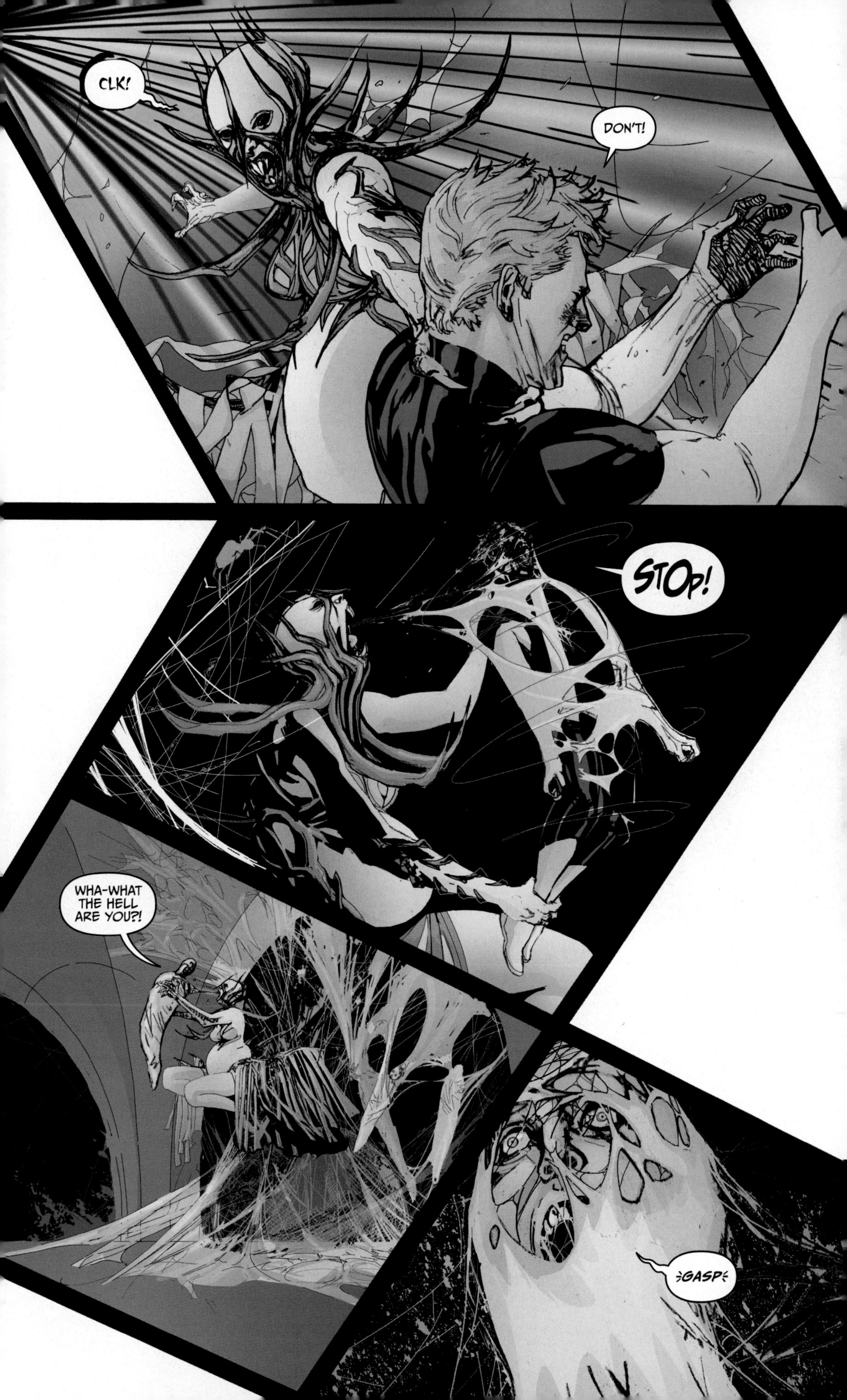
CLK!
DON'T!
STOP!
WHA-WHAT THE HELL ARE YOU?!
GASP

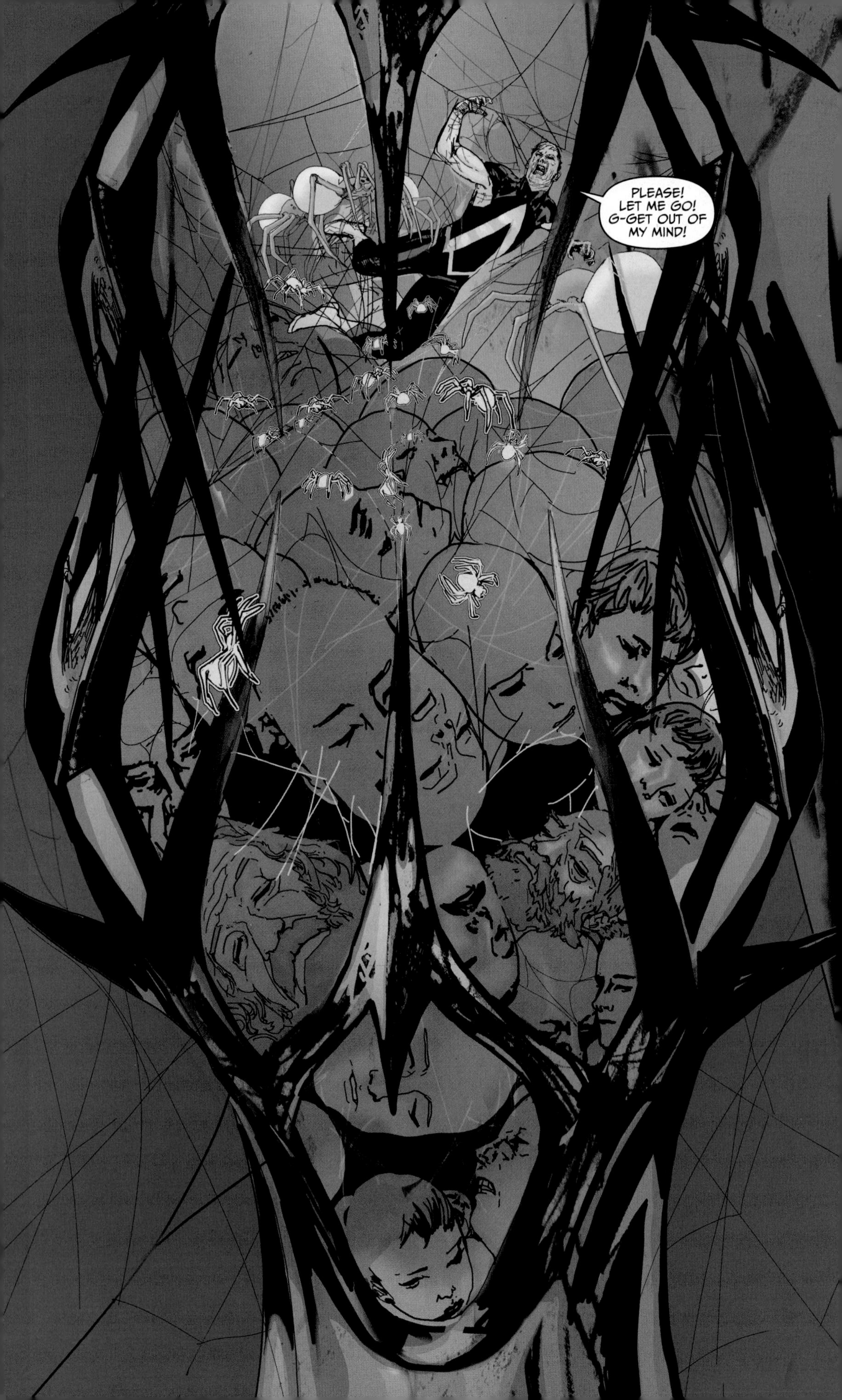
PLEASE! LET ME GO! G-GET OUT OF MY MIND!

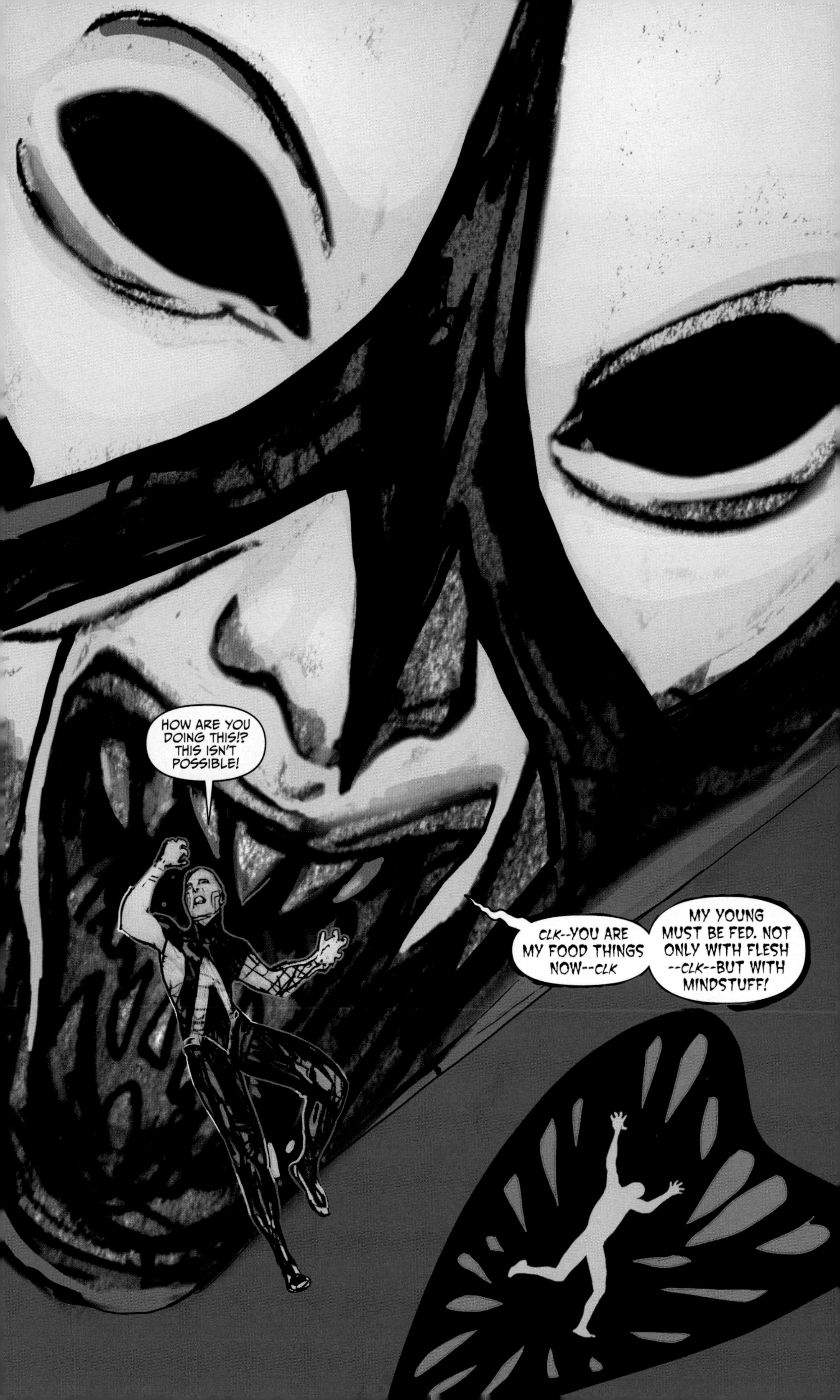

HOW ARE YOU DOING THIS!? THIS ISN'T POSSIBLE!
CLK--YOU ARE MY FOOD THINGS NOW--CLK
MY YOUNG MUST BE FED. NOT ONLY WITH FLESH --CLK--BUT WITH MINDSTUFF!

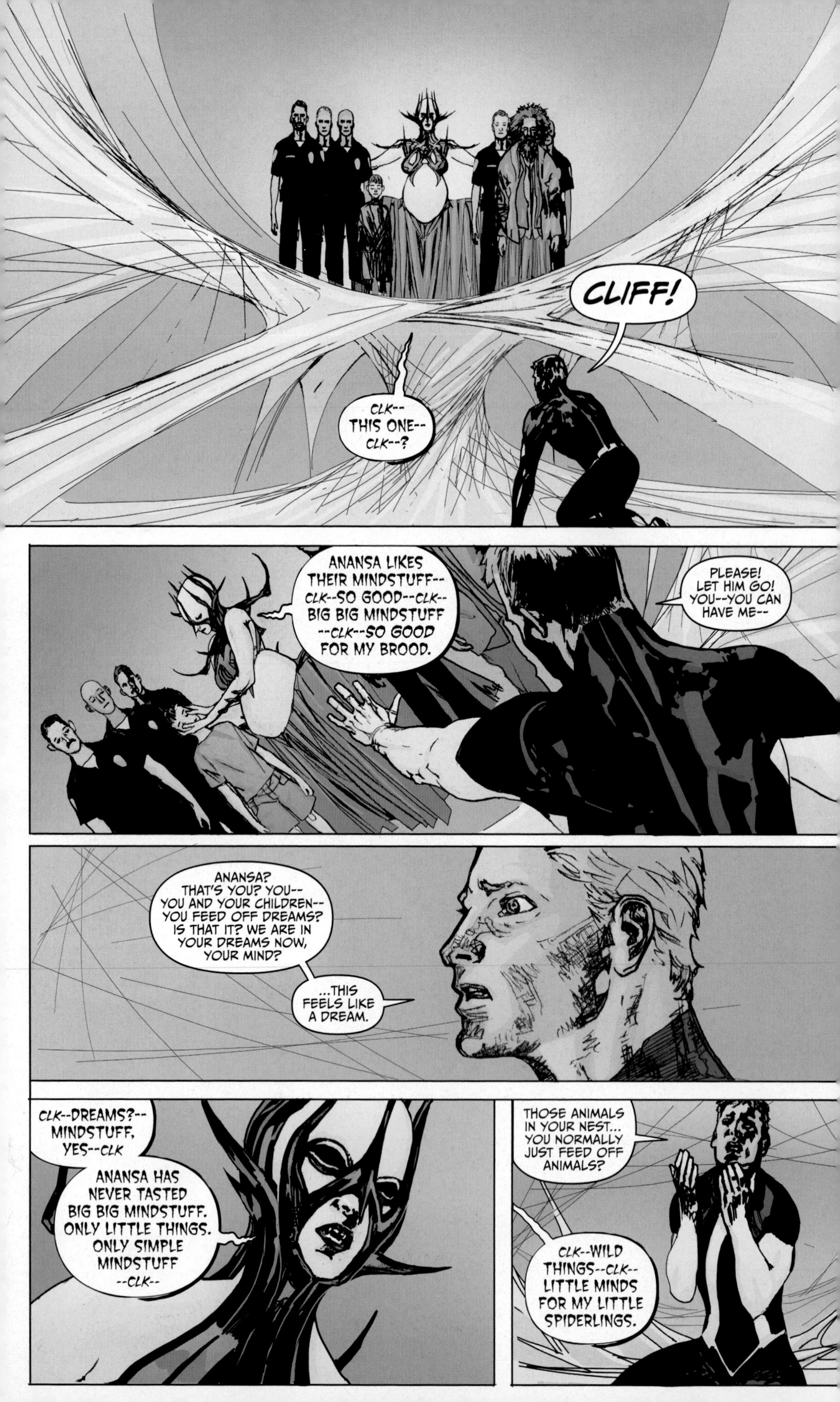
CLIFF!
CLK-- THIS ONE-- CLK--?
ANANSA LIKES THEIR MINDSTUFF-- CLK--SO GOOD--CLK-- BIG BIG MINDSTUFF --CLK--SO GOOD FOR MY BROOD.
PLEASE! LET HIM GO! YOU--YOU CAN HAVE ME--
ANANSA? THAT'S YOU? YOU-- YOU AND YOUR CHILDREN-- YOU FEED OFF DREAMS? IS THAT IT? WE ARE IN YOUR DREAMS NOW, YOUR MIND?
...THIS FEELS LIKE A DREAM.
CLK--DREAMS?-- MINDSTUFF, YES--CLK
ANANSA HAS NEVER TASTED BIG BIG MINDSTUFF. ONLY LITTLE THINGS. ONLY SIMPLE MINDSTUFF --CLK--
THOSE ANIMALS IN YOUR NEST... YOU NORMALLY JUST FEED OFF ANIMALS?
CLK--WILD THINGS--CLK-- LITTLE MINDS FOR MY LITTLE SPIDERLINGS.

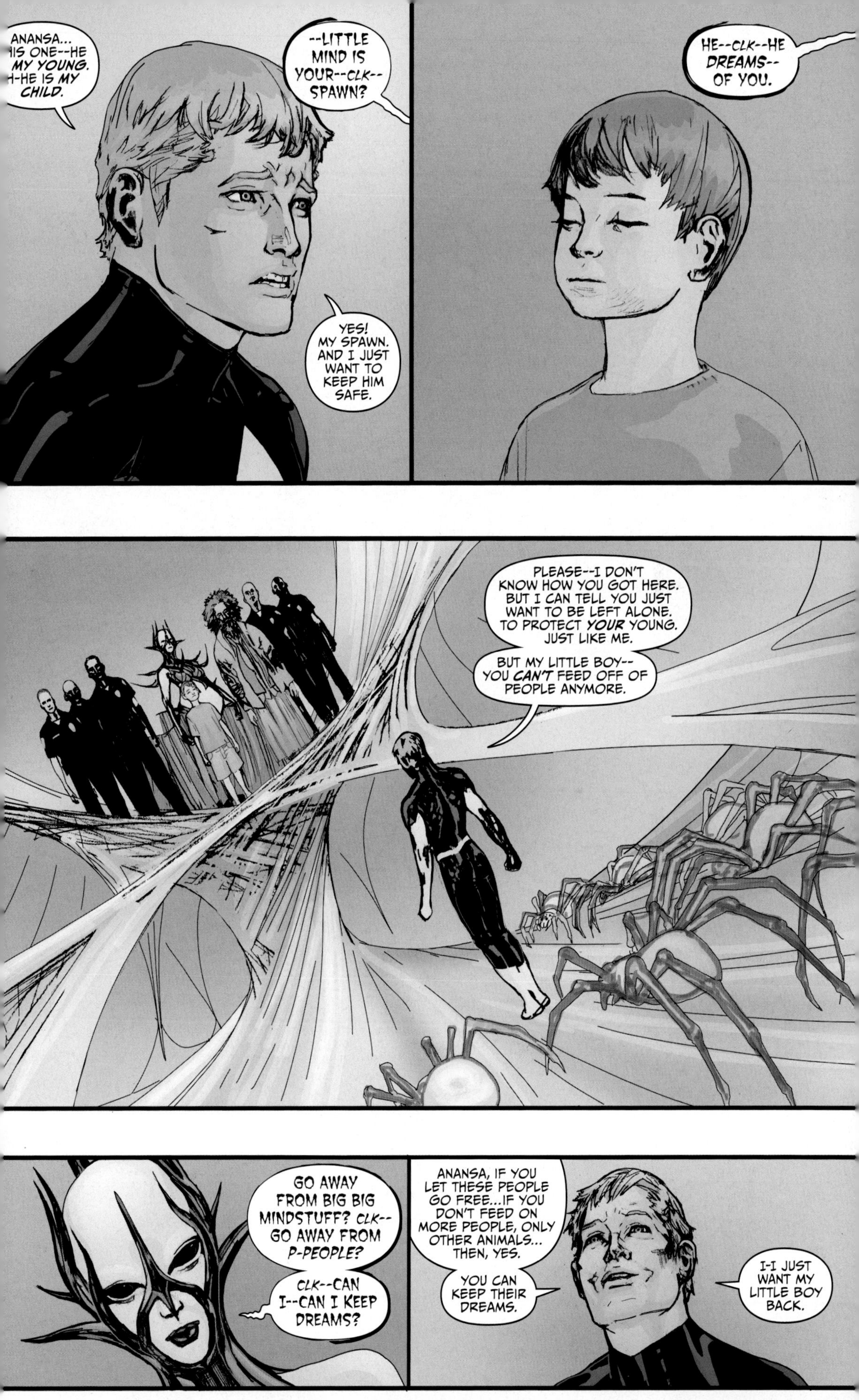

ANANSA... HIS ONE--HE MY YOUNG. H-HE IS MY CHILD.
--LITTLE MIND IS YOUR--CLK-- SPAWN?
YES! MY SPAWN. AND I JUST WANT TO KEEP HIM SAFE.
HE--CLK--HE DREAMS-- OF YOU.
PLEASE--I DON'T KNOW HOW YOU GOT HERE. BUT I CAN TELL YOU JUST WANT TO BE LEFT ALONE. TO PROTECT YOUR YOUNG. JUST LIKE ME.
BUT MY LITTLE BOY-- YOU CAN'T FEED OFF OF PEOPLE ANYMORE.
GO AWAY FROM BIG BIG MINDSTUFF? CLK-- GO AWAY FROM P-PEOPLE?
CLK--CAN I--CAN I KEEP DREAMS?
ANANSA, IF YOU LET THESE PEOPLE GO FREE...IF YOU DON'T FEED ON MORE PEOPLE, ONLY OTHER ANIMALS... THEN, YES.
YOU CAN KEEP THEIR DREAMS.
I-I JUST WANT MY LITTLE BOY BACK.

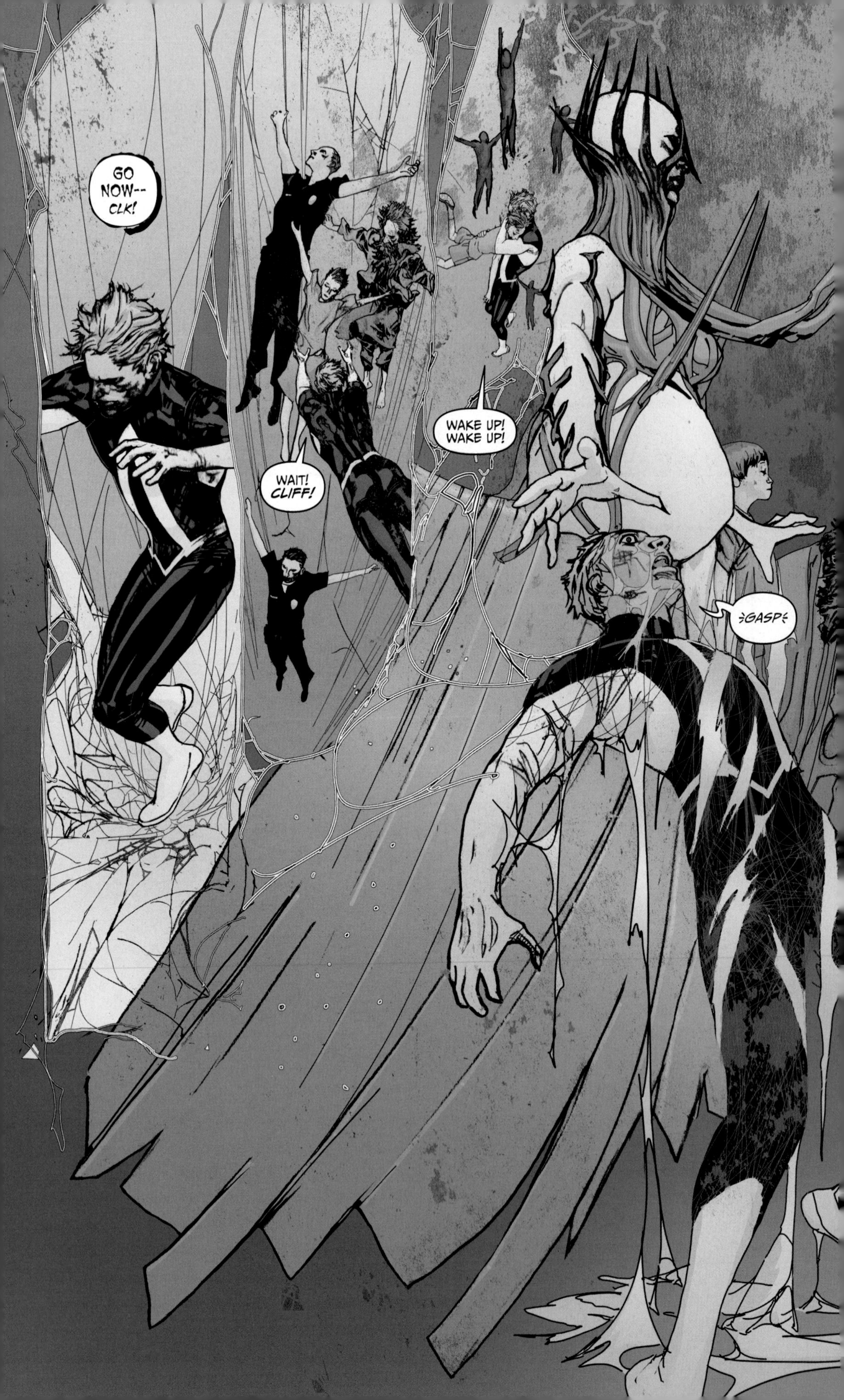
GO NOW-- CLK!
WAIT! CLIFF!
WAKE UP! WAKE UP!
GASP

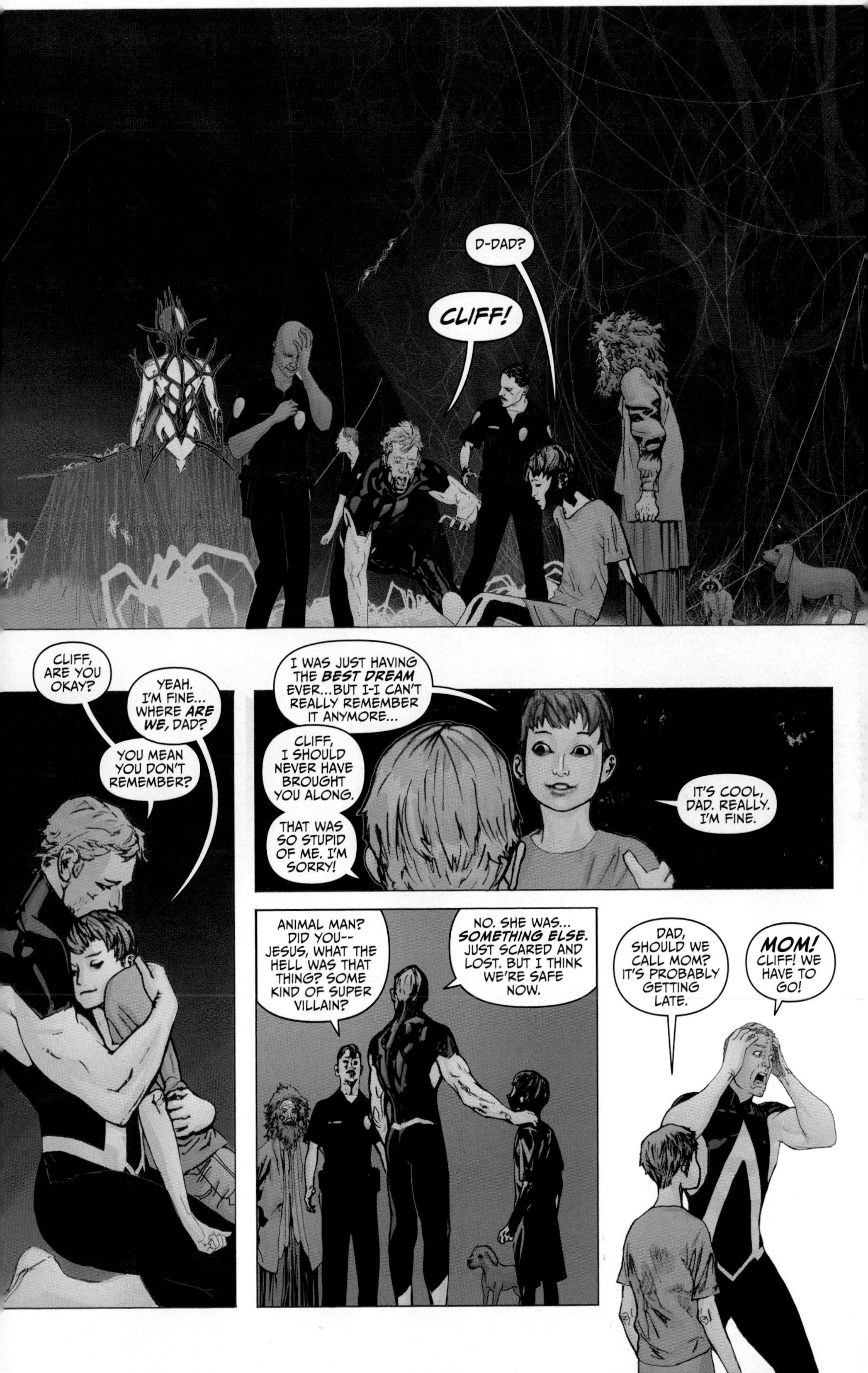
D-DAD?
CLIFF!
CLIFF, ARE YOU OKAY?
YEAH. I'M FINE... WHERE ARE WE, DAD?
YOU MEAN YOU DON'T REMEMBER?
I WAS JUST HAVING THE BEST DREAM EVER...BUT I-I CAN'T REALLY REMEMBER IT ANYMORE...
CLIFF, I SHOULD NEVER HAVE BROUGHT YOU ALONG.
THAT WAS SO STUPID OF ME. I'M SORRY!
IT'S COOL, DAD. REALLY. I'M FINE.
ANIMAL MAN? DID YOU-- JESUS, WHAT THE HELL WAS THAT THING? SOME KIND OF SUPER VILLAIN?
NO. SHE WAS... SOMETHING ELSE. JUST SCARED AND LOST. BUT I THINK WE'RE SAFE NOW.
DAD, SHOULD WE CALL MOM? IT'S PROBABLY GETTING LATE.
MOM! CLIFF! WE HAVE TO GO!

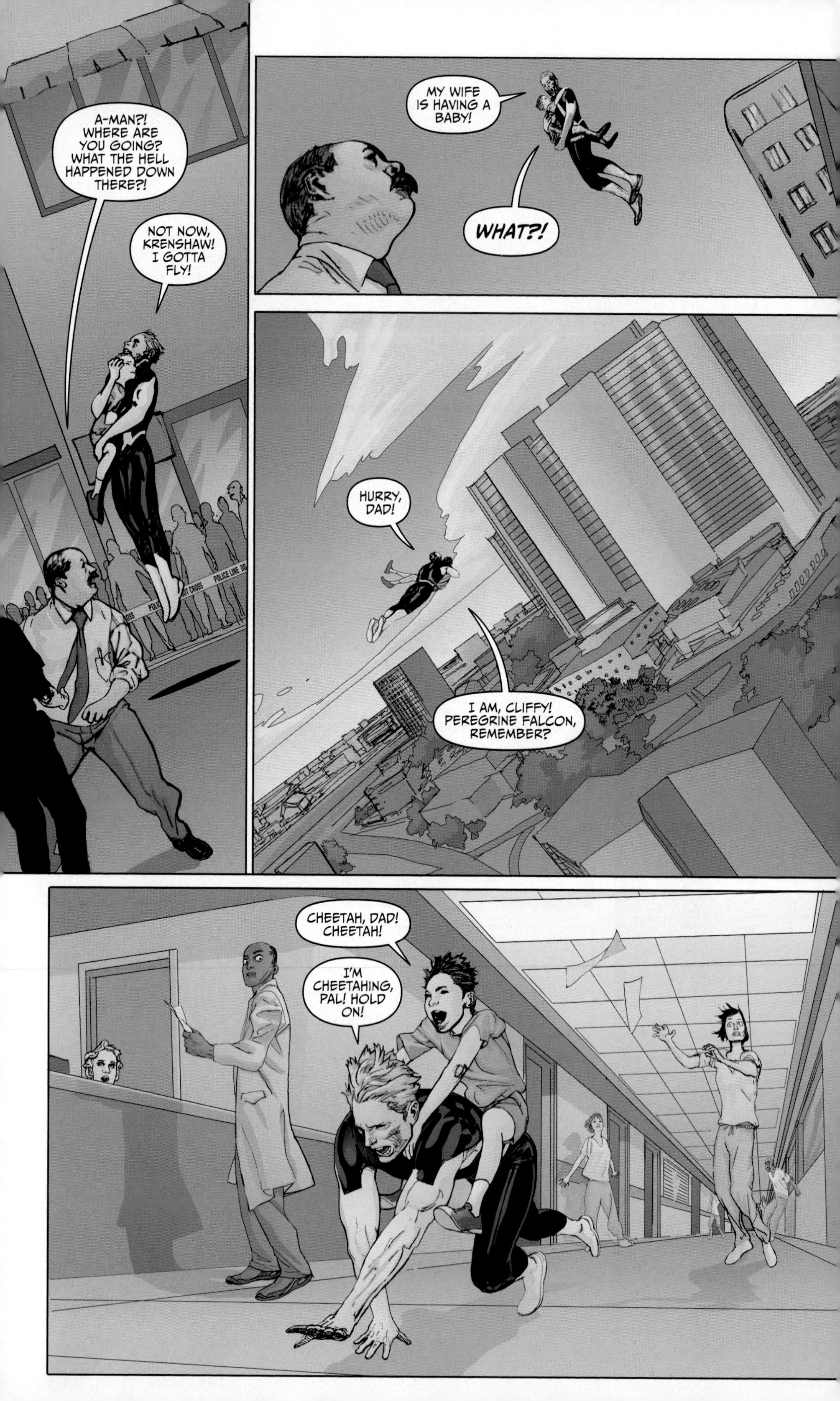
A-MAN?! WHERE ARE YOU GOING? WHAT THE HELL HAPPENED DOWN THERE?!
NOT NOW, KRENSHAW! I GOTTA FLY!
POLICE LINE DO NOT CROSS
MY WIFE IS HAVING A BABY!
WHAT?!
HURRY, DAD!
I AM, CLIFFY! PEREGRINE FALCON, REMEMBER?
CHEETAH, DAD! CHEETAH!
I'M CHEETAHING, PAL! HOLD ON!

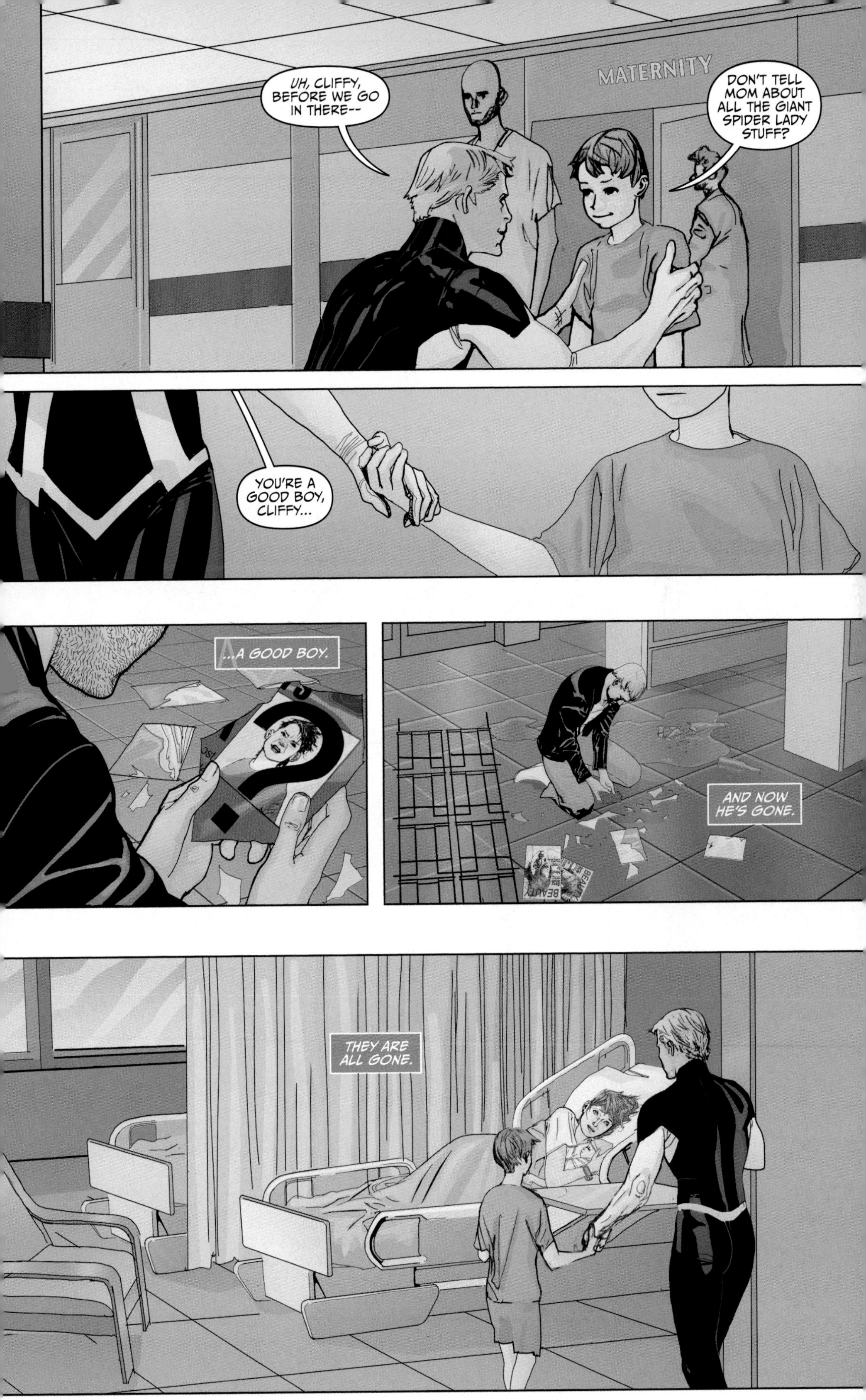
MATERNITY
UH, CLIFFY, BEFORE WE GO IN THERE--
DON'T TELL MOM ABOUT ALL THE GIANT SPIDER LADY STUFF?
YOU'RE A GOOD BOY, CLIFFY...
...A GOOD BOY.
AND NOW HE'S GONE.
THEY ARE ALL GONE.

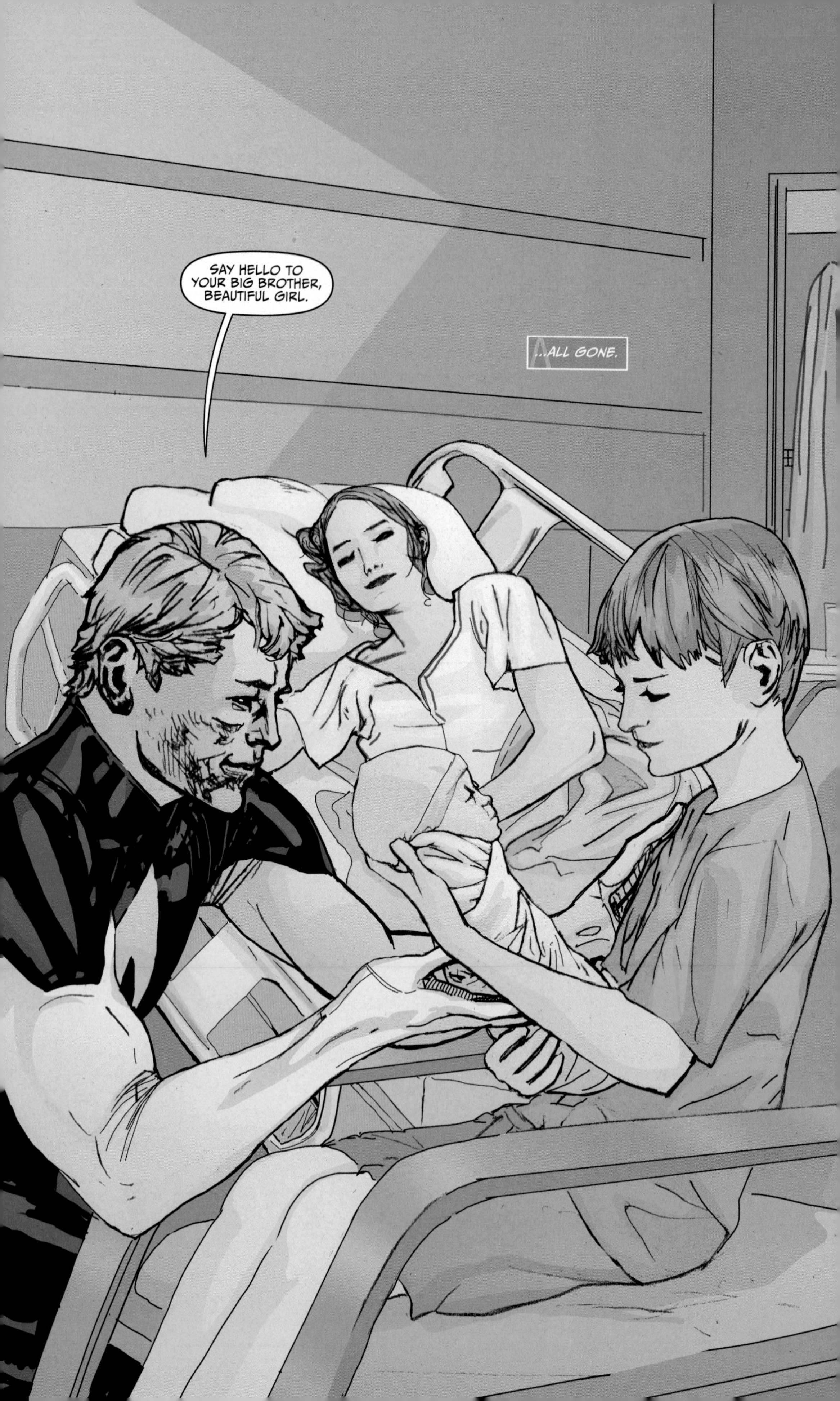
SAY HELLO TO YOUR BIG BROTHER, BEAUTIFUL GIRL.
...ALL GONE.

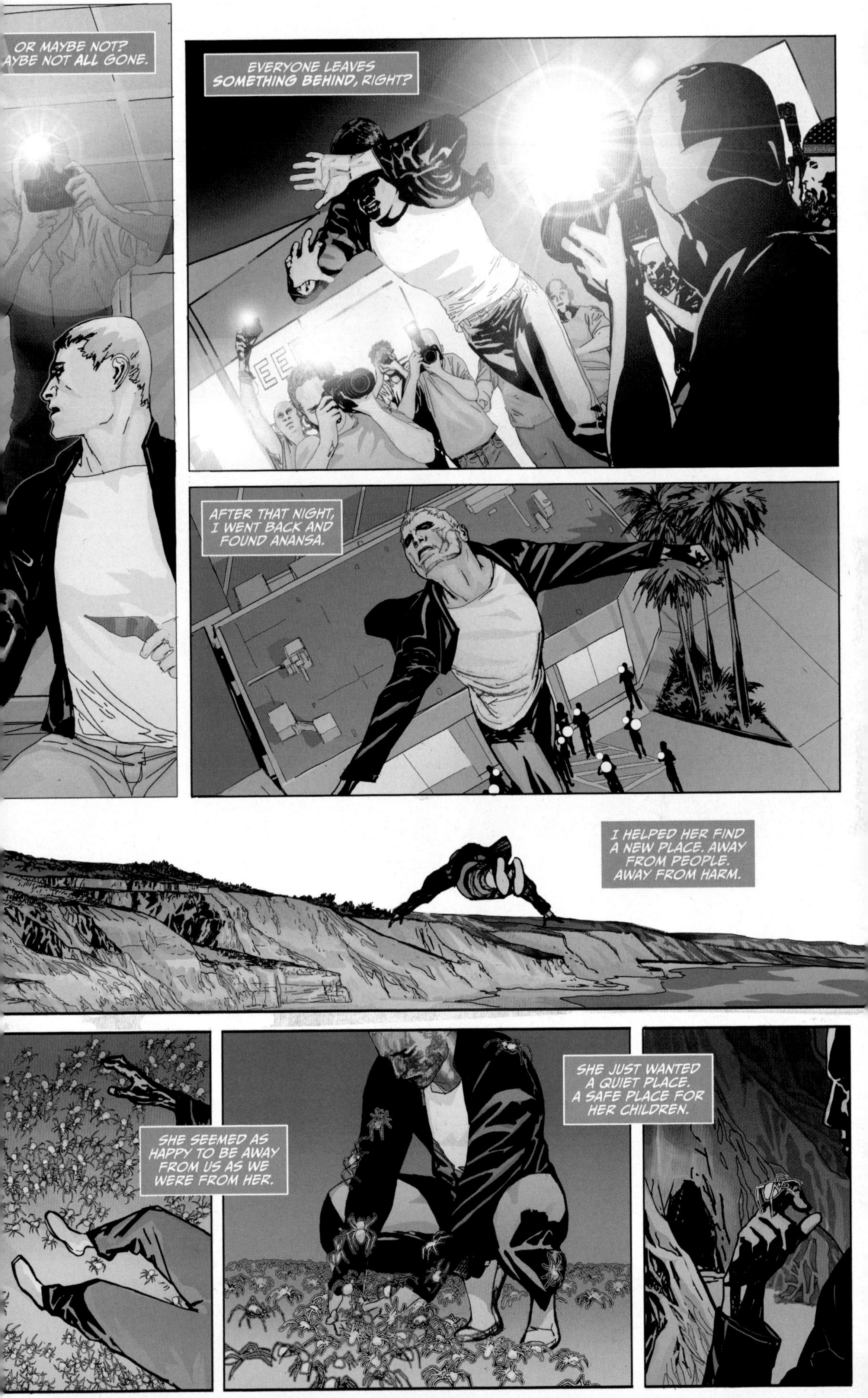
OR MAYBE NOT?
AYBE NOT ALL GONE.
EVERYONE LEAVES SOMETHING BEHIND, RIGHT?
AFTER THAT NIGHT, I WENT BACK AND FOUND ANANSA.
I HELPED HER FIND A NEW PLACE. AWAY FROM PEOPLE. AWAY FROM HARM.
SHE SEEMED AS HAPPY TO BE AWAY FROM US AS WE WERE FROM HER.
SHE JUST WANTED A QUIET PLACE. A SAFE PLACE FOR HER CHILDREN.

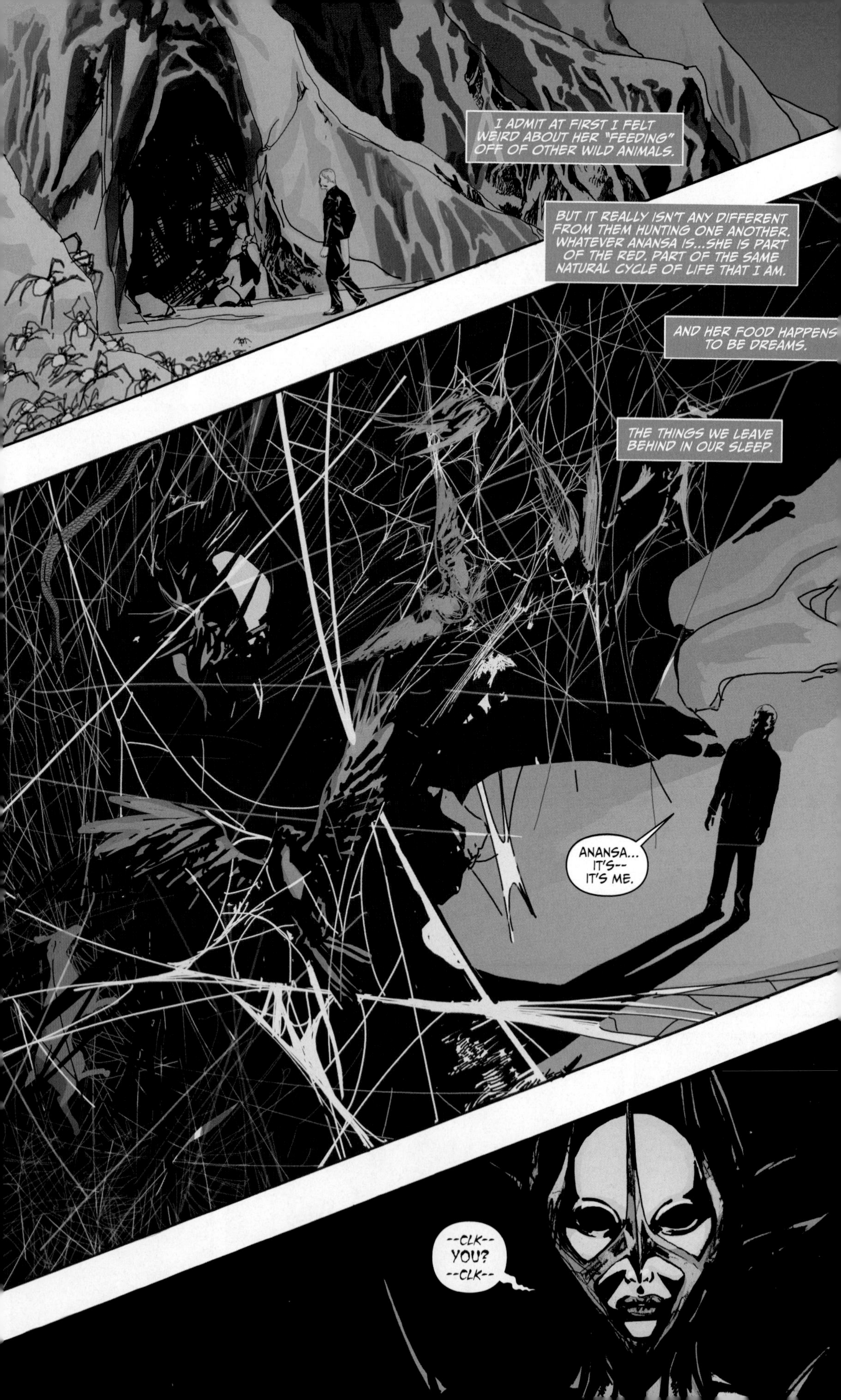

I ADMIT AT FIRST I FELT WEIRD ABOUT HER "FEEDING" OFF OF OTHER WILD ANIMALS.
BUT IT REALLY ISN'T ANY DIFFERENT FROM THEM HUNTING ONE ANOTHER. WHATEVER ANANSA IS...SHE IS PART OF THE RED. PART OF THE SAME NATURAL CYCLE OF LIFE THAT I AM.
AND HER FOOD HAPPENS TO BE DREAMS.
THE THINGS WE LEAVE BEHIND IN OUR SLEEP.
ANANSA... IT'S-- IT'S ME.
--CLK-- YOU? --CLK--

...YOU!

YES. DO YOU REMEMBER?

--CLK-- REMEMBER-- YES--ANANSA REMEMBER --CLK--

I--MY CHILD. MY LITTLE ONE. HE IS GONE. I--I COULDN'T PROTECT HIM. I LOST HIM.

--CLK-- LITTLE SPAWN IS GONE --CLK--

PLEASE. I--I JUST NEED TO HAVE *SOMETHING* OF HIM.

I THOUGHT--

--CLK-- YOU WANT HIS MINDSTUFF--YOU WANT HIS DREAM?

Y-YES...

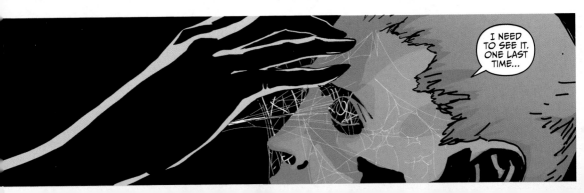

I NEED TO SEE IT. ONE LAST TIME...

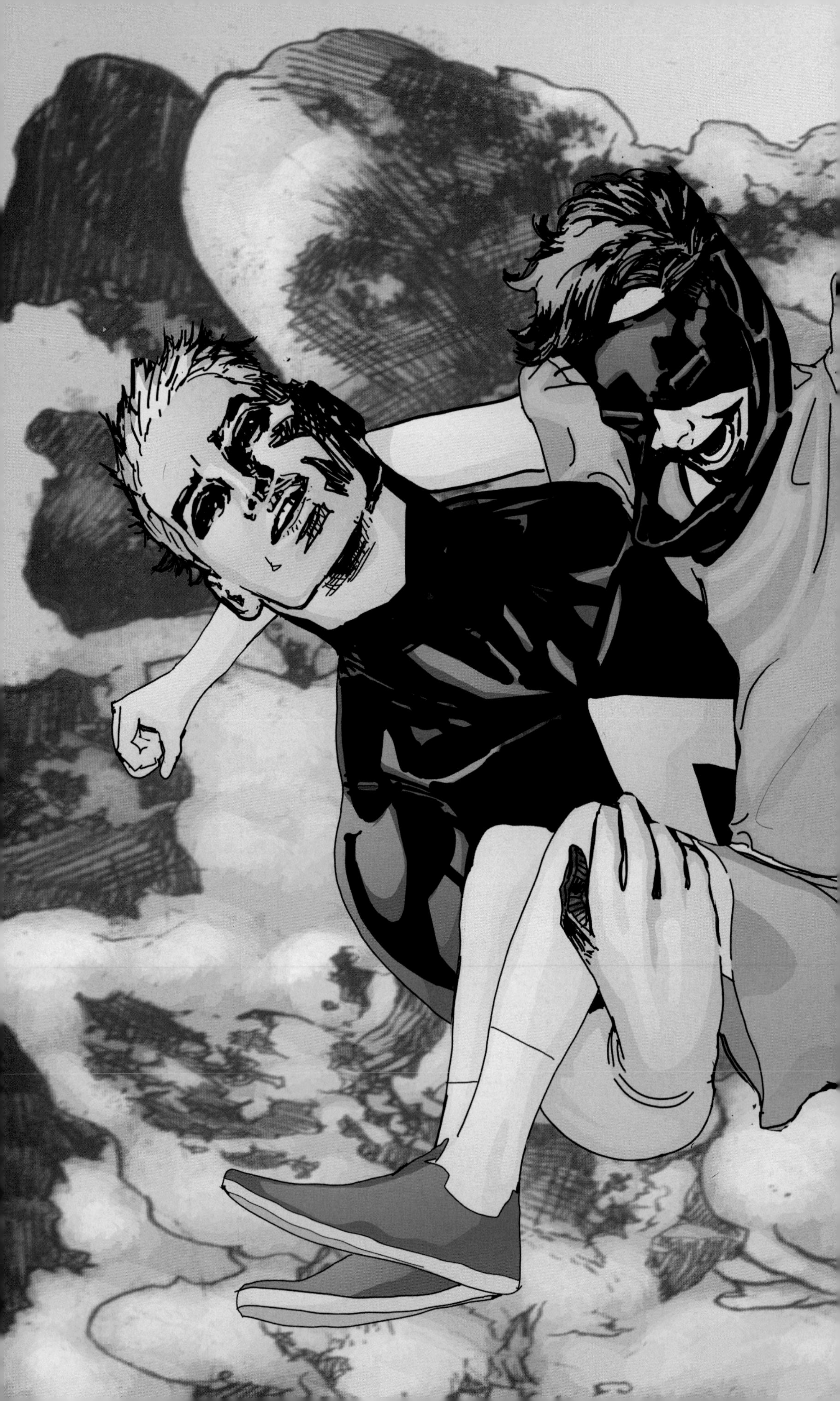

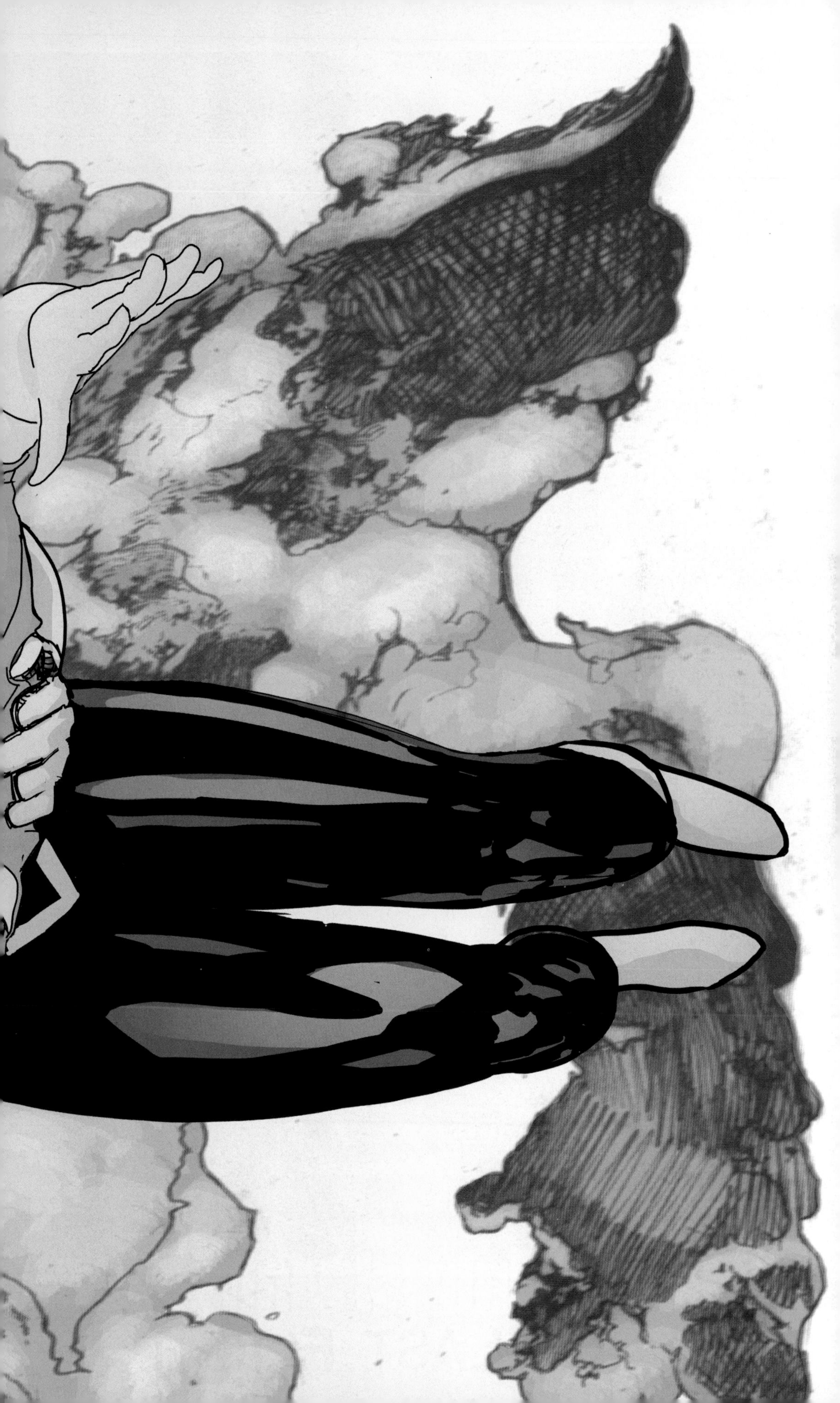

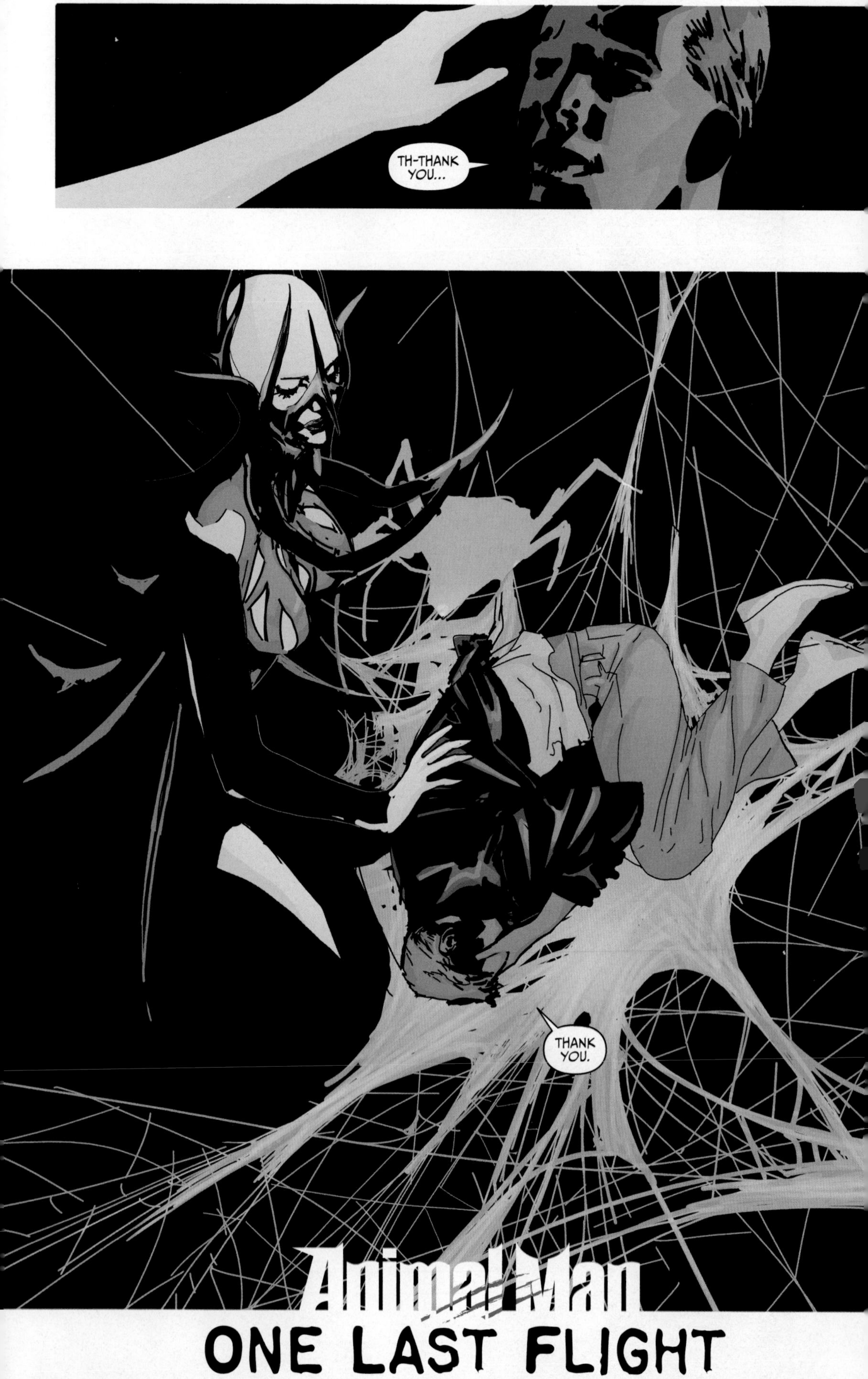
TH-THANK YOU...
THANK YOU.
Animal Man
ONE LAST FLIGHT

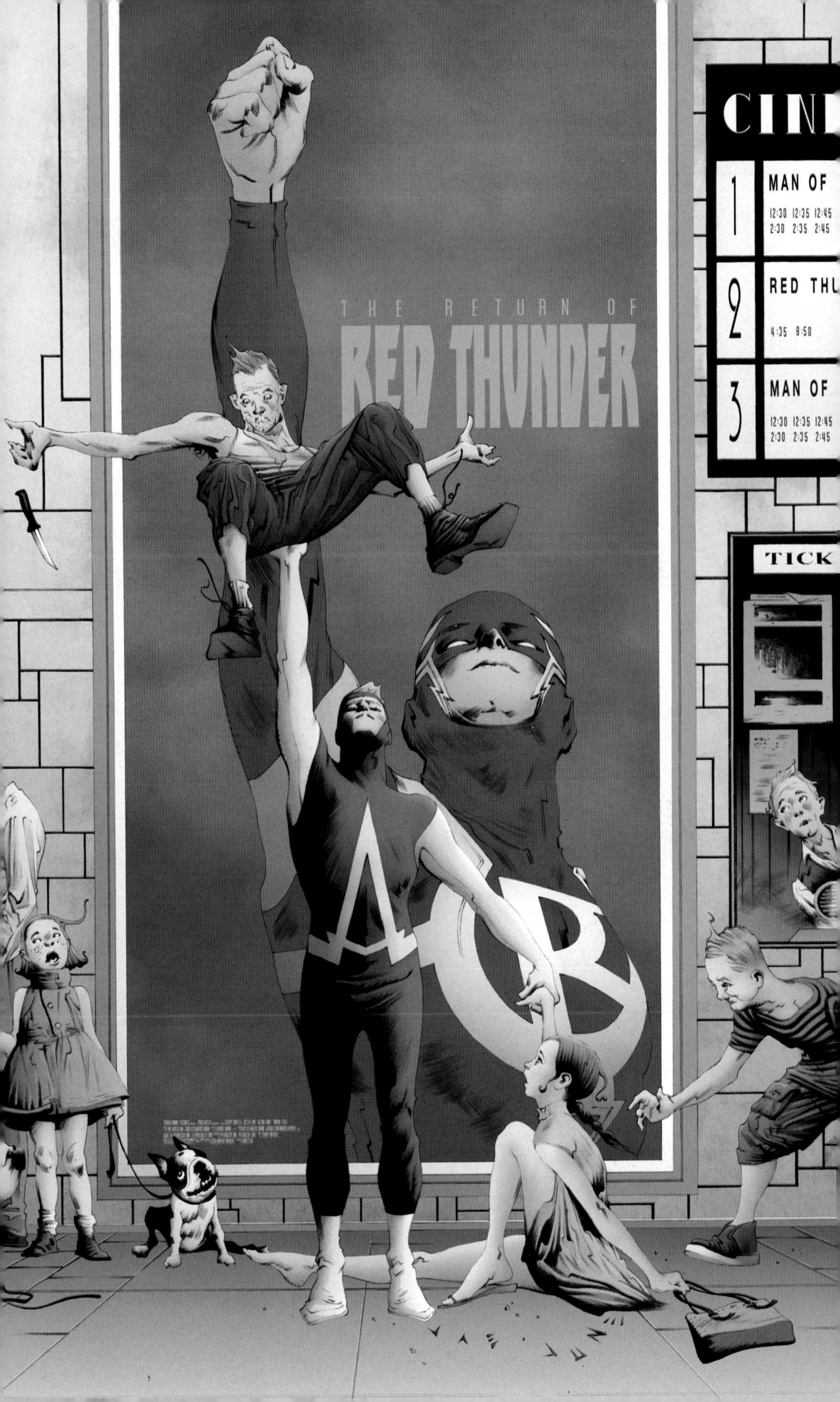
THE RETURN OF
RED THUNDER
CIN
1
MAN OF
12:30 12:35 12:45
2:30 2:35 2:45
2
RED THU
4:35 9:50
3
MAN OF
12:30 12:35 12:45
2:30 2:35 2:45
TICK

JEFF LEMIRE
writer

JOHN PAUL LEON
artist

TIMOTHY GREEN II & JOSEPH SILVER
additional art

JAE LEE with JUNE CHUNG
cover artists

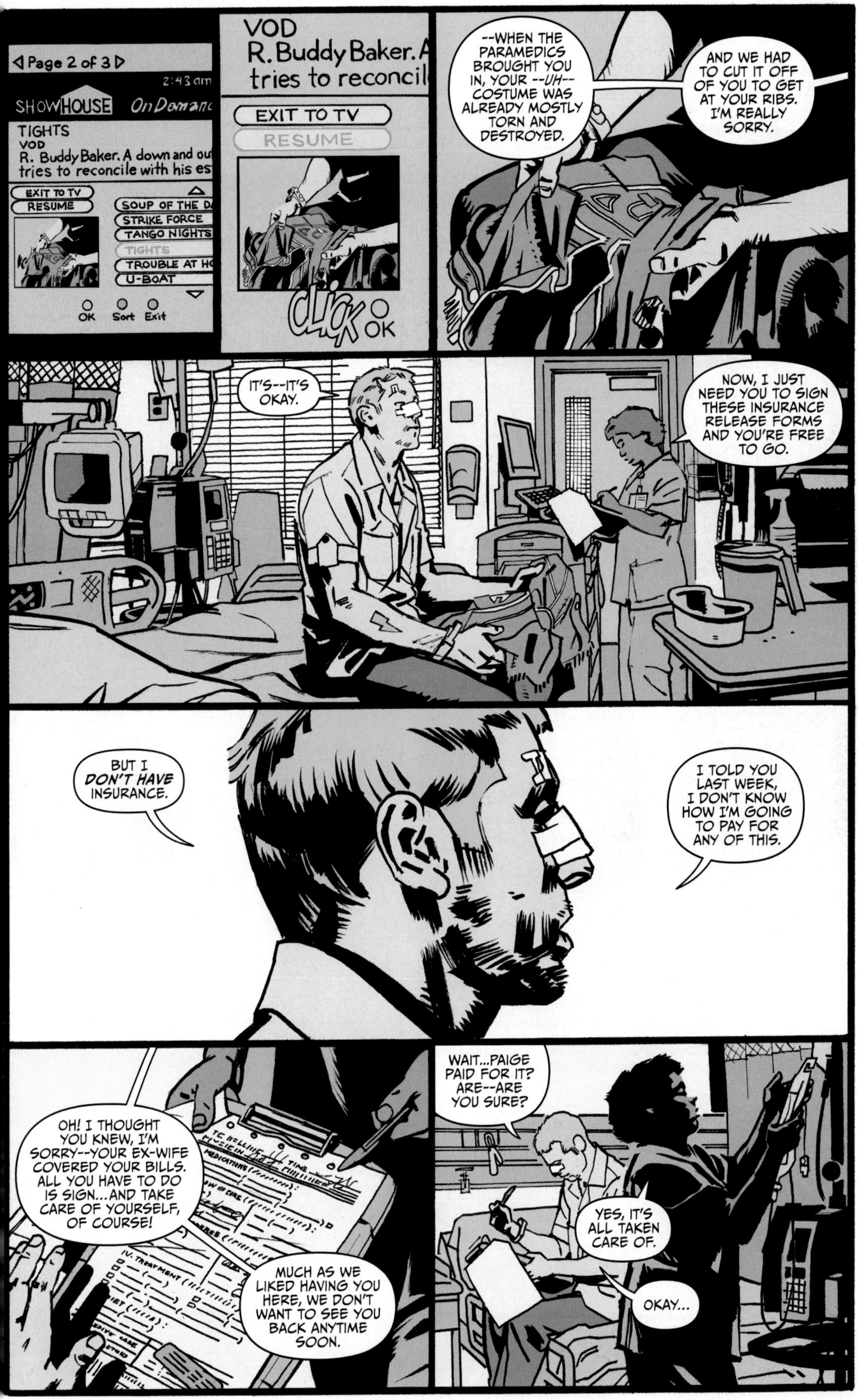
◁ Page 2 of 3 ▷
2:43 am
SHOWHOUSE On Demand
TIGHTS
VOD
R. Buddy Baker. A down and ou
tries to reconcile with his es
EXIT TO TV
RESUME
SOUP OF THE DA
STRIKE FORCE
TANGO NIGHTS
TIGHTS
TROUBLE AT HO
U-BOAT
OK Sort Exit
VOD
R. Buddy Baker. A
tries to reconcil
EXIT TO TV
RESUME
CLICK
OK
--WHEN THE PARAMEDICS BROUGHT YOU IN, YOUR --UH-- COSTUME WAS ALREADY MOSTLY TORN AND DESTROYED.
AND WE HAD TO CUT IT OFF OF YOU TO GET AT YOUR RIBS. I'M REALLY SORRY.
IT'S--IT'S OKAY.
NOW, I JUST NEED YOU TO SIGN THESE INSURANCE RELEASE FORMS AND YOU'RE FREE TO GO.
BUT I *DON'T HAVE* INSURANCE.
I TOLD YOU LAST WEEK, I DON'T KNOW HOW I'M GOING TO PAY FOR ANY OF THIS.
OH! I THOUGHT YOU KNEW, I'M SORRY--YOUR EX-WIFE COVERED YOUR BILLS. ALL YOU HAVE TO DO IS SIGN...AND TAKE CARE OF YOURSELF, OF COURSE!
MUCH AS WE LIKED HAVING YOU HERE, WE DON'T WANT TO SEE YOU BACK ANYTIME SOON.
WAIT...PAIGE PAID FOR IT? ARE--ARE YOU SURE?
YES, IT'S ALL TAKEN CARE OF.
OKAY...

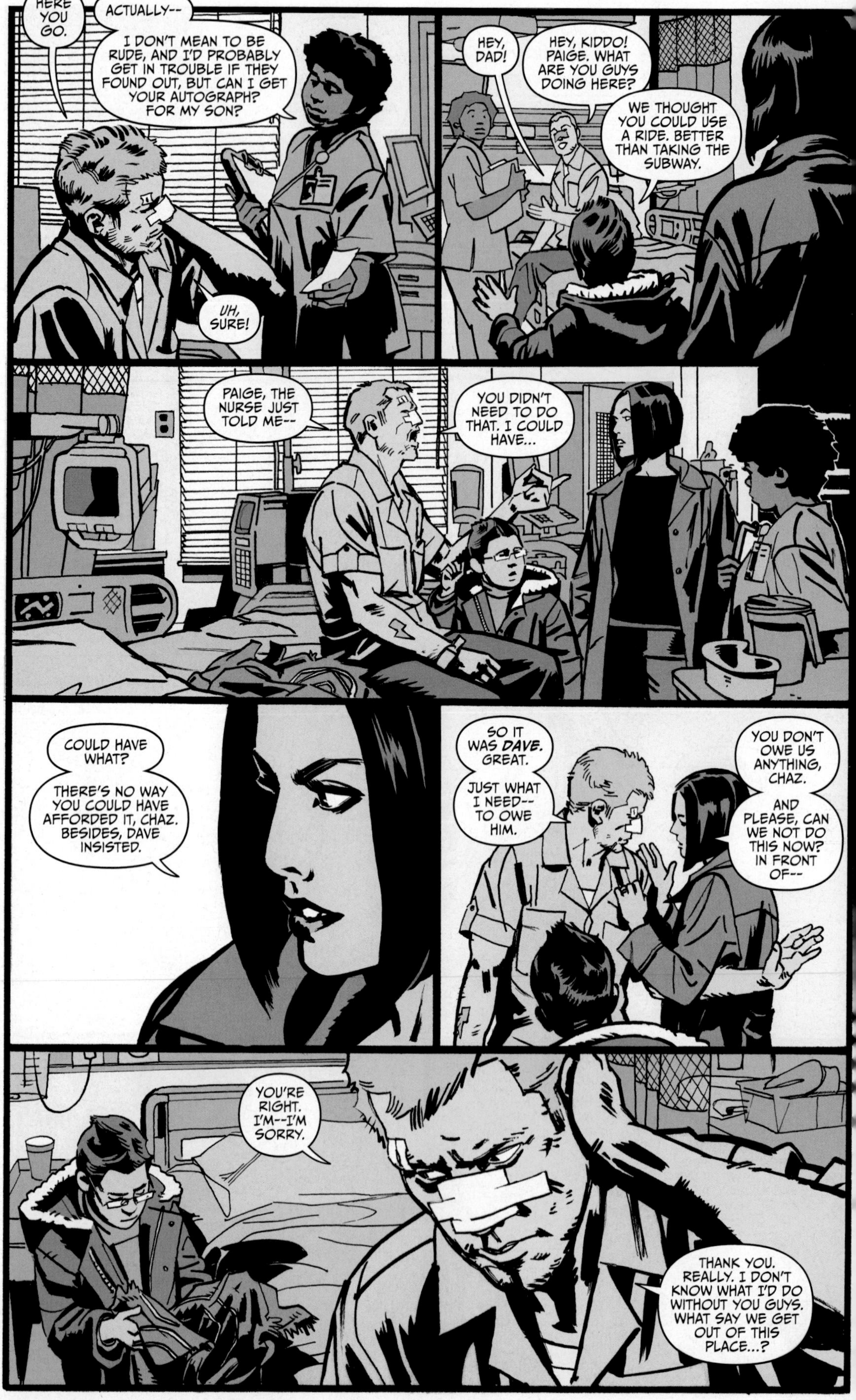
HERE YOU GO.
ACTUALLY--
I DON'T MEAN TO BE RUDE, AND I'D PROBABLY GET IN TROUBLE IF THEY FOUND OUT, BUT CAN I GET YOUR AUTOGRAPH? FOR MY SON?
UH, SURE!
HEY, DAD!
HEY, KIDDO! PAIGE. WHAT ARE YOU GUYS DOING HERE?
WE THOUGHT YOU COULD USE A RIDE. BETTER THAN TAKING THE SUBWAY.
PAIGE, THE NURSE JUST TOLD ME--
YOU DIDN'T NEED TO DO THAT. I COULD HAVE...
COULD HAVE WHAT?
THERE'S NO WAY YOU COULD HAVE AFFORDED IT, CHAZ. BESIDES, DAVE INSISTED.
SO IT WAS DAVE. GREAT.
JUST WHAT I NEED-- TO OWE HIM.
YOU DON'T OWE US ANYTHING, CHAZ.
AND PLEASE, CAN WE NOT DO THIS NOW? IN FRONT OF--
YOU'RE RIGHT. I'M--I'M SORRY.
THANK YOU. REALLY. I DON'T KNOW WHAT I'D DO WITHOUT YOU GUYS. WHAT SAY WE GET OUT OF THIS PLACE...?

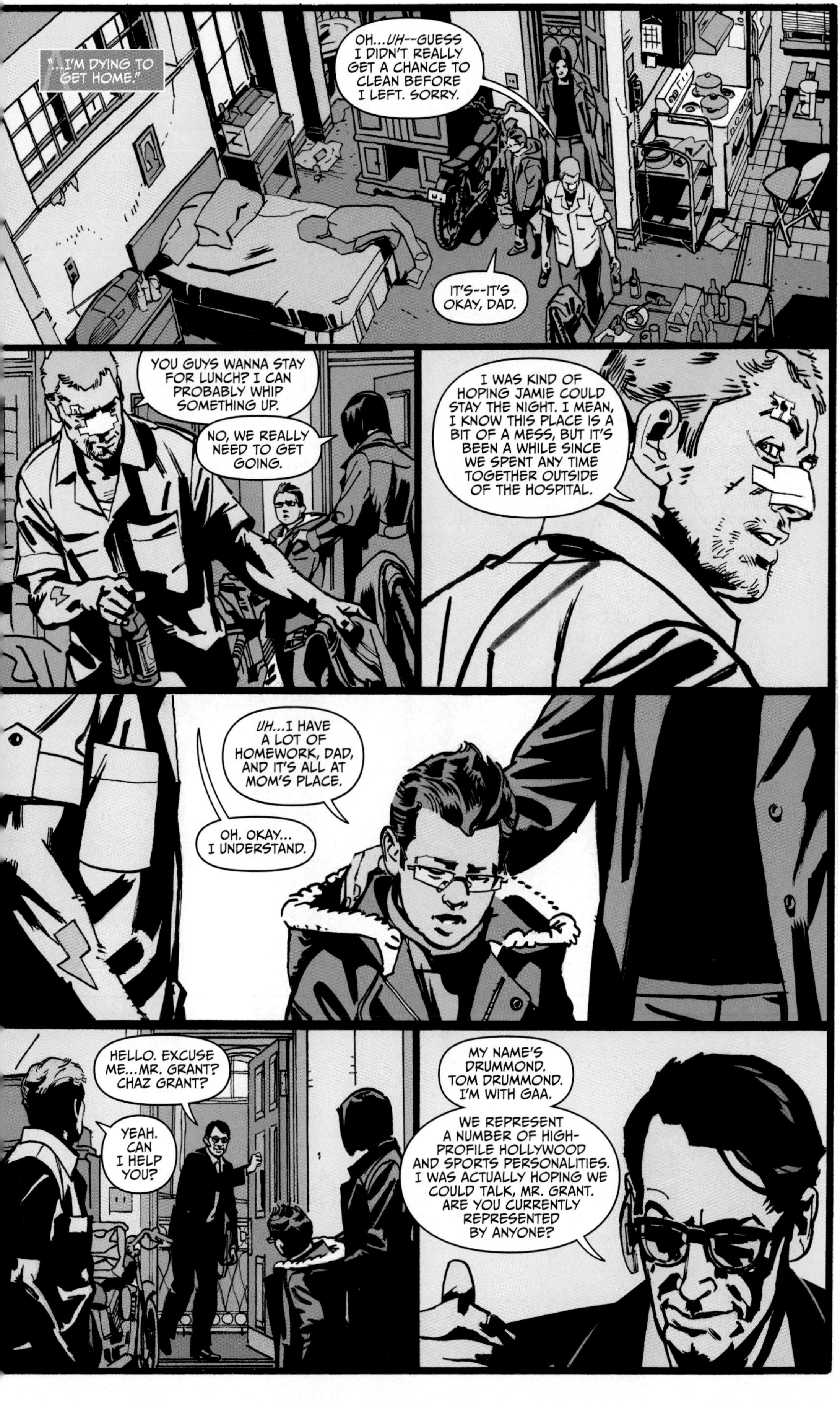

"...I'M DYING TO GET HOME."
OH...UH--GUESS I DIDN'T REALLY GET A CHANCE TO CLEAN BEFORE I LEFT. SORRY.
IT'S--IT'S OKAY, DAD.
YOU GUYS WANNA STAY FOR LUNCH? I CAN PROBABLY WHIP SOMETHING UP.
NO, WE REALLY NEED TO GET GOING.
I WAS KIND OF HOPING JAMIE COULD STAY THE NIGHT. I MEAN, I KNOW THIS PLACE IS A BIT OF A MESS, BUT IT'S BEEN A WHILE SINCE WE SPENT ANY TIME TOGETHER OUTSIDE OF THE HOSPITAL.
UH...I HAVE A LOT OF HOMEWORK, DAD, AND IT'S ALL AT MOM'S PLACE.
OH. OKAY... I UNDERSTAND.
HELLO. EXCUSE ME...MR. GRANT? CHAZ GRANT?
YEAH. CAN I HELP YOU?
MY NAME'S DRUMMOND. TOM DRUMMOND. I'M WITH GAA.
WE REPRESENT A NUMBER OF HIGH-PROFILE HOLLYWOOD AND SPORTS PERSONALITIES. I WAS ACTUALLY HOPING WE COULD TALK, MR. GRANT. ARE YOU CURRENTLY REPRESENTED BY ANYONE?

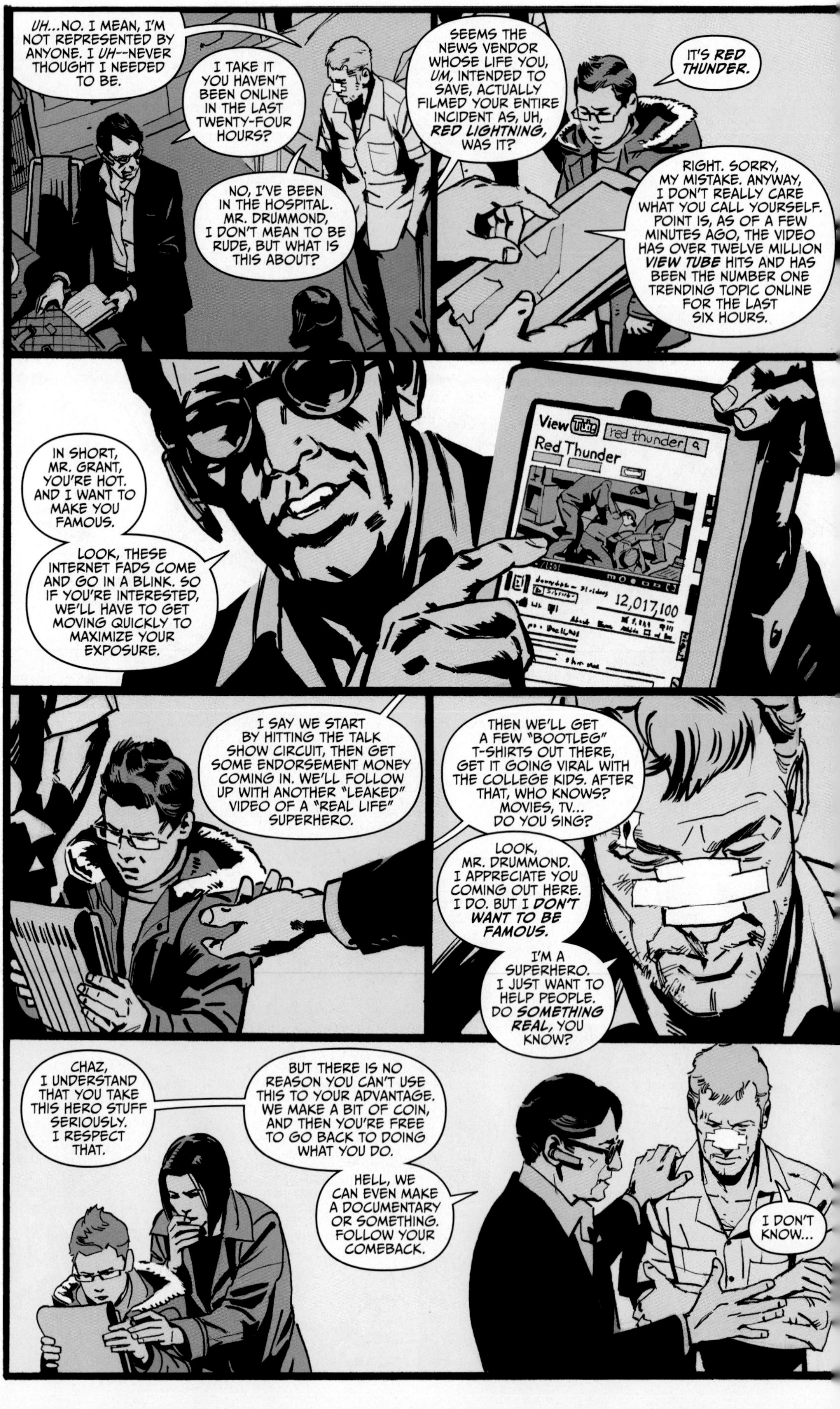
UH...NO. I MEAN, I'M NOT REPRESENTED BY ANYONE. I UH--NEVER THOUGHT I NEEDED TO BE.
I TAKE IT YOU HAVEN'T BEEN ONLINE IN THE LAST TWENTY-FOUR HOURS?
NO, I'VE BEEN IN THE HOSPITAL. MR. DRUMMOND, I DON'T MEAN TO BE RUDE, BUT WHAT IS THIS ABOUT?
SEEMS THE NEWS VENDOR WHOSE LIFE YOU, UM, INTENDED TO SAVE, ACTUALLY FILMED YOUR ENTIRE INCIDENT AS, UH, RED LIGHTNING, WAS IT?
IT'S RED THUNDER.
RIGHT. SORRY, MY MISTAKE. ANYWAY, I DON'T REALLY CARE WHAT YOU CALL YOURSELF. POINT IS, AS OF A FEW MINUTES AGO, THE VIDEO HAS OVER TWELVE MILLION VIEW TUBE HITS AND HAS BEEN THE NUMBER ONE TRENDING TOPIC ONLINE FOR THE LAST SIX HOURS.
IN SHORT, MR. GRANT, YOU'RE HOT. AND I WANT TO MAKE YOU FAMOUS.
LOOK, THESE INTERNET FADS COME AND GO IN A BLINK. SO IF YOU'RE INTERESTED, WE'LL HAVE TO GET MOVING QUICKLY TO MAXIMIZE YOUR EXPOSURE.
View Tube
red thunder
Red Thunder
12,017,100
I SAY WE START BY HITTING THE TALK SHOW CIRCUIT, THEN GET SOME ENDORSEMENT MONEY COMING IN. WE'LL FOLLOW UP WITH ANOTHER "LEAKED" VIDEO OF A "REAL LIFE" SUPERHERO.
THEN WE'LL GET A FEW "BOOTLEG" T-SHIRTS OUT THERE, GET IT GOING VIRAL WITH THE COLLEGE KIDS. AFTER THAT, WHO KNOWS? MOVIES, TV... DO YOU SING?
LOOK, MR. DRUMMOND. I APPRECIATE YOU COMING OUT HERE. I DO. BUT I DON'T WANT TO BE FAMOUS.
I'M A SUPERHERO. I JUST WANT TO HELP PEOPLE. DO SOMETHING REAL, YOU KNOW?
CHAZ, I UNDERSTAND THAT YOU TAKE THIS HERO STUFF SERIOUSLY. I RESPECT THAT.
BUT THERE IS NO REASON YOU CAN'T USE THIS TO YOUR ADVANTAGE. WE MAKE A BIT OF COIN, AND THEN YOU'RE FREE TO GO BACK TO DOING WHAT YOU DO.
HELL, WE CAN EVEN MAKE A DOCUMENTARY OR SOMETHING. FOLLOW YOUR COMEBACK.
I DON'T KNOW...

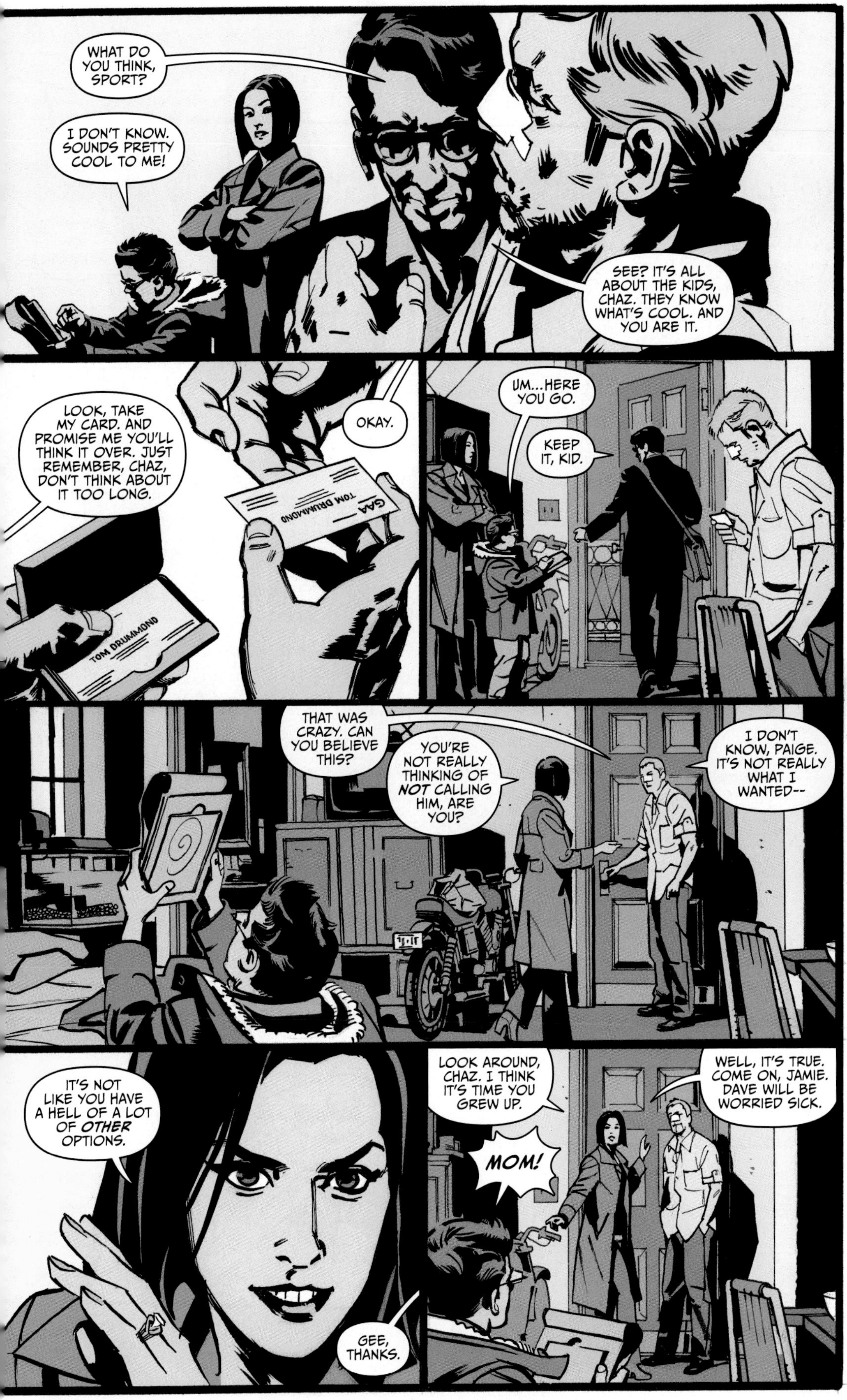

WHAT DO YOU THINK, SPORT?
I DON'T KNOW. SOUNDS PRETTY COOL TO ME!
SEE? IT'S ALL ABOUT THE KIDS, CHAZ. THEY KNOW WHAT'S COOL. AND YOU ARE IT.
LOOK, TAKE MY CARD. AND PROMISE ME YOU'LL THINK IT OVER. JUST REMEMBER, CHAZ, DON'T THINK ABOUT IT TOO LONG.
OKAY.
GAA
TOM DRUMMOND
TOM DRUMMOND
UM...HERE YOU GO.
KEEP IT, KID.
THAT WAS CRAZY. CAN YOU BELIEVE THIS?
YOU'RE NOT REALLY THINKING OF *NOT* CALLING HIM, ARE YOU?
I DON'T KNOW, PAIGE. IT'S NOT REALLY WHAT I WANTED--
IT'S NOT LIKE YOU HAVE A HELL OF A LOT OF *OTHER* OPTIONS.
GEE, THANKS.
LOOK AROUND, CHAZ. I THINK IT'S TIME YOU GREW UP.
WELL, IT'S TRUE. COME ON, JAMIE. DAVE WILL BE WORRIED SICK.
MOM!

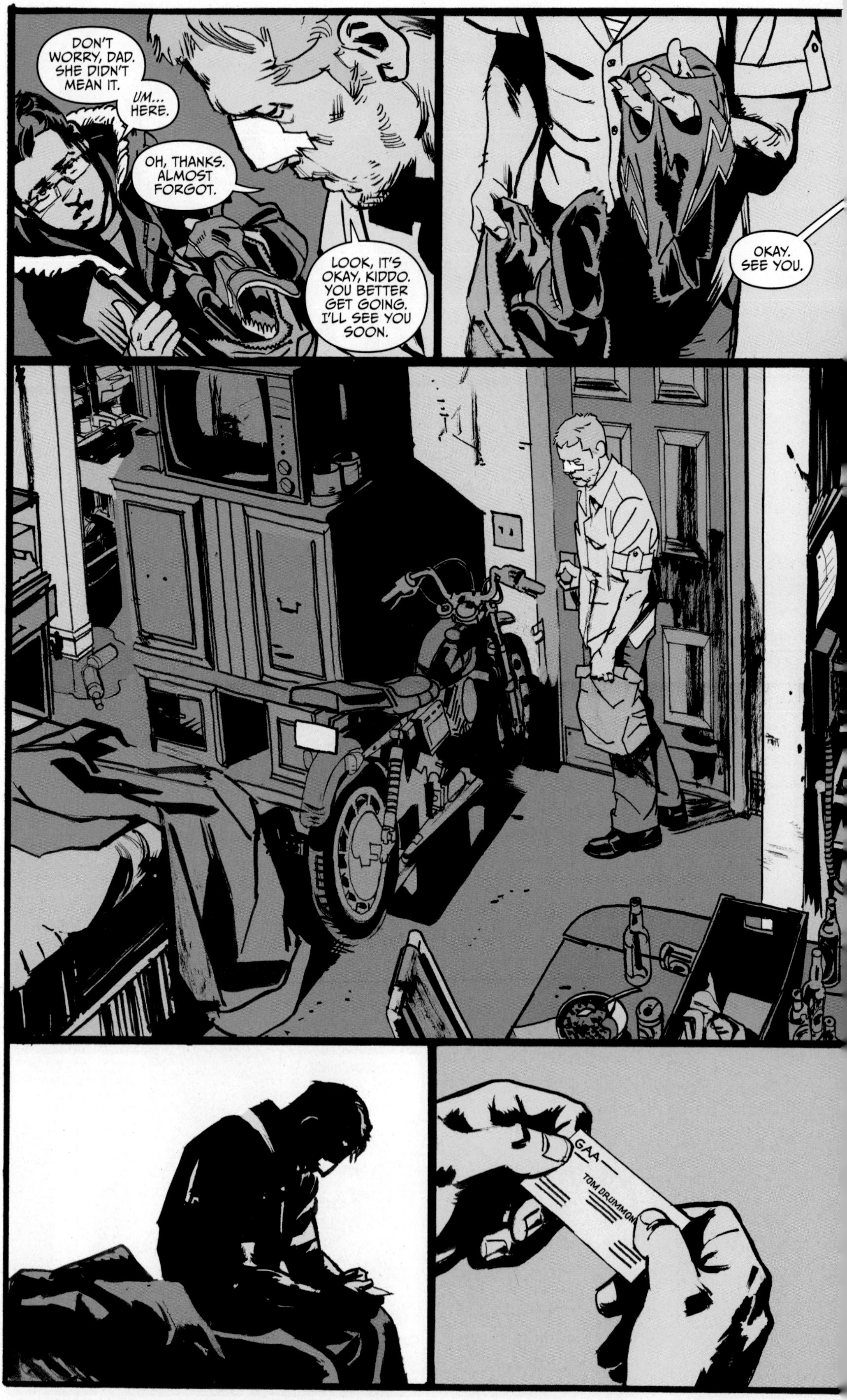

DON'T WORRY, DAD. SHE DIDN'T MEAN IT.
UM... HERE.
OH, THANKS. ALMOST FORGOT.
LOOK, IT'S OKAY, KIDDO. YOU BETTER GET GOING. I'LL SEE YOU SOON.
OKAY. SEE YOU.
GAA
TOM DRUMMON

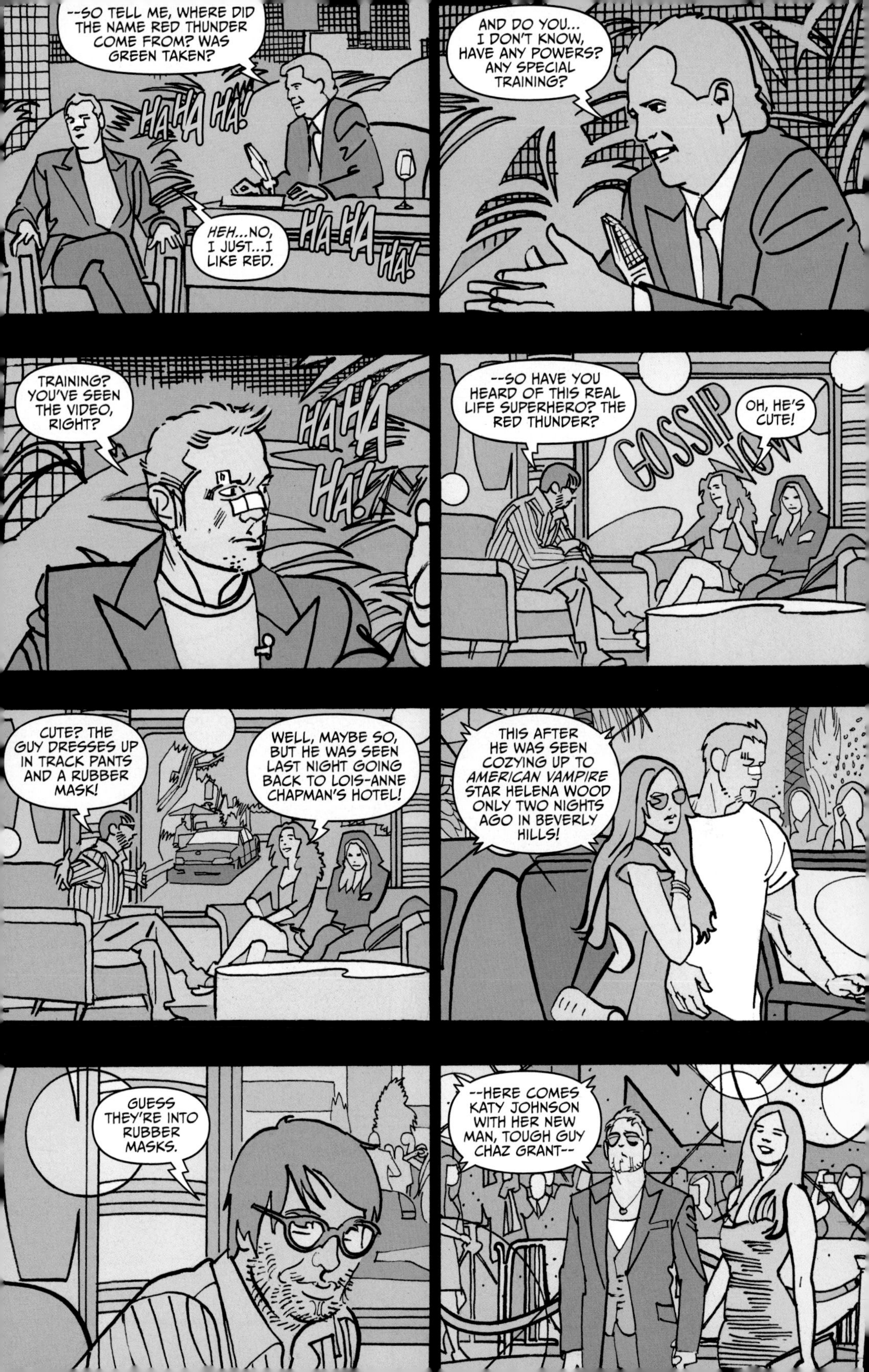
--SO TELL ME, WHERE DID THE NAME RED THUNDER COME FROM? WAS GREEN TAKEN?
HA HA HA!
HEH...NO, I JUST...I LIKE RED.
HA HA HA HA!
AND DO YOU... I DON'T KNOW, HAVE ANY POWERS? ANY SPECIAL TRAINING?
TRAINING? YOU'VE SEEN THE VIDEO, RIGHT?
HA HA HA!
--SO HAVE YOU HEARD OF THIS REAL LIFE SUPERHERO? THE RED THUNDER?
GOSSIP NOW
OH, HE'S CUTE!
CUTE? THE GUY DRESSES UP IN TRACK PANTS AND A RUBBER MASK!
WELL, MAYBE SO, BUT HE WAS SEEN LAST NIGHT GOING BACK TO LOIS-ANNE CHAPMAN'S HOTEL!
THIS AFTER HE WAS SEEN COZYING UP TO *AMERICAN VAMPIRE* STAR HELENA WOOD ONLY TWO NIGHTS AGO IN BEVERLY HILLS!
GUESS THEY'RE INTO RUBBER MASKS.
--HERE COMES KATY JOHNSON WITH HER NEW MAN, TOUGH GUY CHAZ GRANT--

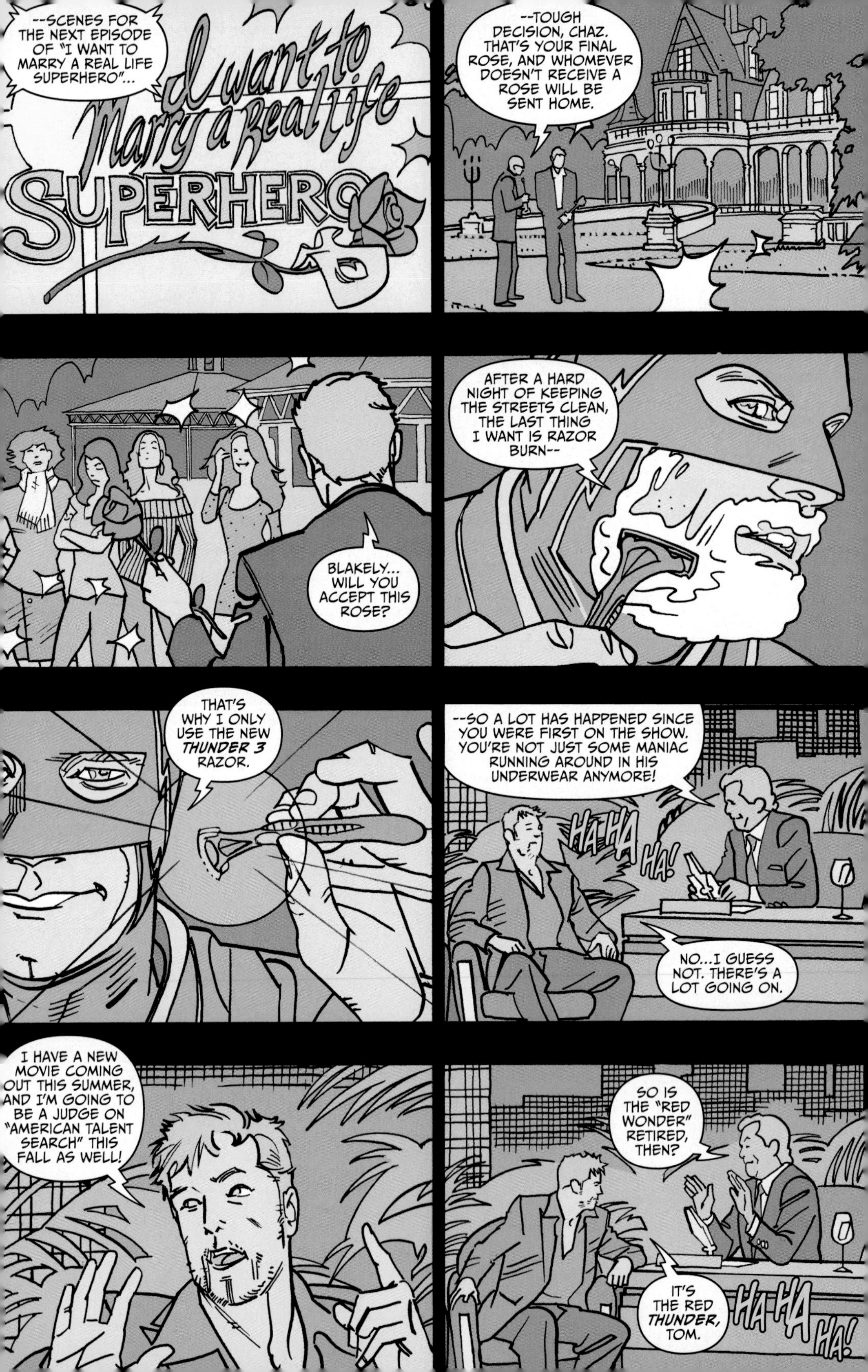
--SCENES FOR THE NEXT EPISODE OF "I WANT TO MARRY A REAL LIFE SUPERHERO"...
I want to Marry a Real Life SUPERHERO
--TOUGH DECISION, CHAZ. THAT'S YOUR FINAL ROSE, AND WHOMEVER DOESN'T RECEIVE A ROSE WILL BE SENT HOME.
BLAKELY... WILL YOU ACCEPT THIS ROSE?
AFTER A HARD NIGHT OF KEEPING THE STREETS CLEAN, THE LAST THING I WANT IS RAZOR BURN--
THAT'S WHY I ONLY USE THE NEW THUNDER 3 RAZOR.
--SO A LOT HAS HAPPENED SINCE YOU WERE FIRST ON THE SHOW. YOU'RE NOT JUST SOME MANIAC RUNNING AROUND IN HIS UNDERWEAR ANYMORE!
HA HA HA!
NO...I GUESS NOT. THERE'S A LOT GOING ON.
I HAVE A NEW MOVIE COMING OUT THIS SUMMER, AND I'M GOING TO BE A JUDGE ON "AMERICAN TALENT SEARCH" THIS FALL AS WELL!
SO IS THE "RED WONDER" RETIRED, THEN?
IT'S THE RED THUNDER, TOM.
HA HA HA HA!

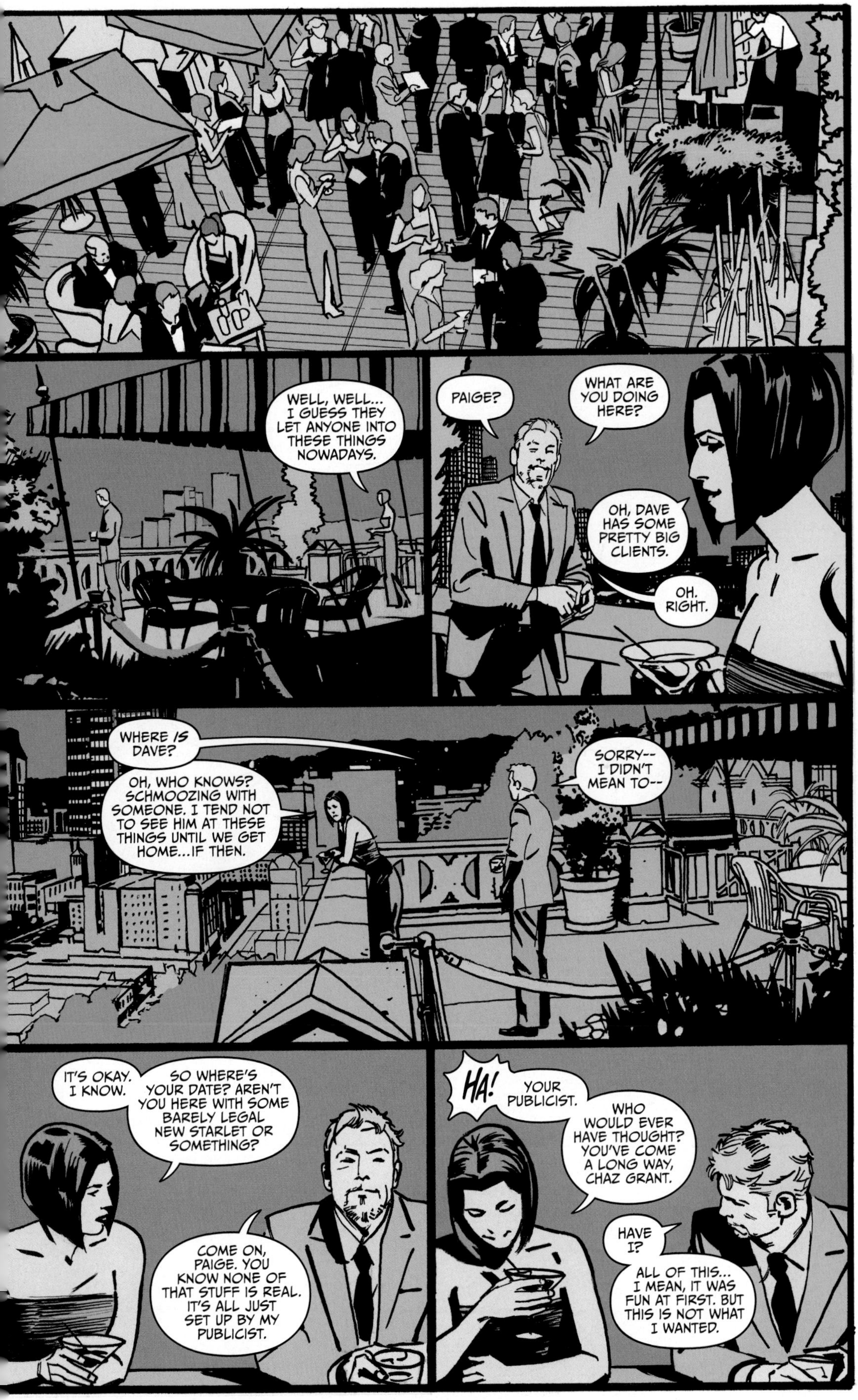
WELL, WELL... I GUESS THEY LET ANYONE INTO THESE THINGS NOWADAYS.
PAIGE?
WHAT ARE YOU DOING HERE?
OH, DAVE HAS SOME PRETTY BIG CLIENTS.
OH. RIGHT.
WHERE IS DAVE?
OH, WHO KNOWS? SCHMOOZING WITH SOMEONE. I TEND NOT TO SEE HIM AT THESE THINGS UNTIL WE GET HOME...IF THEN.
SORRY-- I DIDN'T MEAN TO--
IT'S OKAY. I KNOW.
SO WHERE'S YOUR DATE? AREN'T YOU HERE WITH SOME BARELY LEGAL NEW STARLET OR SOMETHING?
COME ON, PAIGE. YOU KNOW NONE OF THAT STUFF IS REAL. IT'S ALL JUST SET UP BY MY PUBLICIST.
HA!
YOUR PUBLICIST.
WHO WOULD EVER HAVE THOUGHT? YOU'VE COME A LONG WAY, CHAZ GRANT.
HAVE I?
ALL OF THIS... I MEAN, IT WAS FUN AT FIRST. BUT THIS IS NOT WHAT I WANTED.

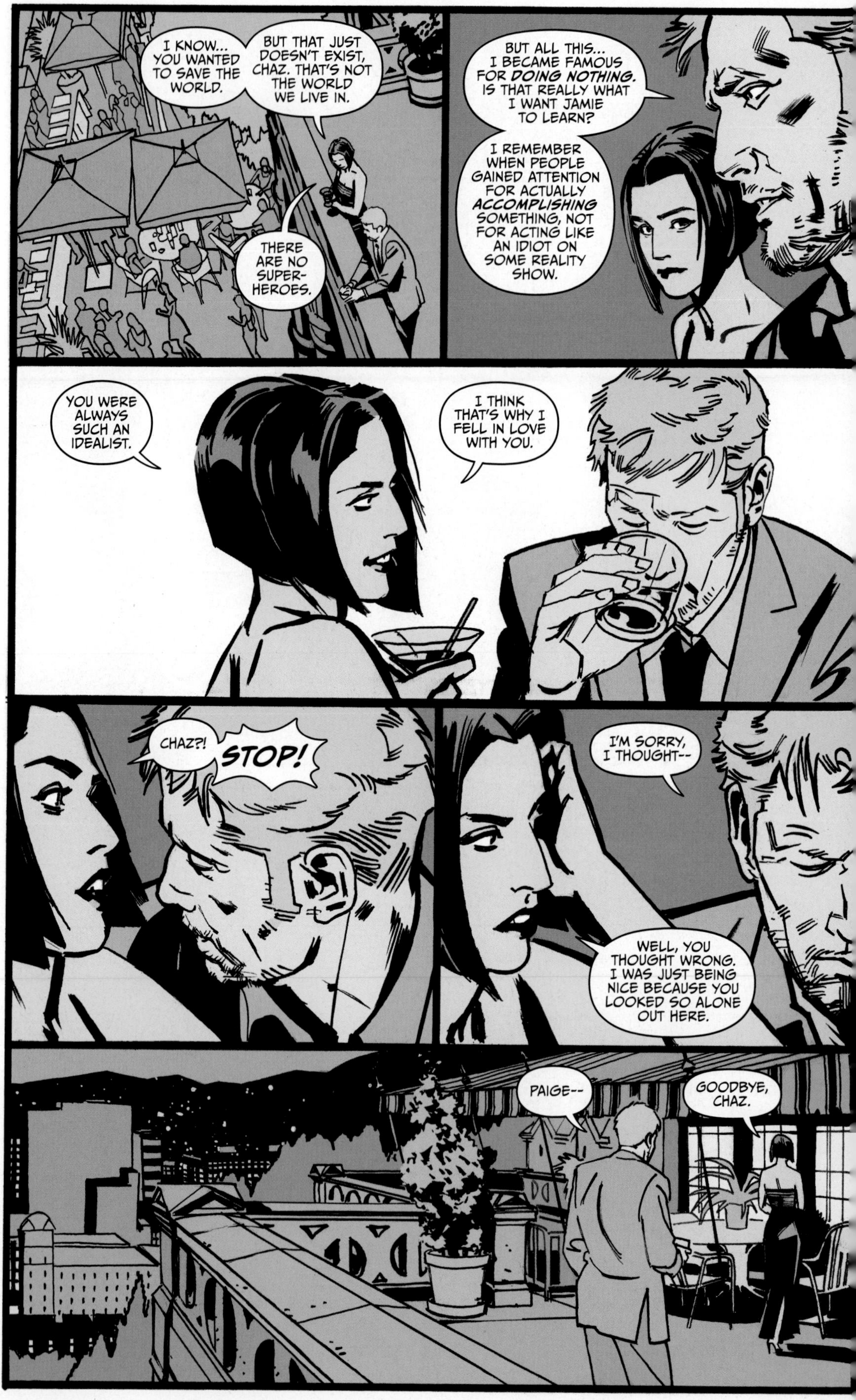
I KNOW... YOU WANTED TO SAVE THE WORLD.
BUT THAT JUST DOESN'T EXIST, CHAZ. THAT'S NOT THE WORLD WE LIVE IN.
THERE ARE NO SUPER-HEROES.
BUT ALL THIS... I BECAME FAMOUS FOR *DOING NOTHING*. IS THAT REALLY WHAT I WANT JAMIE TO LEARN?
I REMEMBER WHEN PEOPLE GAINED ATTENTION FOR ACTUALLY *ACCOMPLISHING* SOMETHING, NOT FOR ACTING LIKE AN IDIOT ON SOME REALITY SHOW.
YOU WERE ALWAYS SUCH AN IDEALIST.
I THINK THAT'S WHY I FELL IN LOVE WITH YOU.
CHAZ?!
STOP!
I'M SORRY, I THOUGHT--
WELL, YOU THOUGHT WRONG. I WAS JUST BEING NICE BECAUSE YOU LOOKED SO ALONE OUT HERE.
PAIGE--
GOODBYE, CHAZ.

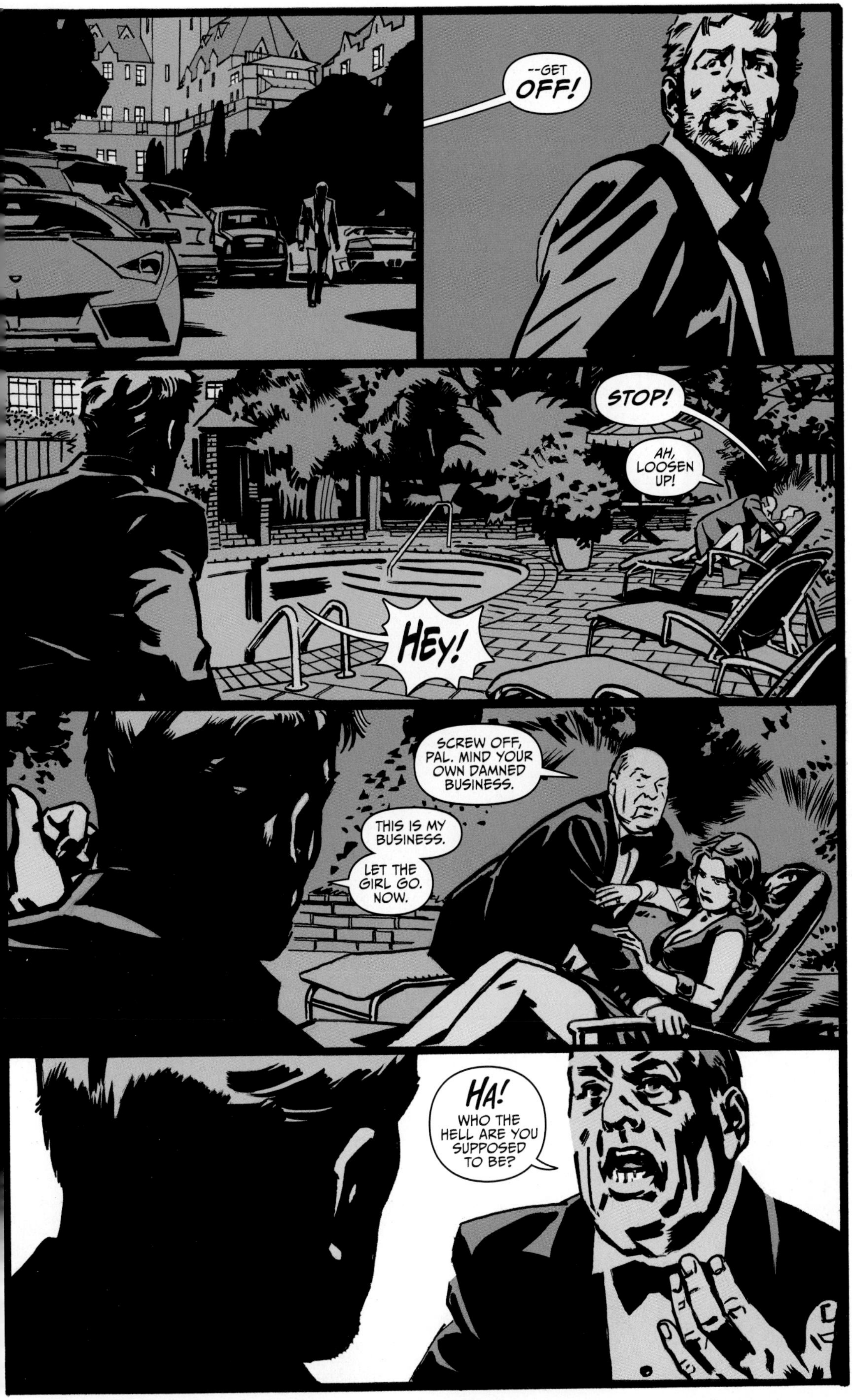
--GET OFF!
STOP!
AH, LOOSEN UP!
HEY!
SCREW OFF, PAL. MIND YOUR OWN DAMNED BUSINESS.
THIS IS MY BUSINESS.
LET THE GIRL GO. NOW.
HA! WHO THE HELL ARE YOU SUPPOSED TO BE?

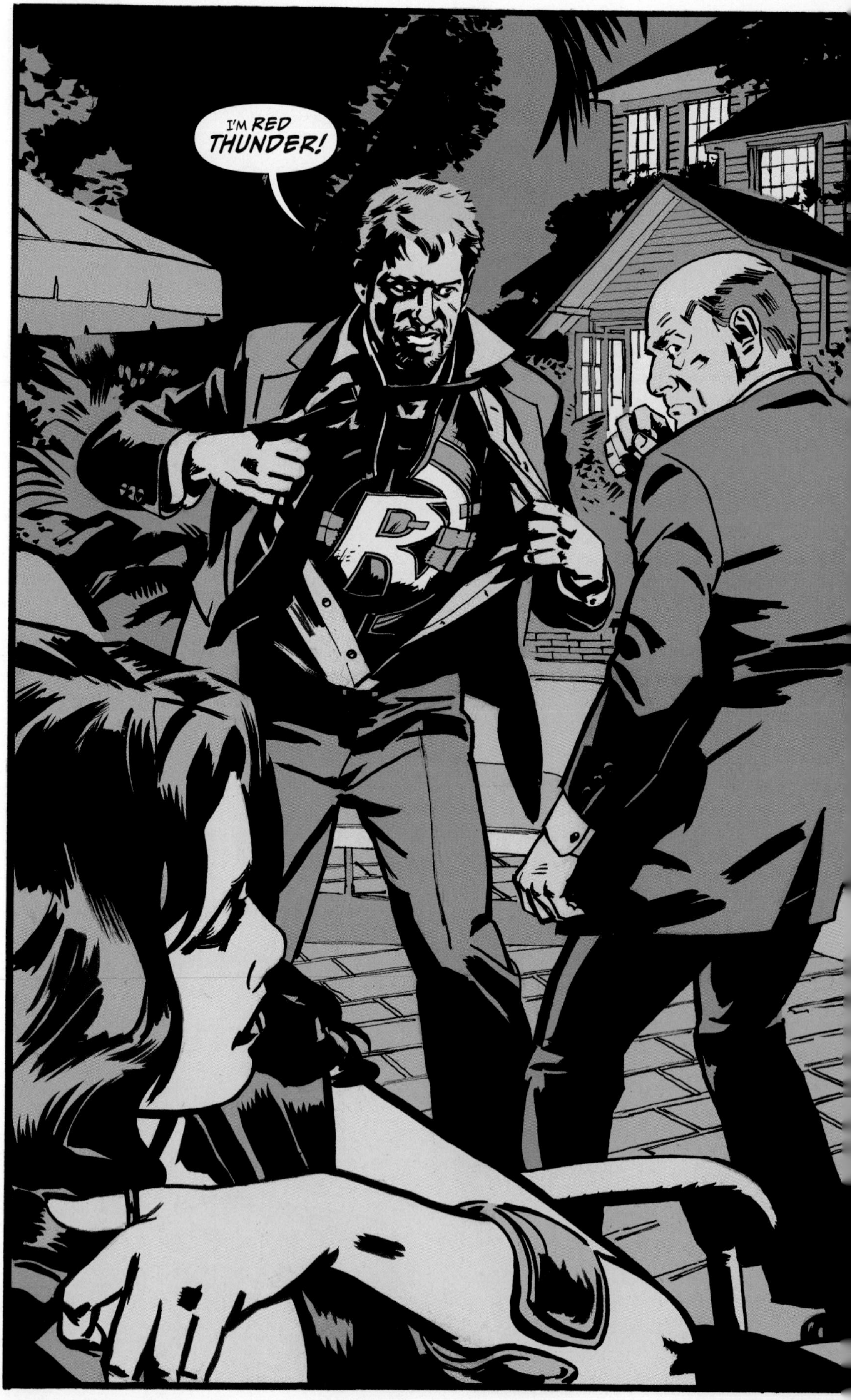
I'M RED THUNDER!

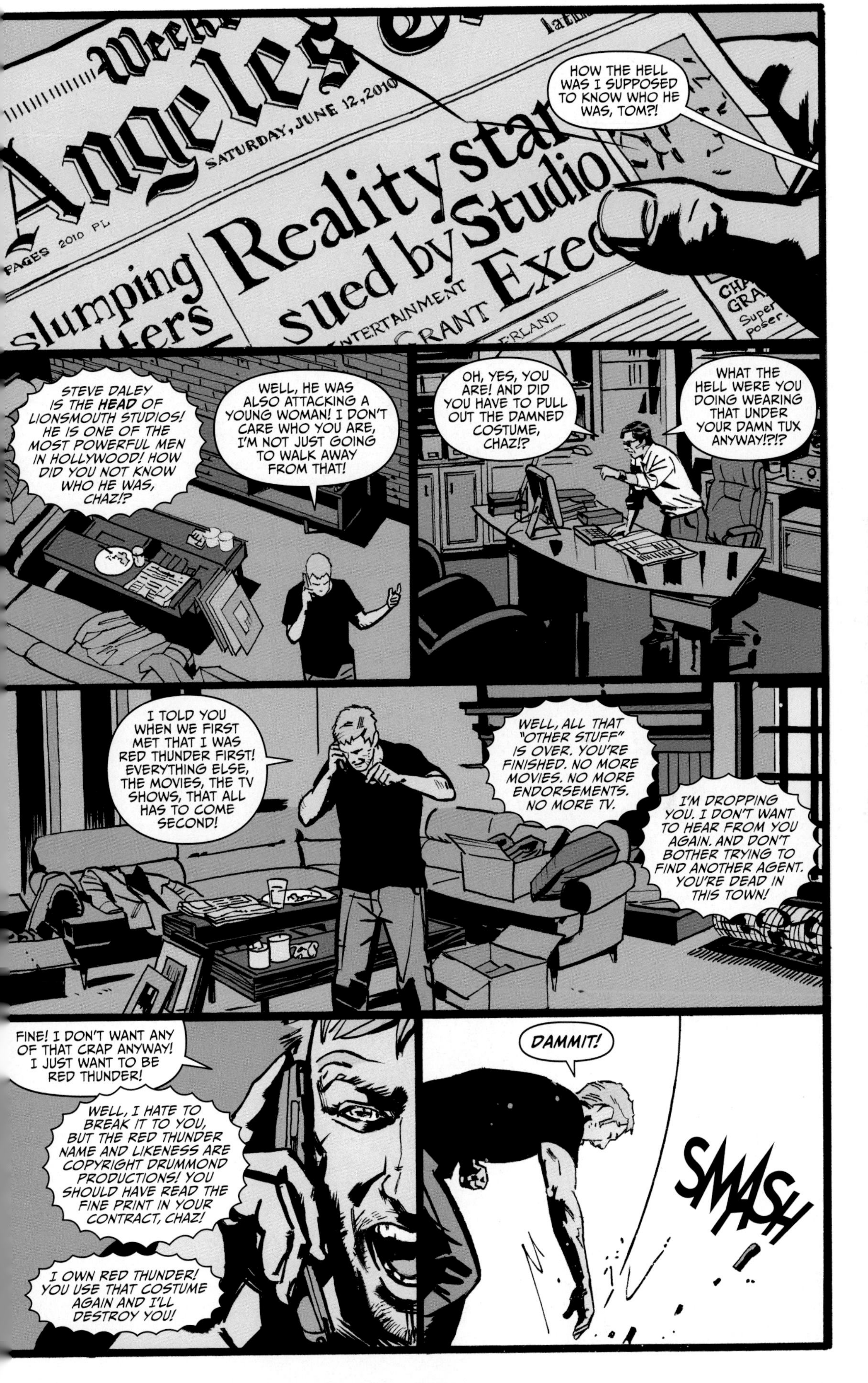
Angeles
SATURDAY, JUNE 12, 2010
PAGES 2010 PL
Reality star sued by Studio Exec
slumping
ENTERTAINMENT
GRANT
HOW THE HELL WAS I SUPPOSED TO KNOW WHO HE WAS, TOM?!
STEVE DALEY IS THE HEAD OF LIONSMOUTH STUDIOS! HE IS ONE OF THE MOST POWERFUL MEN IN HOLLYWOOD! HOW DID YOU NOT KNOW WHO HE WAS, CHAZ!?
WELL, HE WAS ALSO ATTACKING A YOUNG WOMAN! I DON'T CARE WHO YOU ARE, I'M NOT JUST GOING TO WALK AWAY FROM THAT!
OH, YES, YOU ARE! AND DID YOU HAVE TO PULL OUT THE DAMNED COSTUME, CHAZ!?
WHAT THE HELL WERE YOU DOING WEARING THAT UNDER YOUR DAMN TUX ANYWAY!?!?
I TOLD YOU WHEN WE FIRST MET THAT I WAS RED THUNDER FIRST! EVERYTHING ELSE, THE MOVIES, THE TV SHOWS, THAT ALL HAS TO COME SECOND!
WELL, ALL THAT "OTHER STUFF" IS OVER. YOU'RE FINISHED. NO MORE MOVIES. NO MORE ENDORSEMENTS. NO MORE TV.
I'M DROPPING YOU. I DON'T WANT TO HEAR FROM YOU AGAIN. AND DON'T BOTHER TRYING TO FIND ANOTHER AGENT. YOU'RE DEAD IN THIS TOWN!
FINE! I DON'T WANT ANY OF THAT CRAP ANYWAY! I JUST WANT TO BE RED THUNDER!
WELL, I HATE TO BREAK IT TO YOU, BUT THE RED THUNDER NAME AND LIKENESS ARE COPYRIGHT DRUMMOND PRODUCTIONS! YOU SHOULD HAVE READ THE FINE PRINT IN YOUR CONTRACT, CHAZ!
I OWN RED THUNDER! YOU USE THAT COSTUME AGAIN AND I'LL DESTROY YOU!
DAMMIT!
SMASH

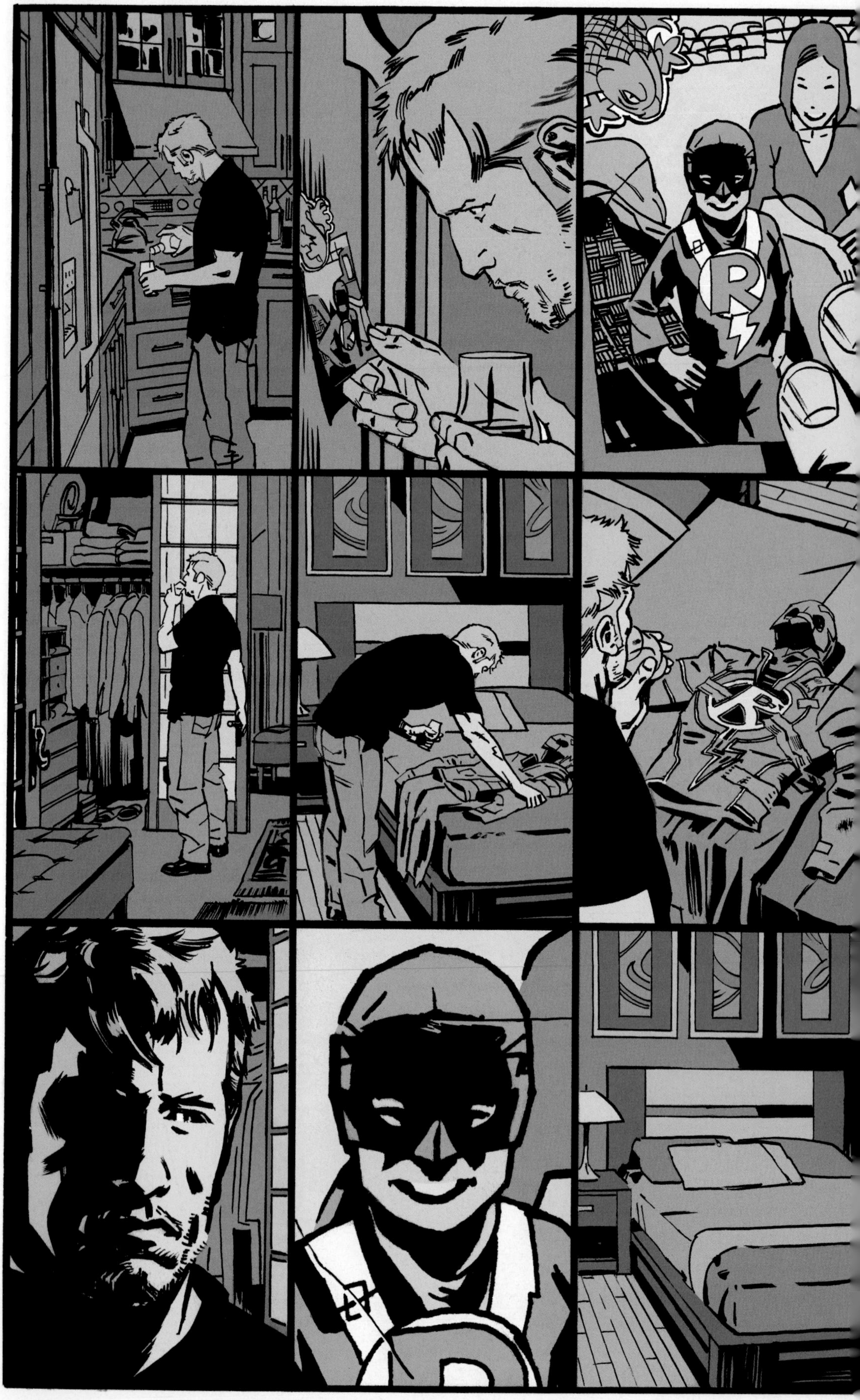

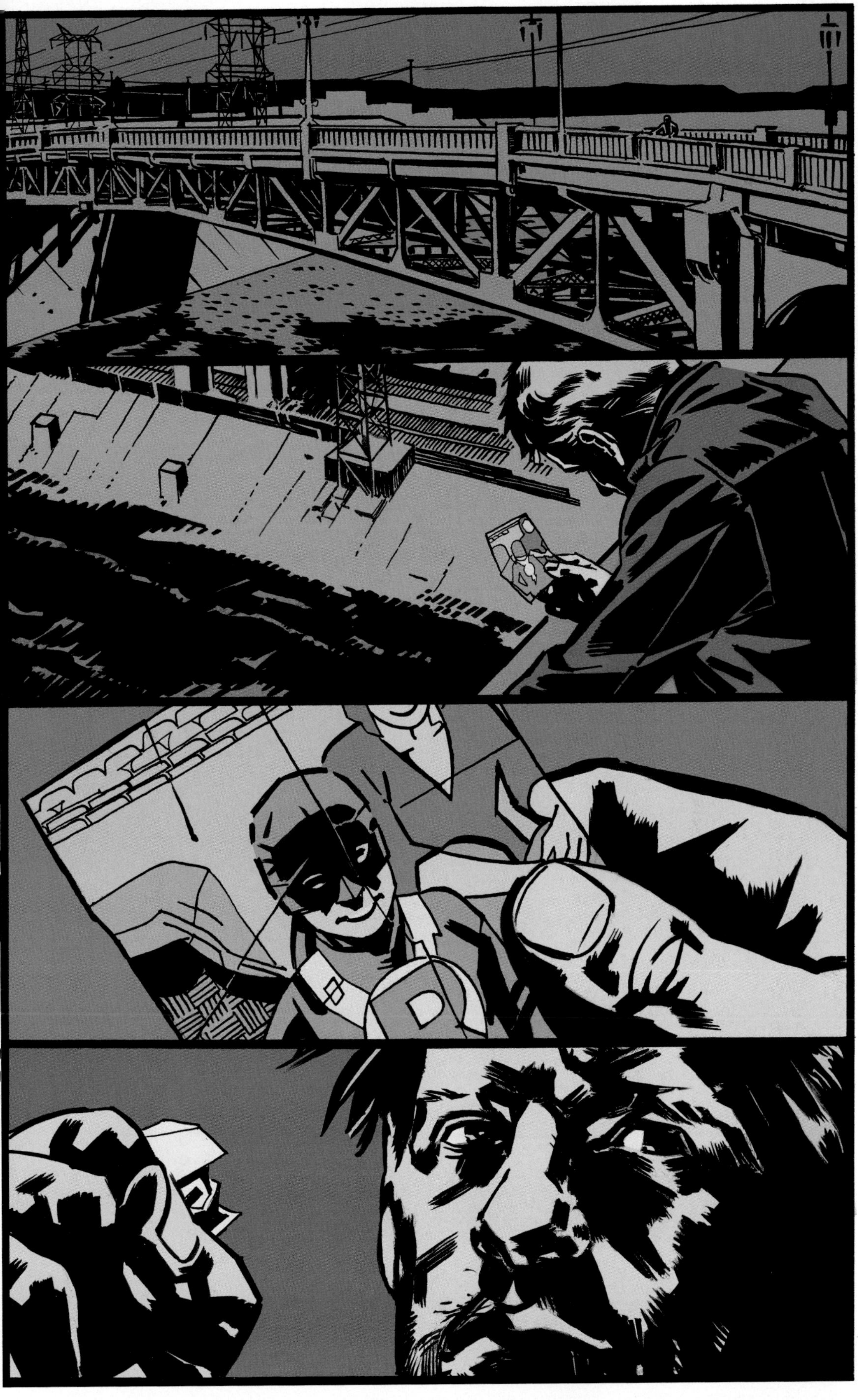

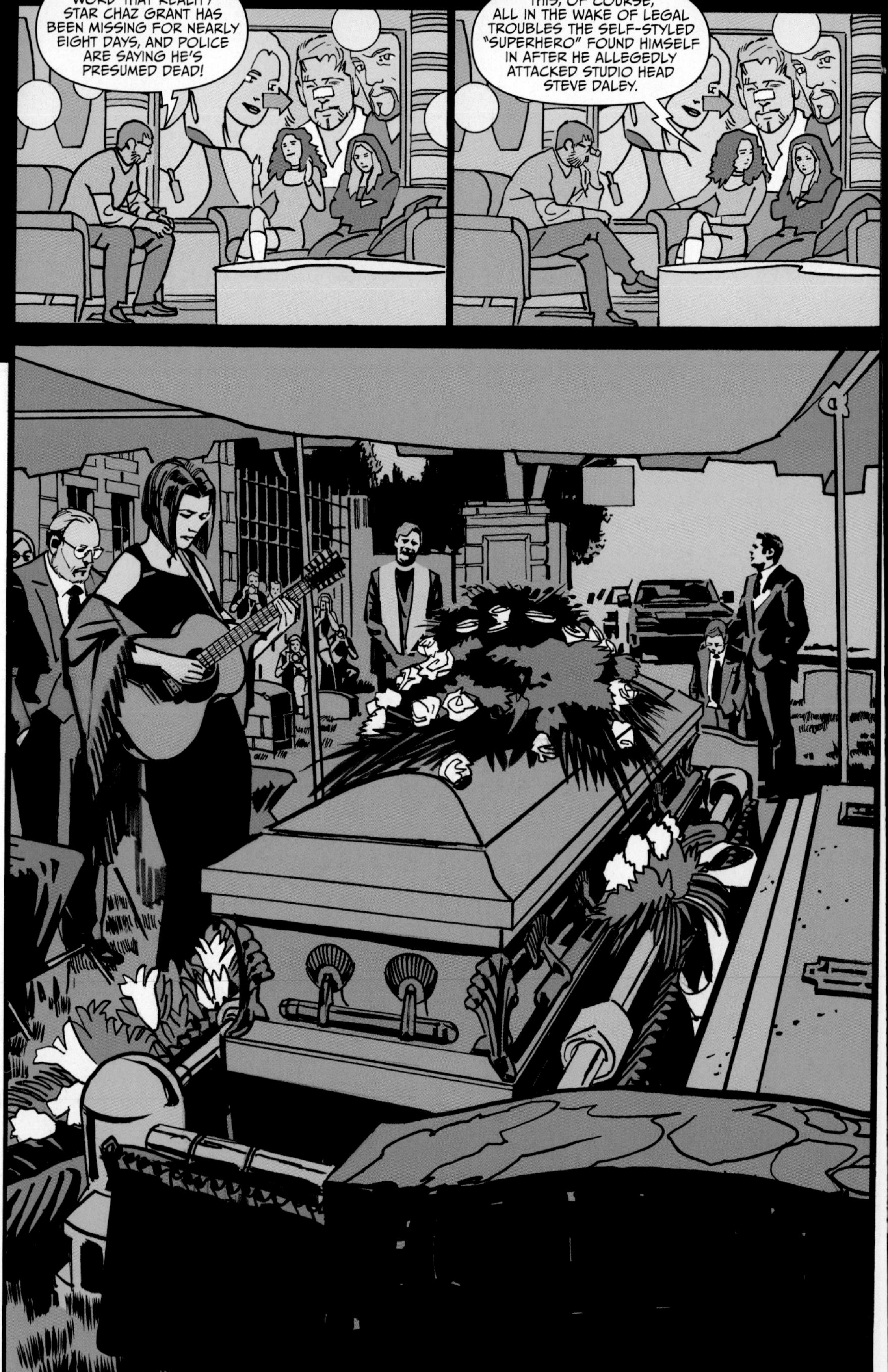
WE JUST GOT WORD THAT REALITY STAR CHAZ GRANT HAS BEEN MISSING FOR NEARLY EIGHT DAYS, AND POLICE ARE SAYING HE'S PRESUMED DEAD!
THIS, OF COURSE, ALL IN THE WAKE OF LEGAL TROUBLES THE SELF-STYLED "SUPERHERO" FOUND HIMSELF IN AFTER HE ALLEGEDLY ATTACKED STUDIO HEAD STEVE DALEY.

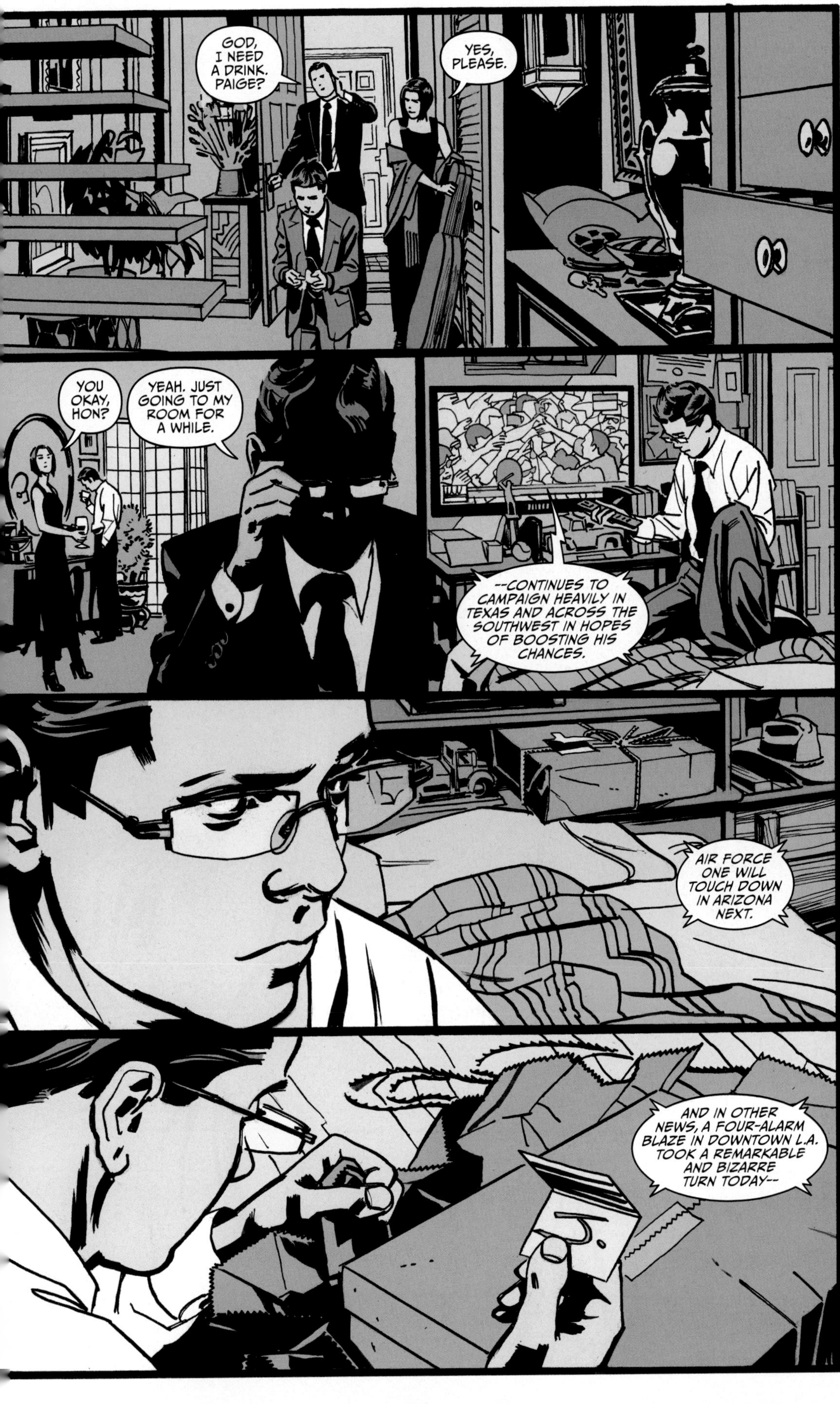
GOD, I NEED A DRINK. PAIGE?
YES, PLEASE.
YOU OKAY, HON?
YEAH. JUST GOING TO MY ROOM FOR A WHILE.
--CONTINUES TO CAMPAIGN HEAVILY IN TEXAS AND ACROSS THE SOUTHWEST IN HOPES OF BOOSTING HIS CHANCES.
AIR FORCE ONE WILL TOUCH DOWN IN ARIZONA NEXT.
AND IN OTHER NEWS, A FOUR-ALARM BLAZE IN DOWNTOWN L.A. TOOK A REMARKABLE AND BIZARRE TURN TODAY--

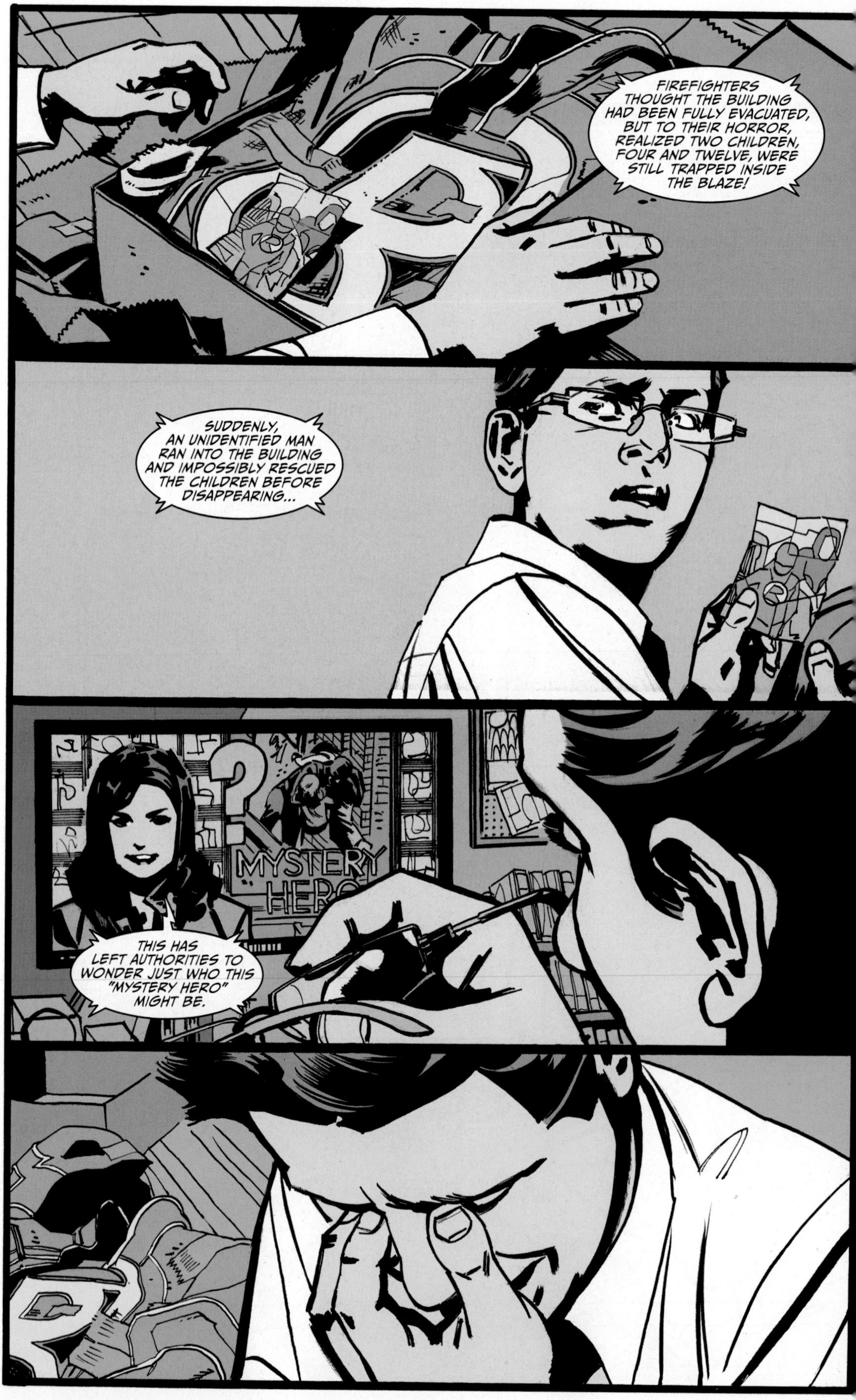
FIREFIGHTERS THOUGHT THE BUILDING HAD BEEN FULLY EVACUATED, BUT TO THEIR HORROR, REALIZED TWO CHILDREN, FOUR AND TWELVE, WERE STILL TRAPPED INSIDE THE BLAZE!
SUDDENLY, AN UNIDENTIFIED MAN RAN INTO THE BUILDING AND IMPOSSIBLY RESCUED THE CHILDREN BEFORE DISAPPEARING...
MYSTERY HERO
THIS HAS LEFT AUTHORITIES TO WONDER JUST WHO THIS "MYSTERY HERO" MIGHT BE.

THIS HAS LEFT AUTHORITIES TO WONDER JUST WHO THIS "MYSTERY HERO" MIGHT BE.

CLICK

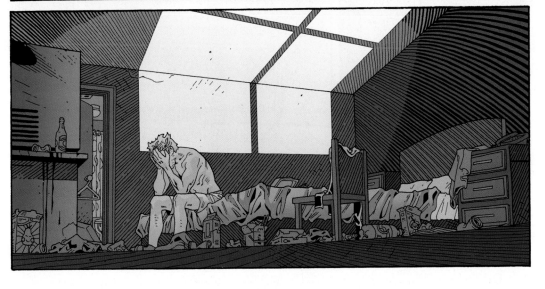

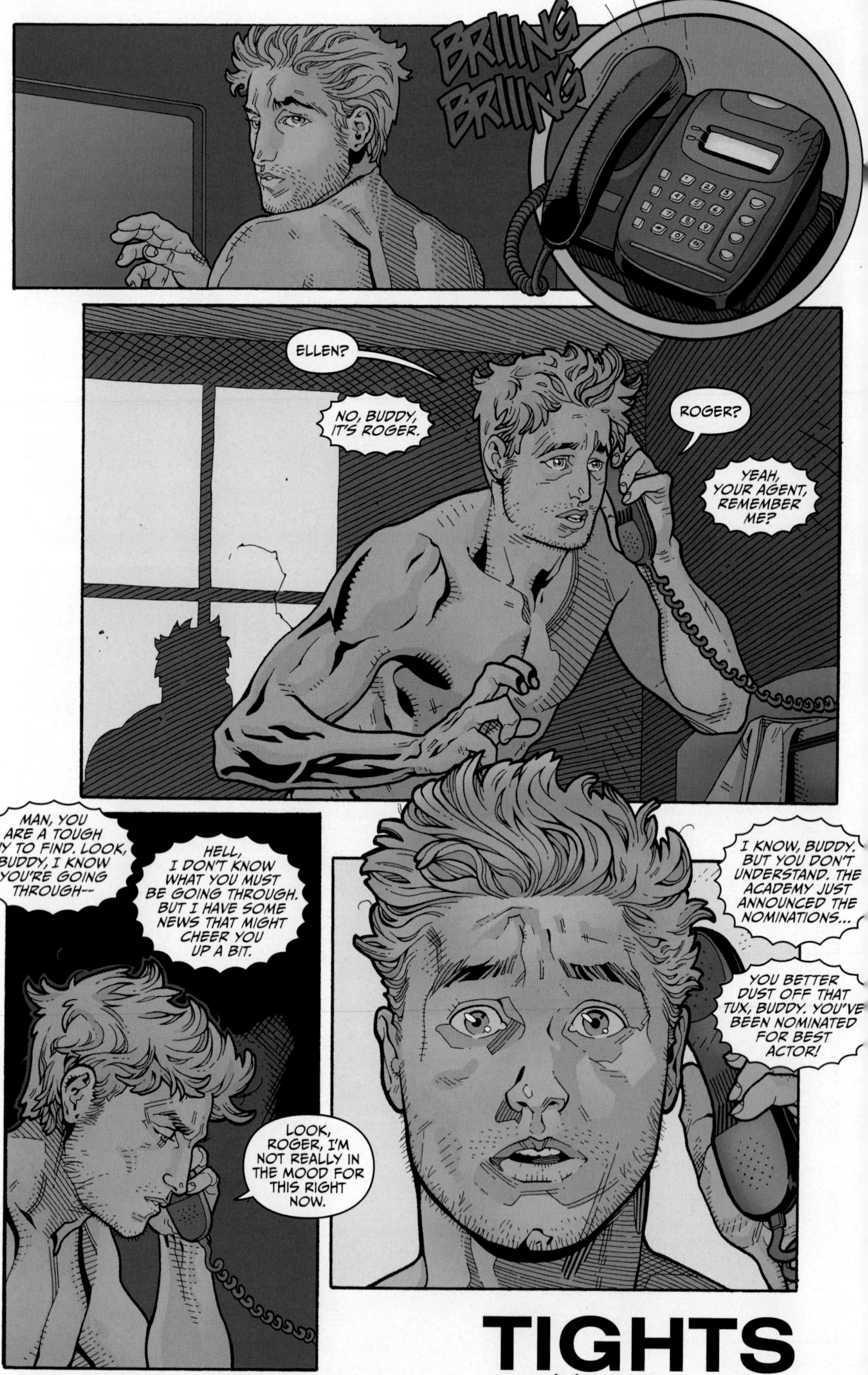
BRIIING
BRIIING
ELLEN?
NO, BUDDY, IT'S ROGER.
ROGER?
YEAH, YOUR AGENT, REMEMBER ME?
MAN, YOU ARE A TOUGH GUY TO FIND. LOOK, BUDDY, I KNOW YOU'RE GOING THROUGH--
HELL, I DON'T KNOW WHAT YOU MUST BE GOING THROUGH. BUT I HAVE SOME NEWS THAT MIGHT CHEER YOU UP A BIT.
LOOK, ROGER, I'M NOT REALLY IN THE MOOD FOR THIS RIGHT NOW.
I KNOW, BUDDY. BUT YOU DON'T UNDERSTAND. THE ACADEMY JUST ANNOUNCED THE NOMINATIONS...
YOU BETTER DUST OFF THAT TUX, BUDDY. YOU'VE BEEN NOMINATED FOR BEST ACTOR!

TIGHTS
part two

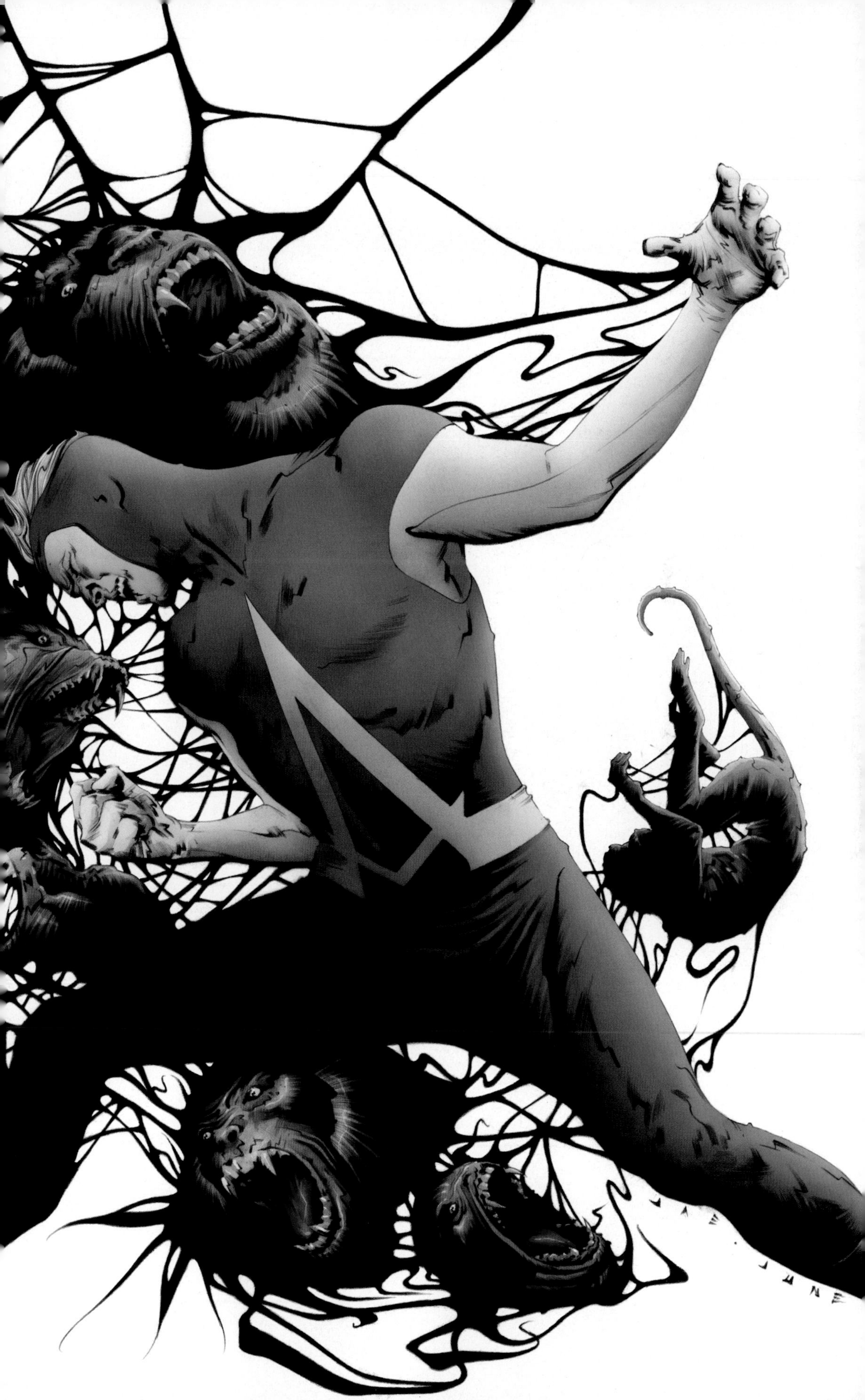
JAE · JUNE

JEFF LEMIRE
writer

STEVE PUGH & FRANCIS PORTELA
artists

JAE LEE with JUNE CHUNG
cover artists

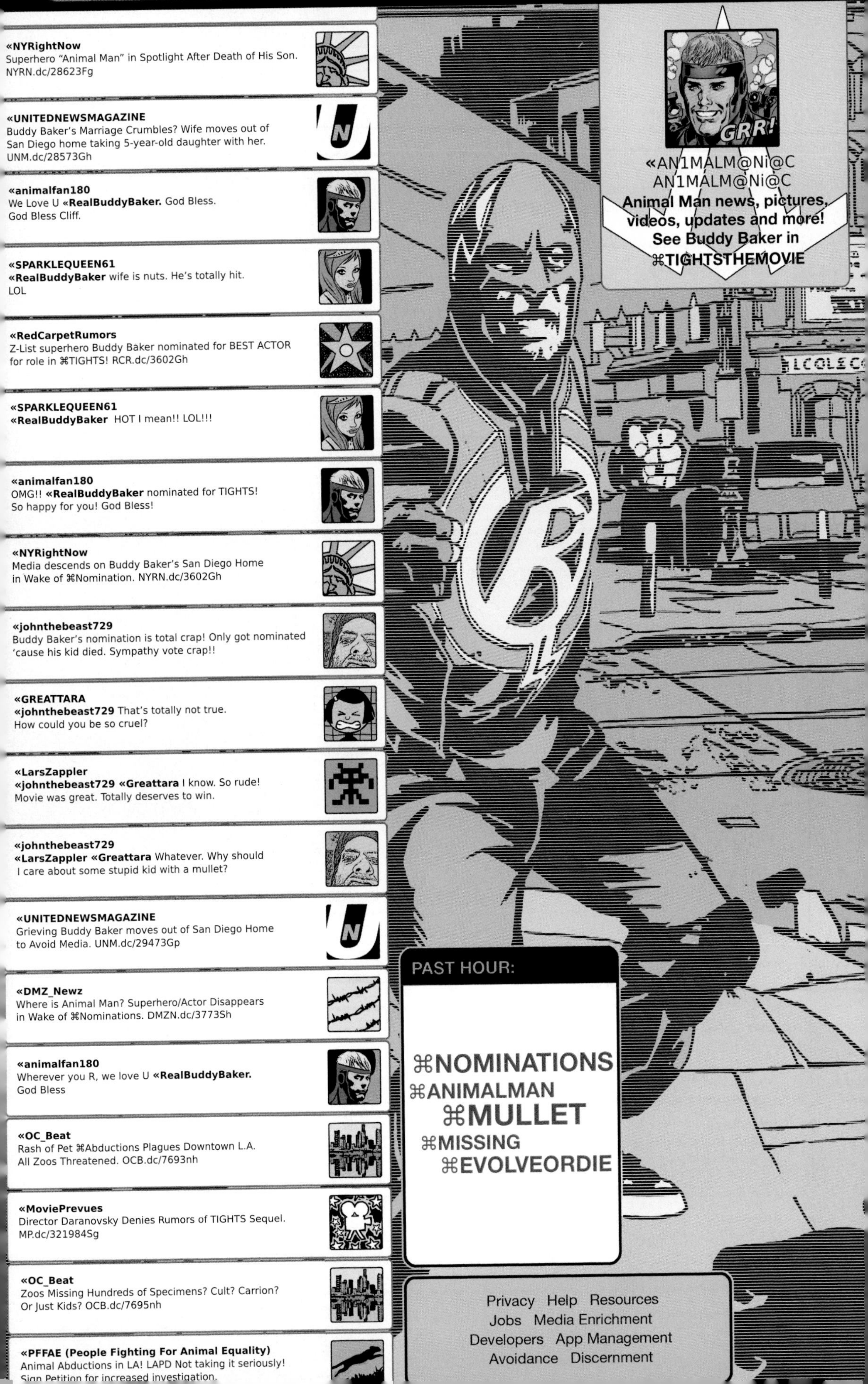
«NYRightNow
Superhero "Animal Man" in Spotlight After Death of His Son.
NYRN.dc/28623Fg
«UNITEDNEWSMAGAZINE
Buddy Baker's Marriage Crumbles? Wife moves out of
San Diego home taking 5-year-old daughter with her.
UNM.dc/28573Gh
«animalfan180
We Love U «RealBuddyBaker. God Bless.
God Bless Cliff.
«SPARKLEQUEEN61
«RealBuddyBaker wife is nuts. He's totally hit.
LOL
«RedCarpetRumors
Z-List superhero Buddy Baker nominated for BEST ACTOR
for role in ⌘TIGHTS! RCR.dc/3602Gh
«SPARKLEQUEEN61
«RealBuddyBaker HOT I mean!! LOL!!!
«animalfan180
OMG!! «RealBuddyBaker nominated for TIGHTS!
So happy for you! God Bless!
«NYRightNow
Media descends on Buddy Baker's San Diego Home
in Wake of ⌘Nomination. NYRN.dc/3602Gh
«johnthebeast729
Buddy Baker's nomination is total crap! Only got nominated
'cause his kid died. Sympathy vote crap!!
«GREATTARA
«johnthebeast729 That's totally not true.
How could you be so cruel?
«LarsZappler
«johnthebeast729 «Greattara I know. So rude!
Movie was great. Totally deserves to win.
«johnthebeast729
«LarsZappler «Greattara Whatever. Why should
I care about some stupid kid with a mullet?
«UNITEDNEWSMAGAZINE
Grieving Buddy Baker moves out of San Diego Home
to Avoid Media. UNM.dc/29473Gp
«DMZ_Newz
Where is Animal Man? Superhero/Actor Disappears
in Wake of ⌘Nominations. DMZN.dc/3773Sh
«animalfan180
Wherever you R, we love U «RealBuddyBaker.
God Bless
«OC_Beat
Rash of Pet ⌘Abductions Plagues Downtown L.A.
All Zoos Threatened. OCB.dc/7693nh
«MoviePrevues
Director Daranovsky Denies Rumors of TIGHTS Sequel.
MP.dc/321984Sg
«OC_Beat
Zoos Missing Hundreds of Specimens? Cult? Carrion?
Or Just Kids? OCB.dc/7695nh
«PFFAE (People Fighting For Animal Equality)
Animal Abductions in LA! LAPD Not taking it seriously!
Sign Petition for increased investigation.
GRR!
«AN1MALM@Ni@C
AN1MALM@Ni@C
Animal Man news, pictures, videos, updates and more!
See Buddy Baker in
⌘TIGHTSTHEMOVIE
PAST HOUR:
⌘NOMINATIONS
⌘ANIMALMAN
⌘MULLET
⌘MISSING
⌘EVOLVEORDIE
Privacy Help Resources
Jobs Media Enrichment
Developers App Management
Avoidance Discernment

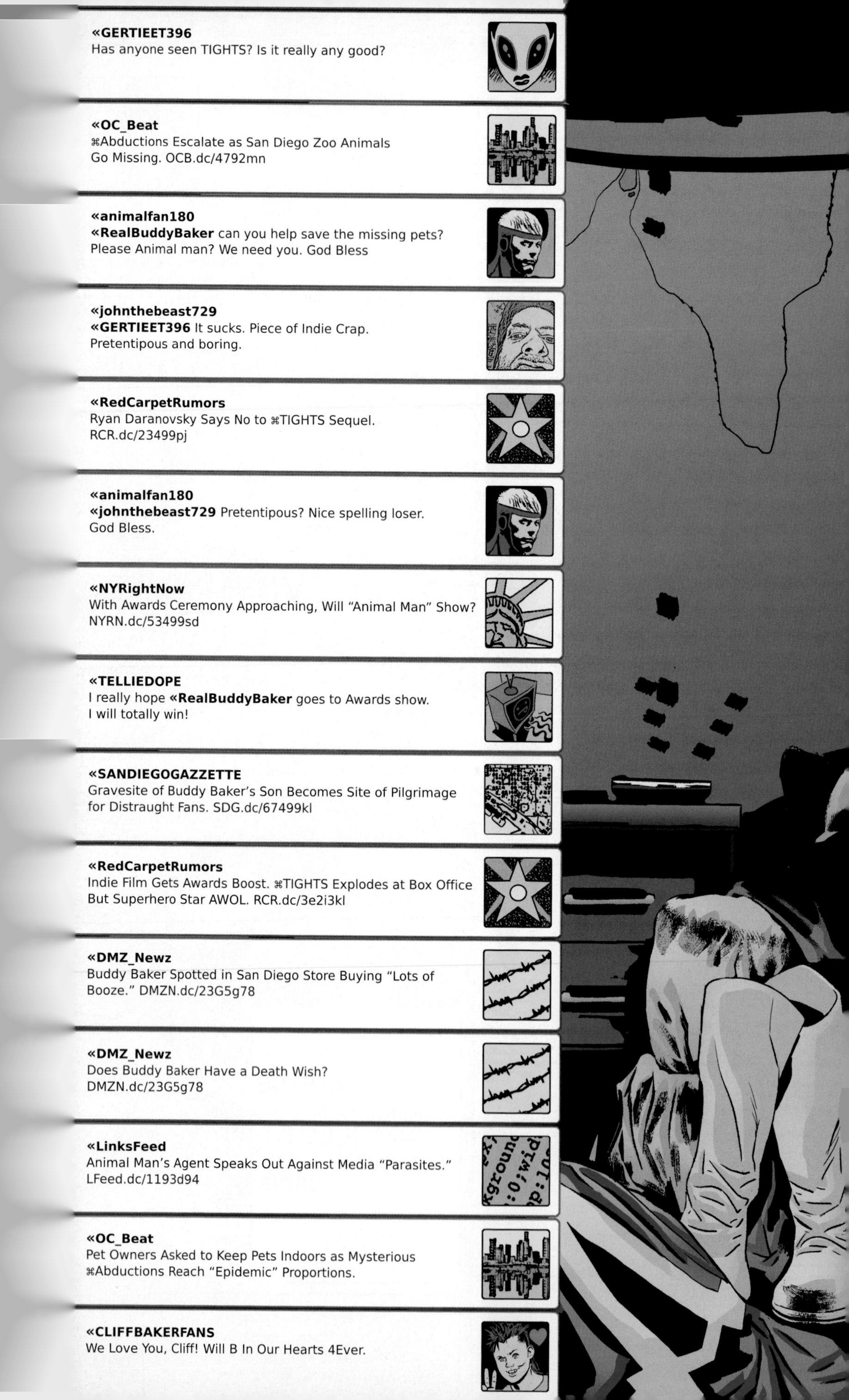
«GERTIEET396
Has anyone seen TIGHTS? Is it really any good?
«OC_Beat
⌘Abductions Escalate as San Diego Zoo Animals Go Missing. OCB.dc/4792mn
«animalfan180
«RealBuddyBaker can you help save the missing pets? Please Animal man? We need you. God Bless
«johnthebeast729
«GERTIEET396 It sucks. Piece of Indie Crap. Pretentipous and boring.
«RedCarpetRumors
Ryan Daranovsky Says No to ⌘TIGHTS Sequel. RCR.dc/23499pj
«animalfan180
«johnthebeast729 Pretentipous? Nice spelling loser. God Bless.
«NYRightNow
With Awards Ceremony Approaching, Will "Animal Man" Show? NYRN.dc/53499sd
«TELLIEDOPE
I really hope «RealBuddyBaker goes to Awards show. I will totally win!
«SANDIEGOGAZZETTE
Gravesite of Buddy Baker's Son Becomes Site of Pilgrimage for Distraught Fans. SDG.dc/67499kl
«RedCarpetRumors
Indie Film Gets Awards Boost. ⌘TIGHTS Explodes at Box Office But Superhero Star AWOL. RCR.dc/3e2i3kl
«DMZ_Newz
Buddy Baker Spotted in San Diego Store Buying "Lots of Booze." DMZN.dc/23G5g78
«DMZ_Newz
Does Buddy Baker Have a Death Wish? DMZN.dc/23G5g78
«LinksFeed
Animal Man's Agent Speaks Out Against Media "Parasites." LFeed.dc/1193d94
«OC_Beat
Pet Owners Asked to Keep Pets Indoors as Mysterious ⌘Abductions Reach "Epidemic" Proportions.
«CLIFFBAKERFANS
We Love You, Cliff! Will B In Our Hearts 4Ever.

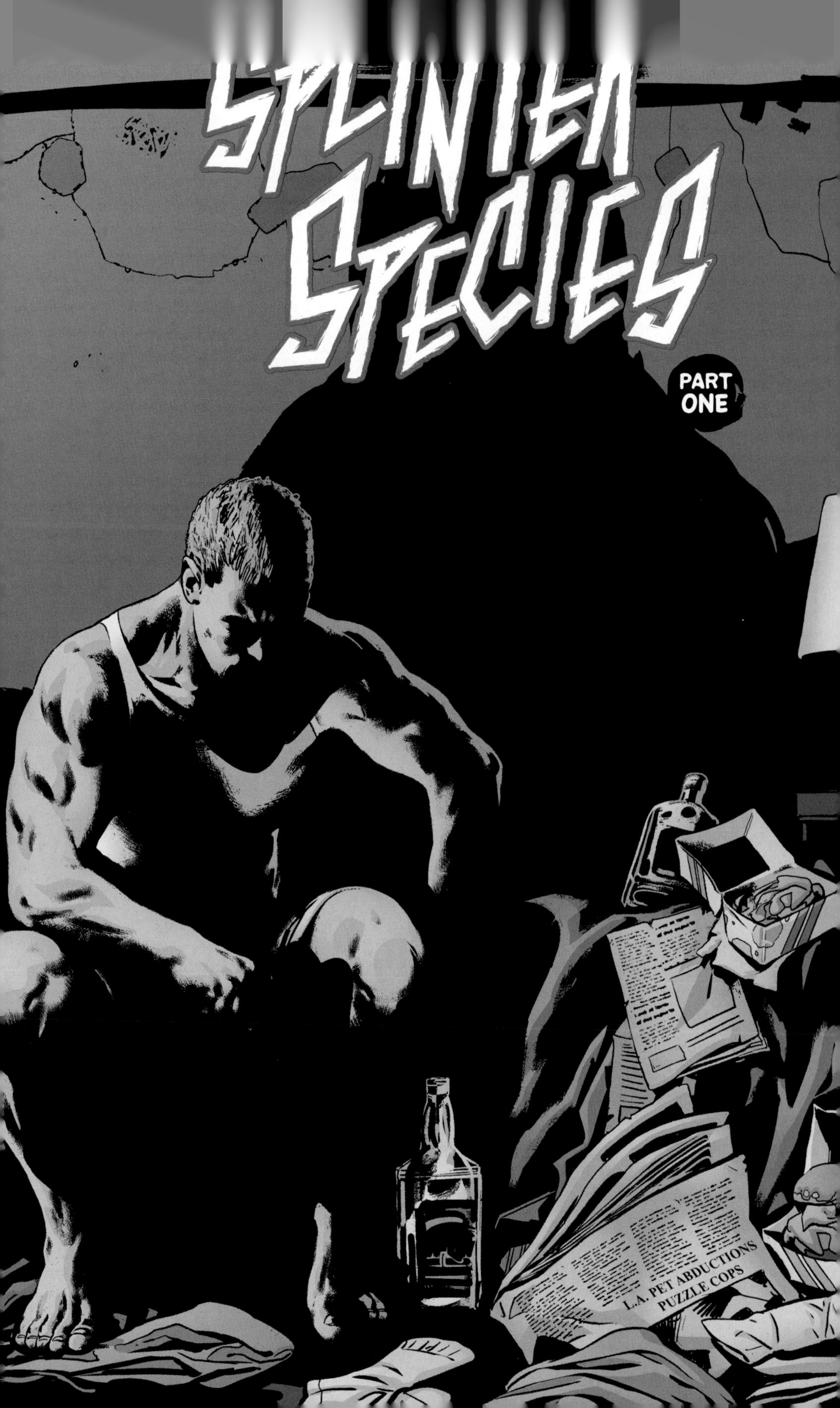
SPECIES
PART ONE
L.A. PET ABDUCTIONS
PUZZLE COPS

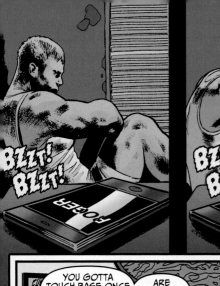

BZZT!
BZZT!

CHRIST.

BZZT!
BZZT!

WHAT DO YOU WANT, ROGER?

BUDDY? JESUS, MAN. I WAS GETTING WORRIED.

YOU GOTTA TOUCH BASE ONCE IN A WHILE, MAN. YOU SCARED ME.

ARE YOU OKAY, MAN?

I'M FINE.

LOOK, MAN. I JUST WANT TO TALK TO YOU ABOUT THE AWARDS SHOW. I KNOW, I KNOW...IT'S THE LAST THING YOU WANT TO THINK ABOUT AFTER CLIFF, BUT--

BUT NOTHING. I COULDN'T CARE LESS ABOUT THE DAMNED MOVIE OR THE AWARDS, ROGER.

BUDDY, LOOK, I'M NOT CALLING AS YOUR AGENT, I'M CALLING AS YOUR FRIEND HERE.

MAYBE YOU NEED TO GET BACK TO WORK. MAYBE THIS IS YOUR CHANCE TO-- I DON'T KNOW, DO SOMETHING TO GET YOUR MIND OFF THINGS.

IT'S BEEN TWO MONTHS. MAYBE IT'S TIME TO...WELL, MAYBE YOU NEED TO KEEP YOURSELF BUSY.

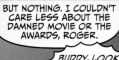

PET ABDUCTIONS
PUZZLE COPS

RIGHT, ROGER. GREAT IDEA. GOING TO A HOLLYWOOD AWARD SHOW, AND BEING ON T. FRONT OF BILLIONS C PEOPLE IS JUST THE W. TO HELP ME FORGET WHAT'S HAPPENED?

MAKE ME FORGET MY WIFE AND DAUGHTER HAVE LEFT ME? MAKE ME FORGET THAT CLIFF IS--

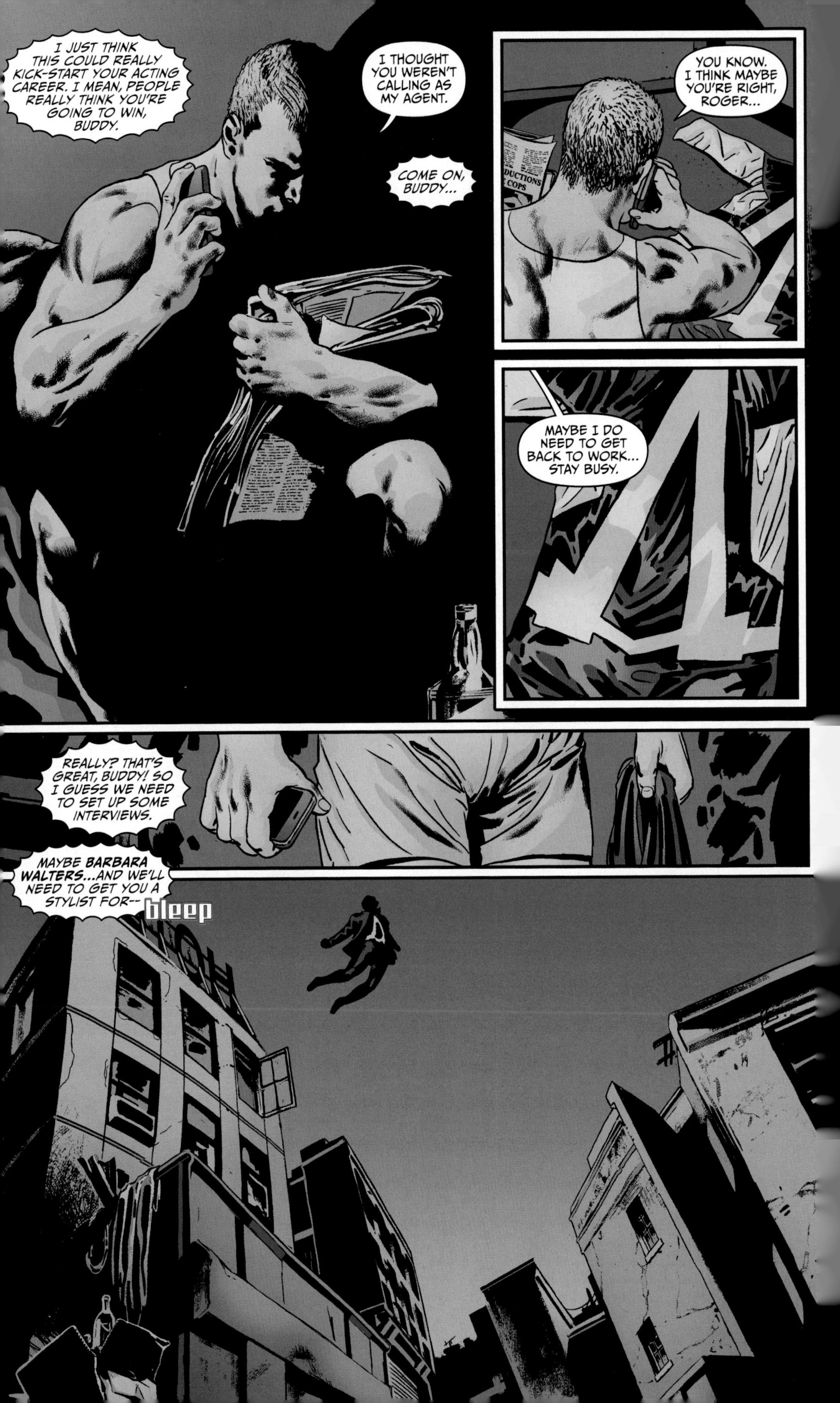

I JUST THINK THIS COULD REALLY KICK-START YOUR ACTING CAREER. I MEAN, PEOPLE REALLY THINK YOU'RE GOING TO WIN, BUDDY.
I THOUGHT YOU WEREN'T CALLING AS MY AGENT.
COME ON, BUDDY...
YOU KNOW. I THINK MAYBE YOU'RE RIGHT, ROGER...
MAYBE I DO NEED TO GET BACK TO WORK... STAY BUSY.
REALLY? THAT'S GREAT, BUDDY! SO I GUESS WE NEED TO SET UP SOME INTERVIEWS.
MAYBE BARBARA WALTERS...AND WE'LL NEED TO GET YOU A STYLIST FOR--
bleep

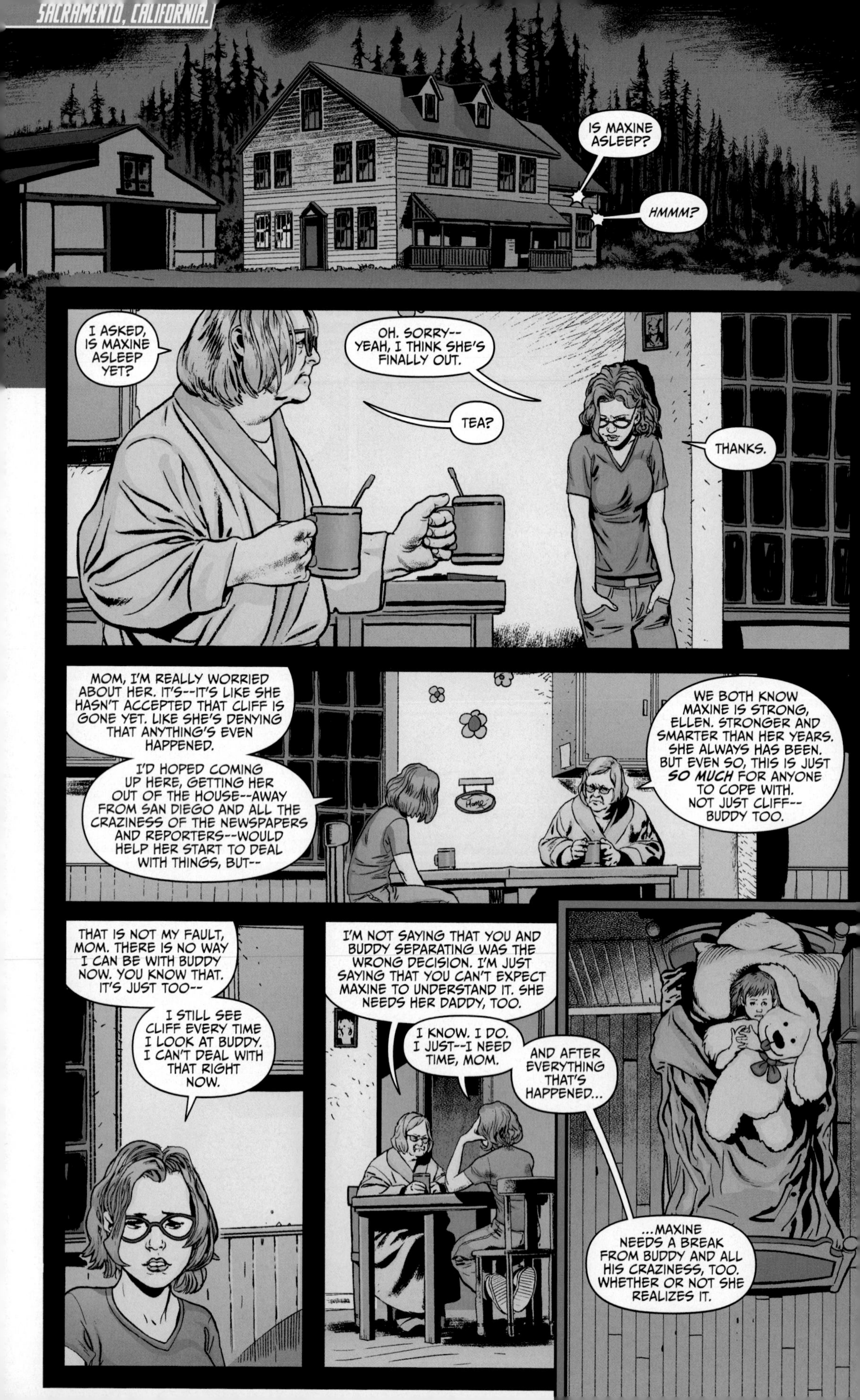
SACRAMENTO, CALIFORNIA.
IS MAXINE ASLEEP?
HMMM?
I ASKED, IS MAXINE ASLEEP YET?
OH. SORRY-- YEAH, I THINK SHE'S FINALLY OUT.
TEA?
THANKS.
MOM, I'M REALLY WORRIED ABOUT HER. IT'S--IT'S LIKE SHE HASN'T ACCEPTED THAT CLIFF IS GONE YET. LIKE SHE'S DENYING THAT ANYTHING'S EVEN HAPPENED.
I'D HOPED COMING UP HERE, GETTING HER OUT OF THE HOUSE--AWAY FROM SAN DIEGO AND ALL THE CRAZINESS OF THE NEWSPAPERS AND REPORTERS--WOULD HELP HER START TO DEAL WITH THINGS, BUT--
WE BOTH KNOW MAXINE IS STRONG, ELLEN. STRONGER AND SMARTER THAN HER YEARS. SHE ALWAYS HAS BEEN. BUT EVEN SO, THIS IS JUST *SO MUCH* FOR ANYONE TO COPE WITH. NOT JUST CLIFF-- BUDDY TOO.
THAT IS NOT MY FAULT, MOM. THERE IS NO WAY I CAN BE WITH BUDDY NOW. YOU KNOW THAT. IT'S JUST TOO--
I STILL SEE CLIFF EVERY TIME I LOOK AT BUDDY. I CAN'T DEAL WITH THAT RIGHT NOW.
I'M NOT SAYING THAT YOU AND BUDDY SEPARATING WAS THE WRONG DECISION. I'M JUST SAYING THAT YOU CAN'T EXPECT MAXINE TO UNDERSTAND IT. SHE NEEDS HER DADDY, TOO.
I KNOW. I DO. I JUST--I NEED TIME, MOM.
AND AFTER EVERYTHING THAT'S HAPPENED...
...MAXINE NEEDS A BREAK FROM BUDDY AND ALL HIS CRAZINESS, TOO. WHETHER OR NOT SHE REALIZES IT.

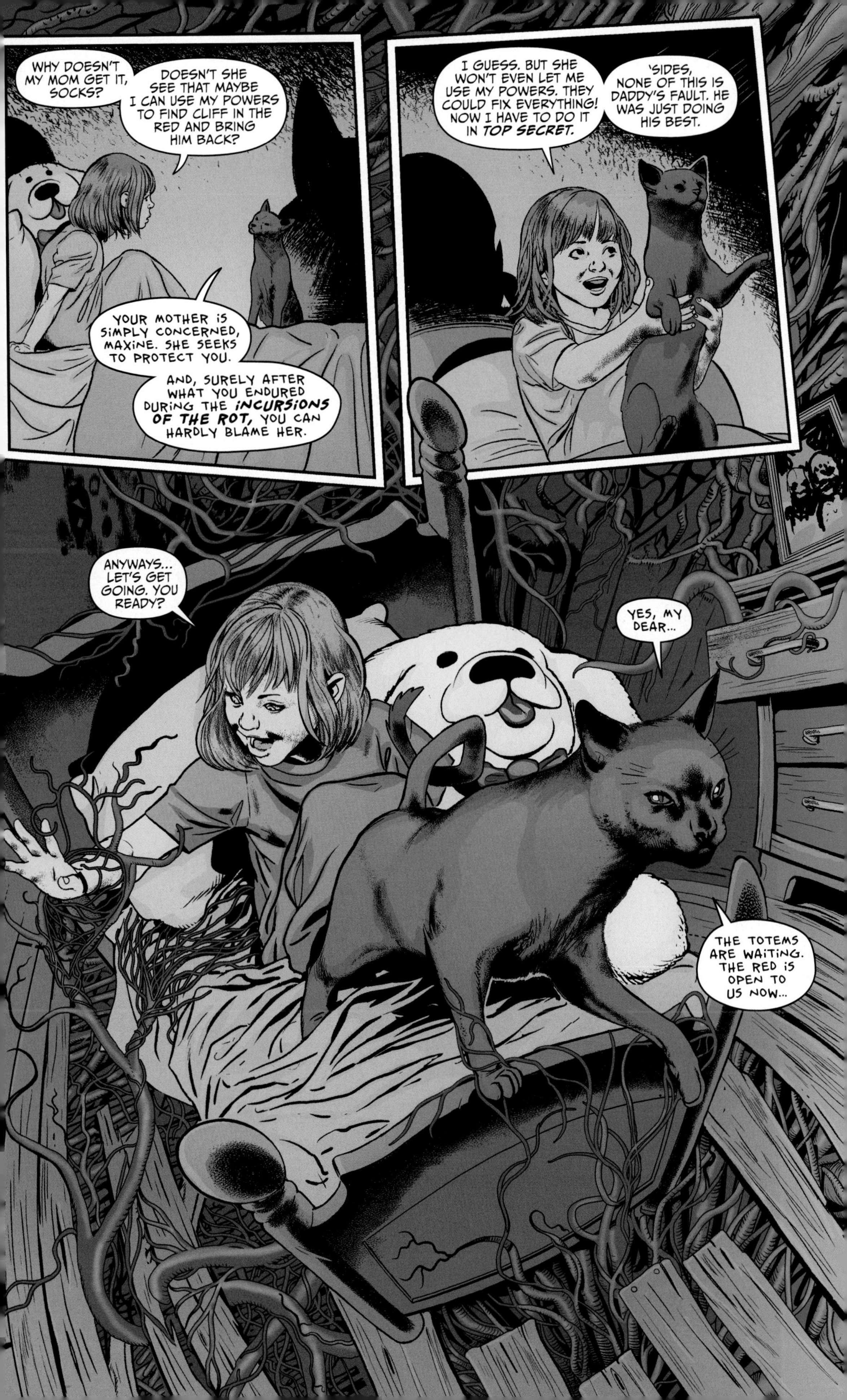
WHY DOESN'T MY MOM GET IT, SOCKS?
DOESN'T SHE SEE THAT MAYBE I CAN USE MY POWERS TO FIND CLIFF IN THE RED AND BRING HIM BACK?
YOUR MOTHER IS SIMPLY CONCERNED, MAXINE. SHE SEEKS TO PROTECT YOU.
AND, SURELY AFTER WHAT YOU ENDURED DURING THE INCURSIONS OF THE ROT, YOU CAN HARDLY BLAME HER.
I GUESS. BUT SHE WON'T EVEN LET ME USE MY POWERS. THEY COULD FIX EVERYTHING! NOW I HAVE TO DO IT IN TOP SECRET.
'SIDES, NONE OF THIS IS DADDY'S FAULT. HE WAS JUST DOING HIS BEST.
ANYWAYS... LET'S GET GOING. YOU READY?
YES, MY DEAR...
THE TOTEMS ARE WAITING. THE RED IS OPEN TO US NOW...

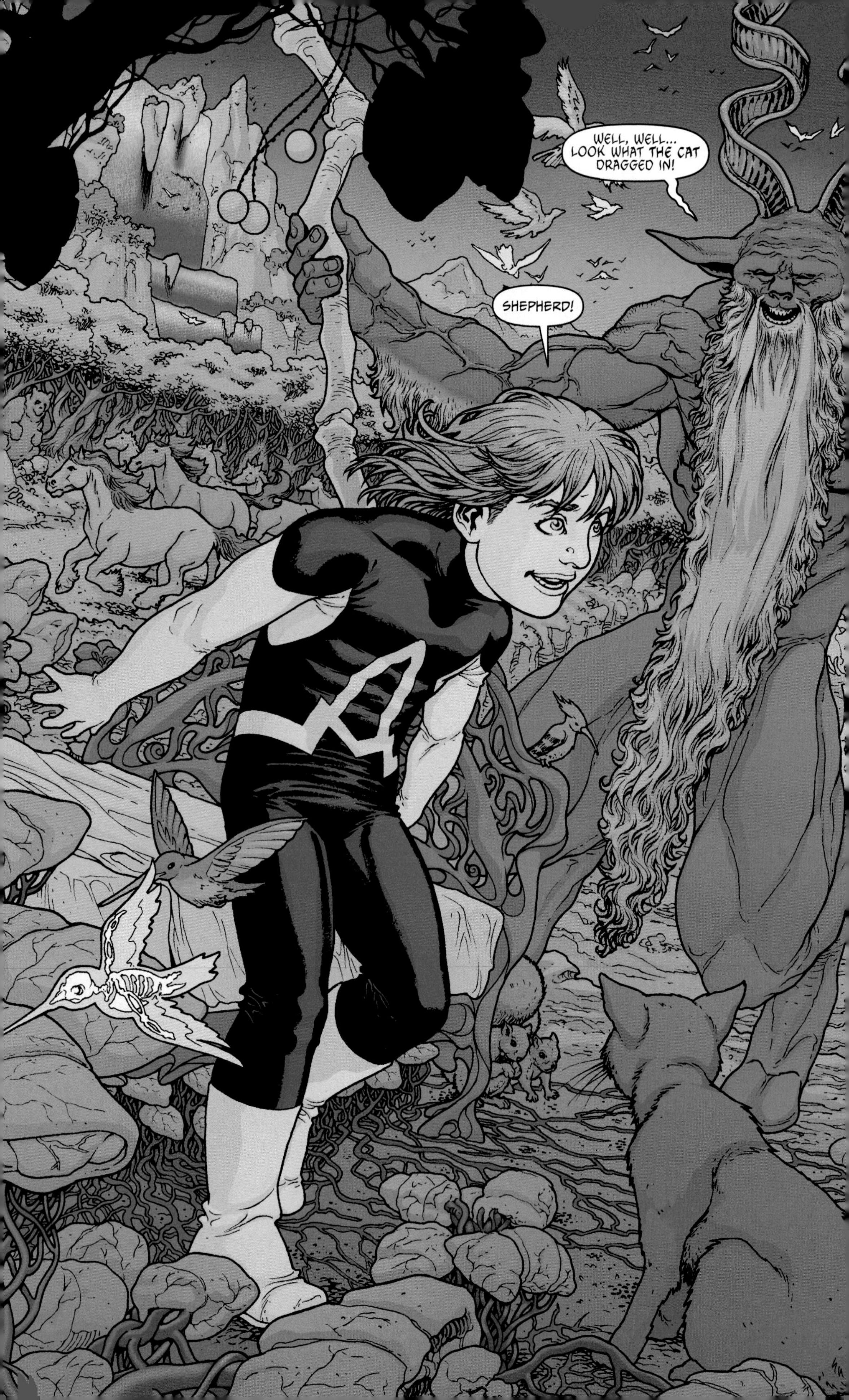
WELL, WELL... LOOK WHAT THE CAT DRAGGED IN!
SHEPHERD!

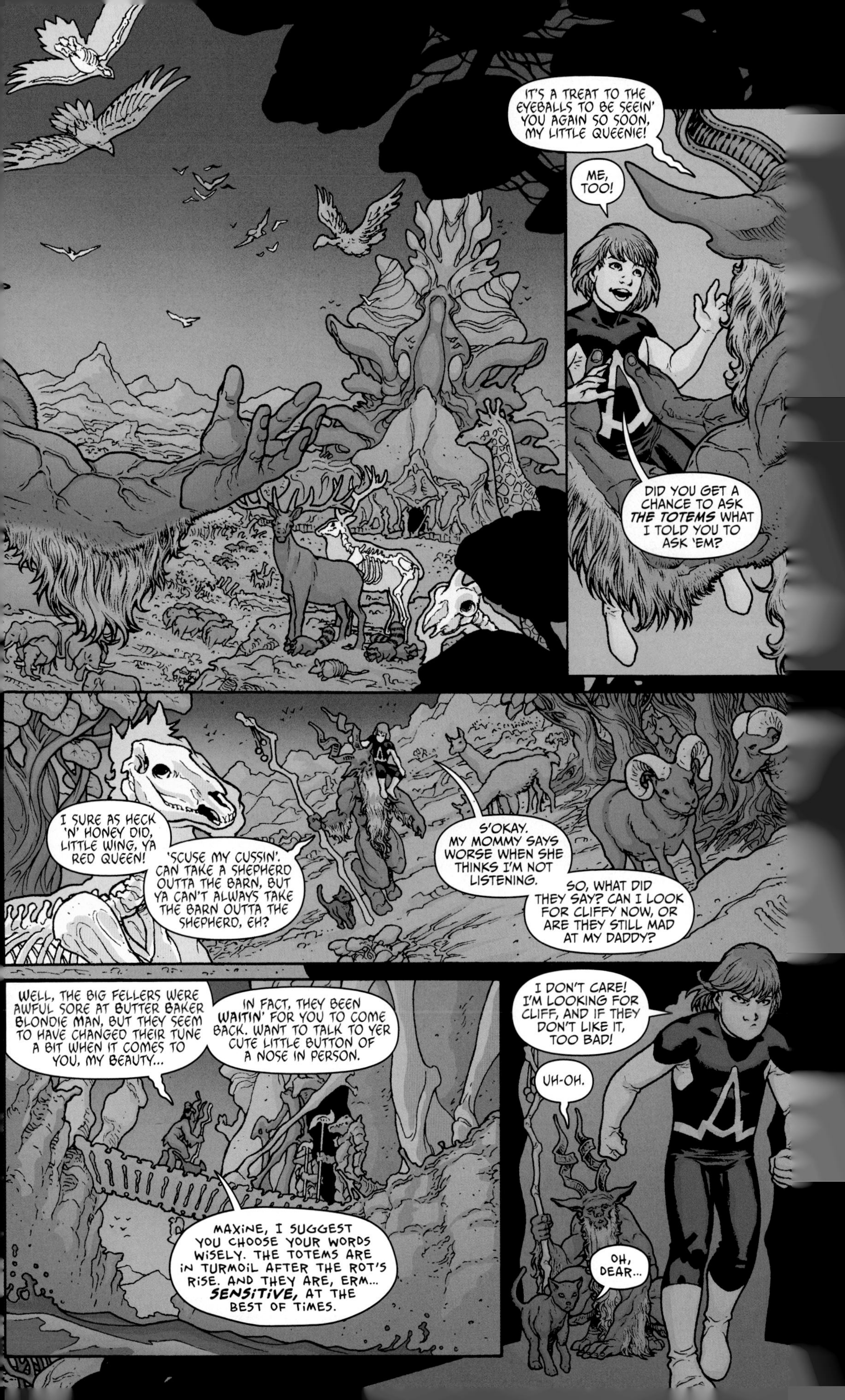

IT'S A TREAT TO THE EYEBALLS TO BE SEEIN' YOU AGAIN SO SOON, MY LITTLE QUEENIE!
ME, TOO!
DID YOU GET A CHANCE TO ASK *THE TOTEMS* WHAT I TOLD YOU TO ASK 'EM?
I SURE AS HECK 'N' HONEY DID, LITTLE WING, YA RED QUEEN!
'SCUSE MY CUSSIN'. CAN TAKE A SHEPHERD OUTTA THE BARN, BUT YA CAN'T ALWAYS TAKE THE BARN OUTTA THE SHEPHERD, EH?
S'OKAY. MY MOMMY SAYS WORSE WHEN SHE THINKS I'M NOT LISTENING.
SO, WHAT DID THEY SAY? CAN I LOOK FOR CLIFFY NOW, OR ARE THEY STILL MAD AT MY DADDY?
WELL, THE BIG FELLERS WERE AWFUL SORE AT BUTTER BAKER BLONDIE MAN, BUT THEY SEEM TO HAVE CHANGED THEIR TUNE A BIT WHEN IT COMES TO YOU, MY BEAUTY...
IN FACT, THEY BEEN **WAITIN'** FOR YOU TO COME BACK. WANT TO TALK TO YER CUTE LITTLE BUTTON OF A NOSE IN PERSON.
MAXINE, I SUGGEST YOU CHOOSE YOUR WORDS WISELY. THE TOTEMS ARE IN TURMOIL AFTER THE ROT'S RISE. AND THEY ARE, ERM... **SENSITIVE,** AT THE BEST OF TIMES.
I DON'T CARE! I'M LOOKING FOR CLIFF, AND IF THEY DON'T LIKE IT, TOO BAD!
UH-OH.
OH, DEAR...

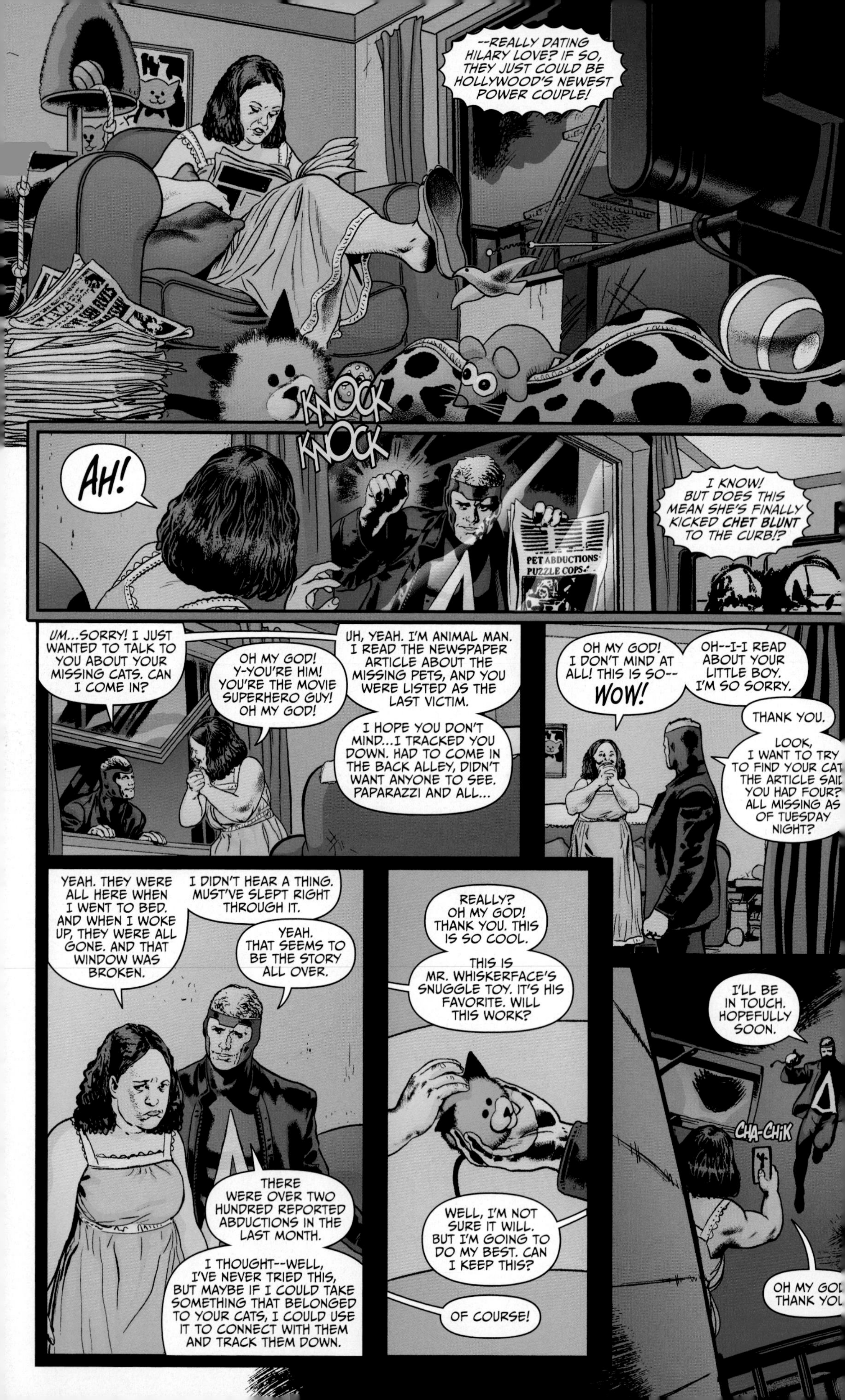
--REALLY DATING HILARY LOVE? IF SO, THEY JUST COULD BE HOLLYWOOD'S NEWEST POWER COUPLE!
KNOCK KNOCK
AH!
I KNOW! BUT DOES THIS MEAN SHE'S FINALLY KICKED CHET BLUNT TO THE CURB!?
PET ABDUCTIONS PUZZLE COPS
UM...SORRY! I JUST WANTED TO TALK TO YOU ABOUT YOUR MISSING CATS. CAN I COME IN?
OH MY GOD! Y-YOU'RE HIM! YOU'RE THE MOVIE SUPERHERO GUY! OH MY GOD!
UH, YEAH. I'M ANIMAL MAN. I READ THE NEWSPAPER ARTICLE ABOUT THE MISSING PETS, AND YOU WERE LISTED AS THE LAST VICTIM.
I HOPE YOU DON'T MIND...I TRACKED YOU DOWN. HAD TO COME IN THE BACK ALLEY, DIDN'T WANT ANYONE TO SEE. PAPARAZZI AND ALL...
OH MY GOD! I DON'T MIND AT ALL! THIS IS SO-- WOW!
OH--I-I READ ABOUT YOUR LITTLE BOY. I'M SO SORRY.
THANK YOU.
LOOK, I WANT TO TRY TO FIND YOUR CAT THE ARTICLE SAID YOU HAD FOUR? ALL MISSING AS OF TUESDAY NIGHT?
YEAH. THEY WERE ALL HERE WHEN I WENT TO BED. AND WHEN I WOKE UP, THEY WERE ALL GONE. AND THAT WINDOW WAS BROKEN.
I DIDN'T HEAR A THING. MUST'VE SLEPT RIGHT THROUGH IT.
YEAH. THAT SEEMS TO BE THE STORY ALL OVER.
THERE WERE OVER TWO HUNDRED REPORTED ABDUCTIONS IN THE LAST MONTH.
I THOUGHT--WELL, I'VE NEVER TRIED THIS, BUT MAYBE IF I COULD TAKE SOMETHING THAT BELONGED TO YOUR CATS, I COULD USE IT TO CONNECT WITH THEM AND TRACK THEM DOWN.
REALLY? OH MY GOD! THANK YOU. THIS IS SO COOL.
THIS IS MR. WHISKERFACE'S SNUGGLE TOY. IT'S HIS FAVORITE. WILL THIS WORK?
WELL, I'M NOT SURE IT WILL. BUT I'M GOING TO DO MY BEST. CAN I KEEP THIS?
OF COURSE!
I'LL BE IN TOUCH. HOPEFULLY SOON.
CHA-CHIK
OH MY GOD THANK YOU

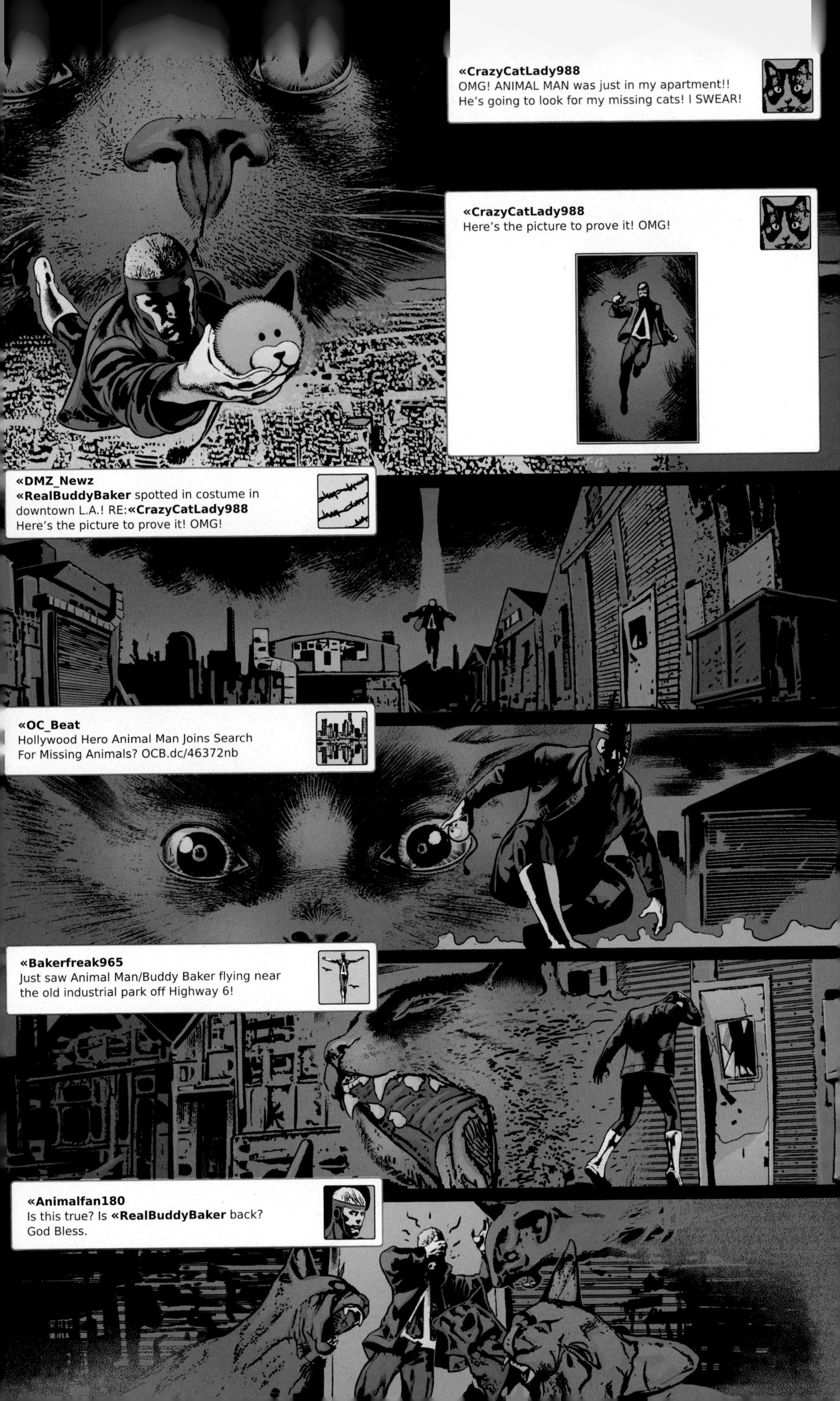

«CrazyCatLady988
OMG! ANIMAL MAN was just in my apartment!! He's going to look for my missing cats! I SWEAR!
«CrazyCatLady988
Here's the picture to prove it! OMG!
«DMZ_Newz
«RealBuddyBaker spotted in costume in downtown L.A.! RE:«CrazyCatLady988 Here's the picture to prove it! OMG!
«OC_Beat
Hollywood Hero Animal Man Joins Search For Missing Animals? OCB.dc/46372nb
«Bakerfreak965
Just saw Animal Man/Buddy Baker flying near the old industrial park off Highway 6!
«Animalfan180
Is this true? Is «RealBuddyBaker back? God Bless.

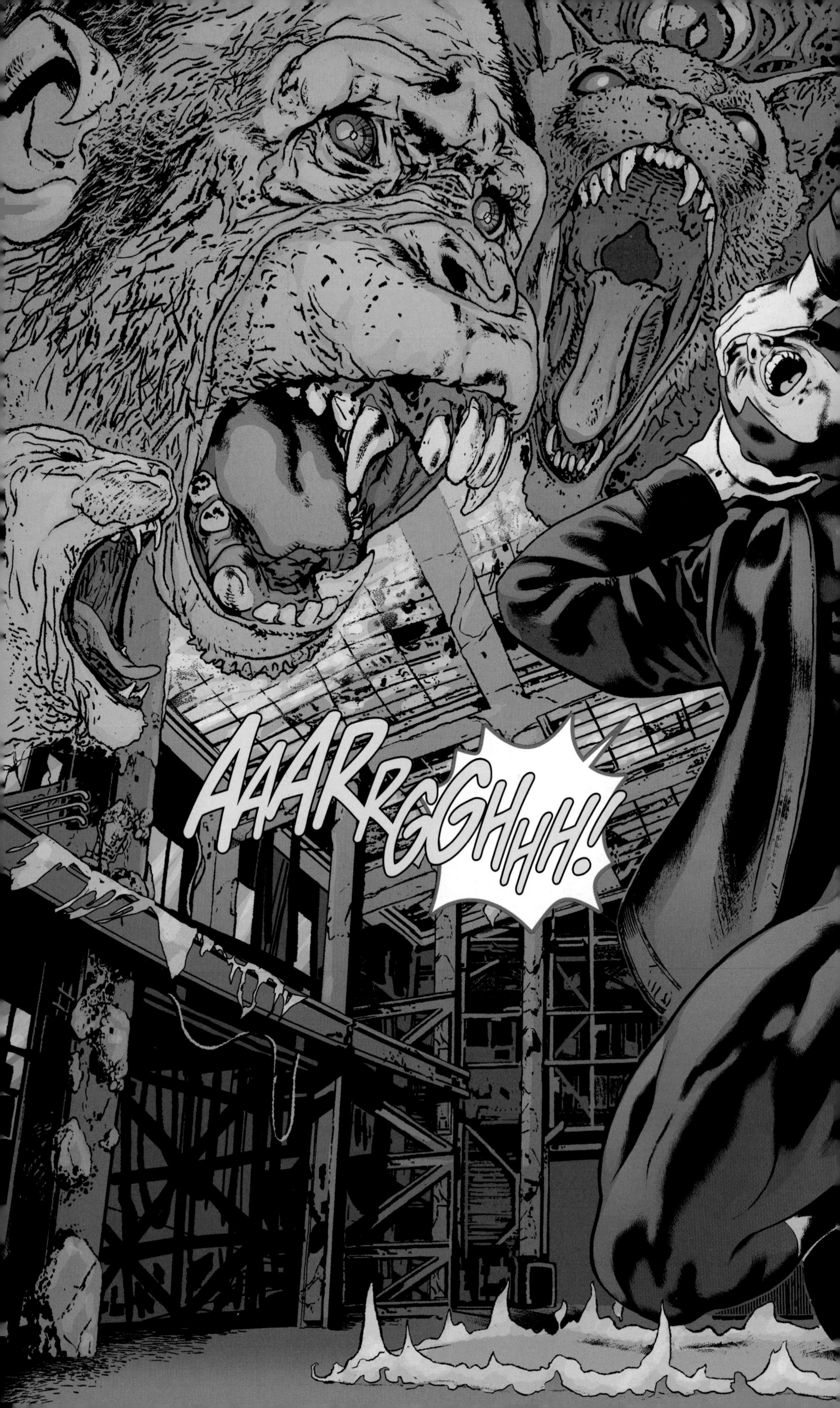
AAARRGGHHH!

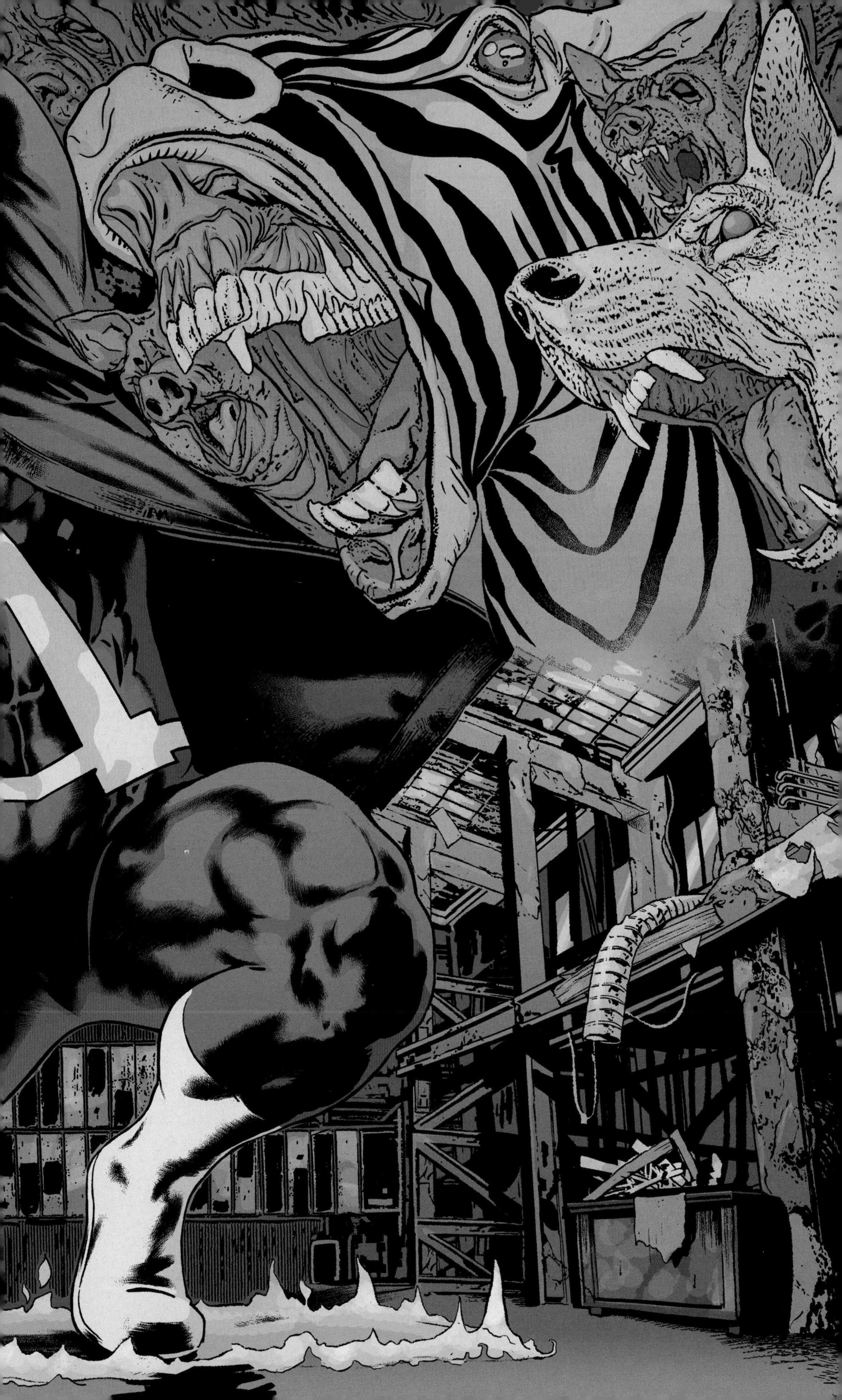

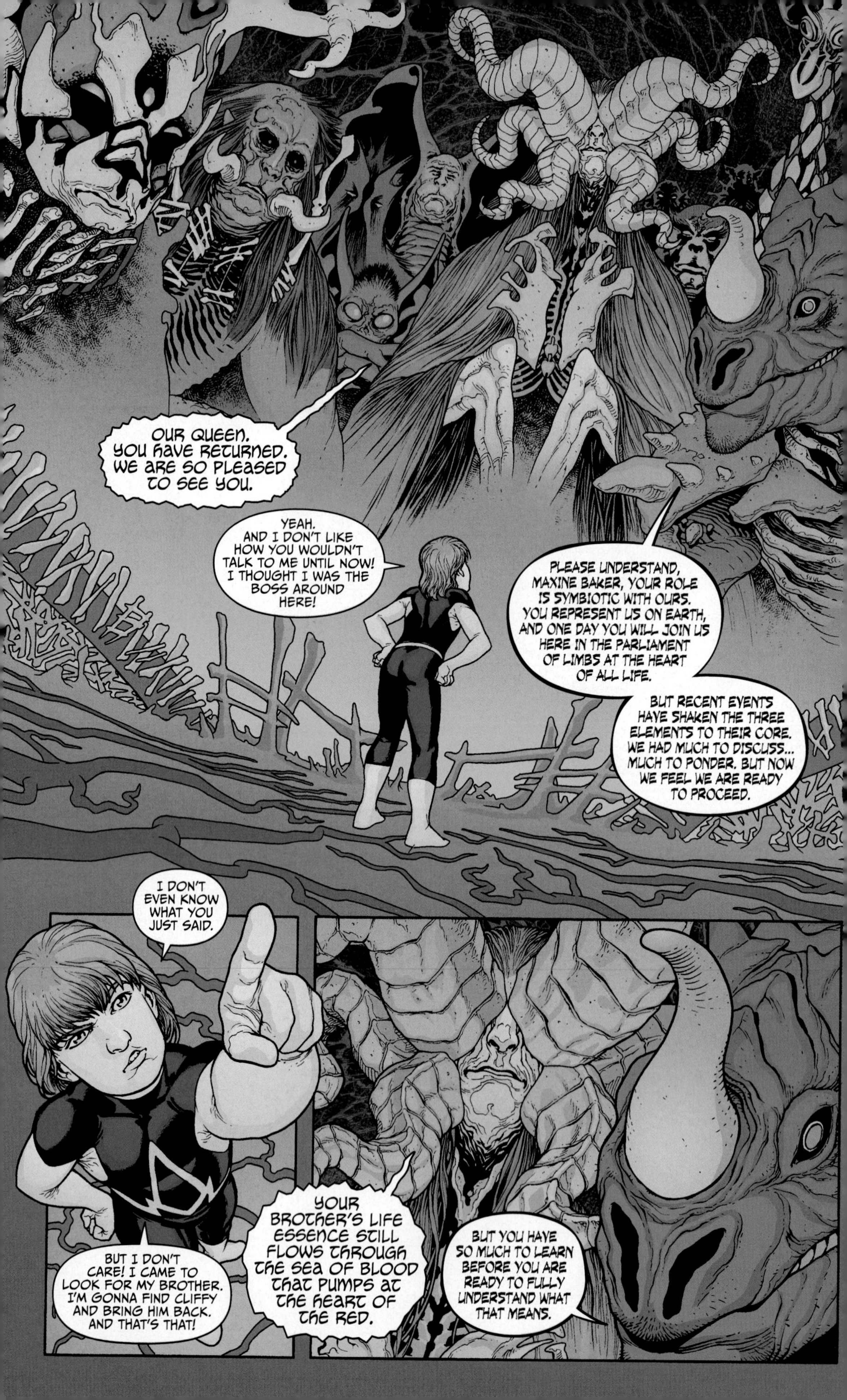
OUR QUEEN. YOU HAVE RETURNED. WE ARE SO PLEASED TO SEE YOU.
YEAH. AND I DON'T LIKE HOW YOU WOULDN'T TALK TO ME UNTIL NOW! I THOUGHT I WAS THE BOSS AROUND HERE!
PLEASE UNDERSTAND, MAXINE BAKER, YOUR ROLE IS SYMBIOTIC WITH OURS. YOU REPRESENT US ON EARTH, AND ONE DAY YOU WILL JOIN US HERE IN THE PARLIAMENT OF LIMBS AT THE HEART OF ALL LIFE.
BUT RECENT EVENTS HAVE SHAKEN THE THREE ELEMENTS TO THEIR CORE. WE HAD MUCH TO DISCUSS... MUCH TO PONDER. BUT NOW WE FEEL WE ARE READY TO PROCEED.
I DON'T EVEN KNOW WHAT YOU JUST SAID.
BUT I DON'T CARE! I CAME TO LOOK FOR MY BROTHER. I'M GONNA FIND CLIFFY AND BRING HIM BACK. AND THAT'S THAT!
YOUR BROTHER'S LIFE ESSENCE STILL FLOWS THROUGH THE SEA OF BLOOD THAT PUMPS AT THE HEART OF THE RED.
BUT YOU HAVE SO MUCH TO LEARN BEFORE YOU ARE READY TO FULLY UNDERSTAND WHAT THAT MEANS.

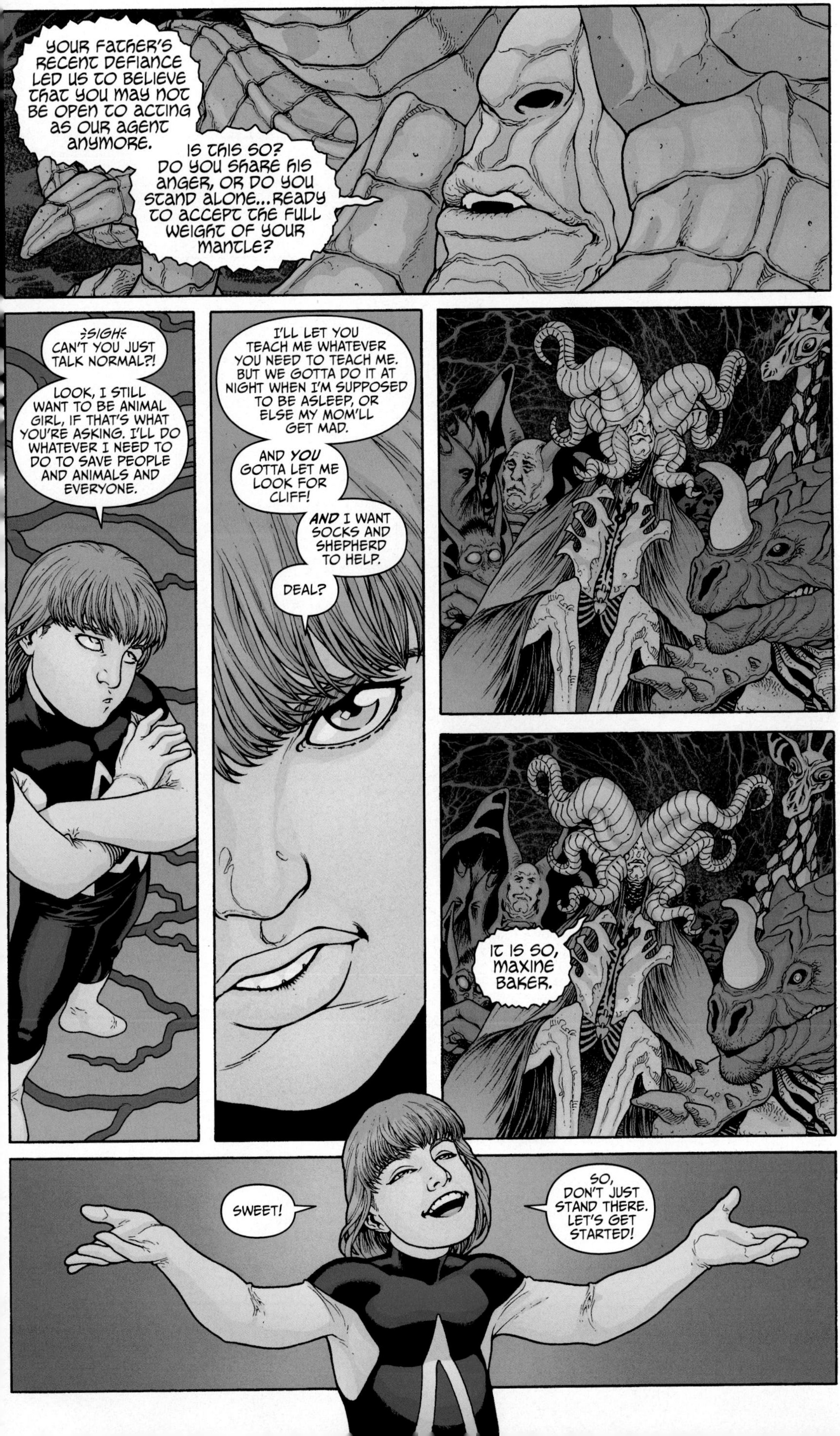

YOUR FATHER'S RECENT DEFIANCE LED US TO BELIEVE THAT YOU MAY NOT BE OPEN TO ACTING AS OUR AGENT ANYMORE.
IS THIS SO? DO YOU SHARE HIS ANGER, OR DO YOU STAND ALONE...READY TO ACCEPT THE FULL WEIGHT OF YOUR MANTLE?
SIGH
CAN'T YOU JUST TALK NORMAL?!
LOOK, I STILL WANT TO BE ANIMAL GIRL, IF THAT'S WHAT YOU'RE ASKING. I'LL DO WHATEVER I NEED TO DO TO SAVE PEOPLE AND ANIMALS AND EVERYONE.
I'LL LET YOU TEACH ME WHATEVER YOU NEED TO TEACH ME. BUT WE GOTTA DO IT AT NIGHT WHEN I'M SUPPOSED TO BE ASLEEP, OR ELSE MY MOM'LL GET MAD.
AND YOU GOTTA LET ME LOOK FOR CLIFF!
AND I WANT SOCKS AND SHEPHERD TO HELP.
DEAL?
IT IS SO, MAXINE BAKER.
SWEET!
SO, DON'T JUST STAND THERE. LET'S GET STARTED!

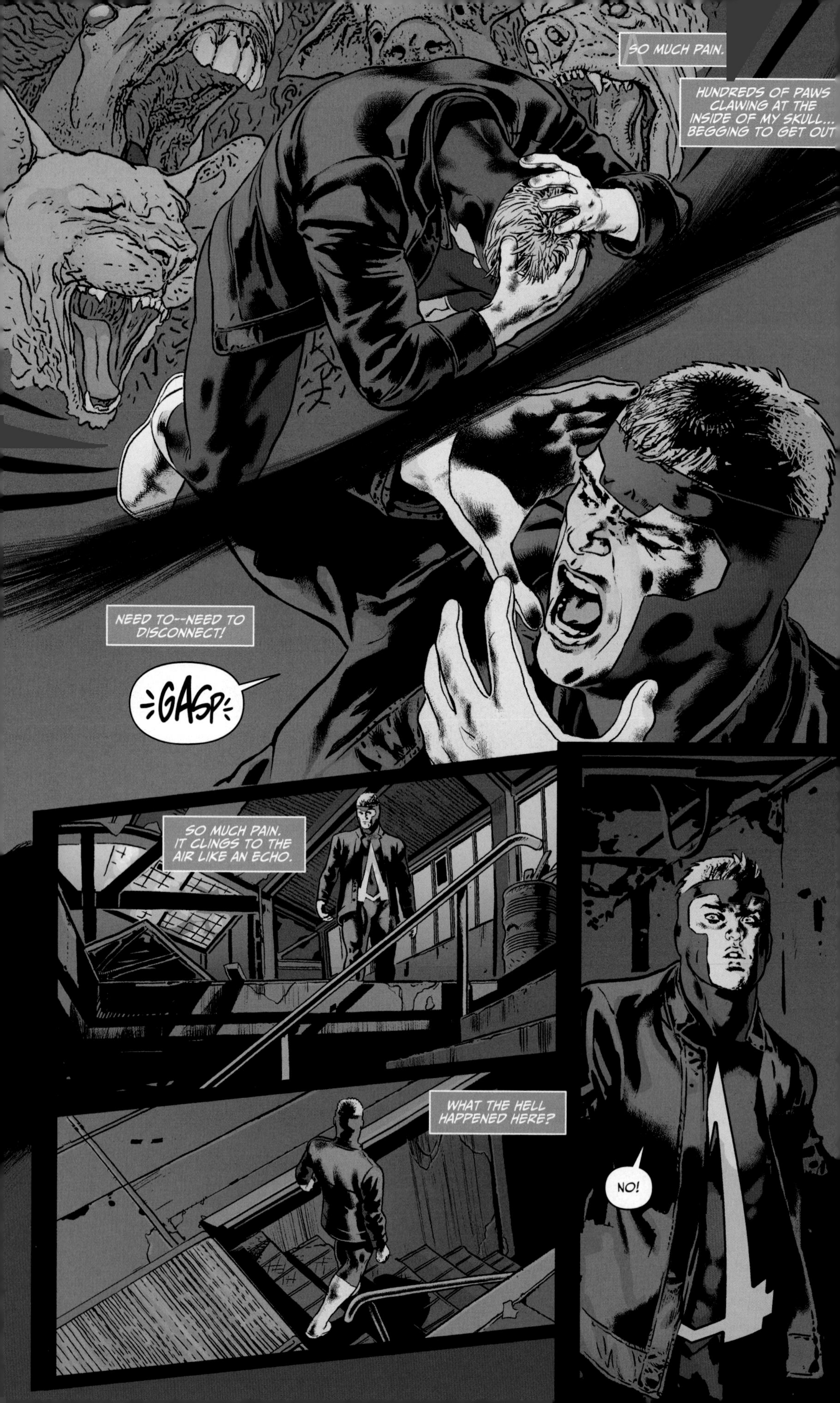
SO MUCH PAIN.
HUNDREDS OF PAWS CLAWING AT THE INSIDE OF MY SKULL... BEGGING TO GET OUT
NEED TO--NEED TO DISCONNECT!
GASP
SO MUCH PAIN. IT CLINGS TO THE AIR LIKE AN ECHO.
WHAT THE HELL HAPPENED HERE?
NO!

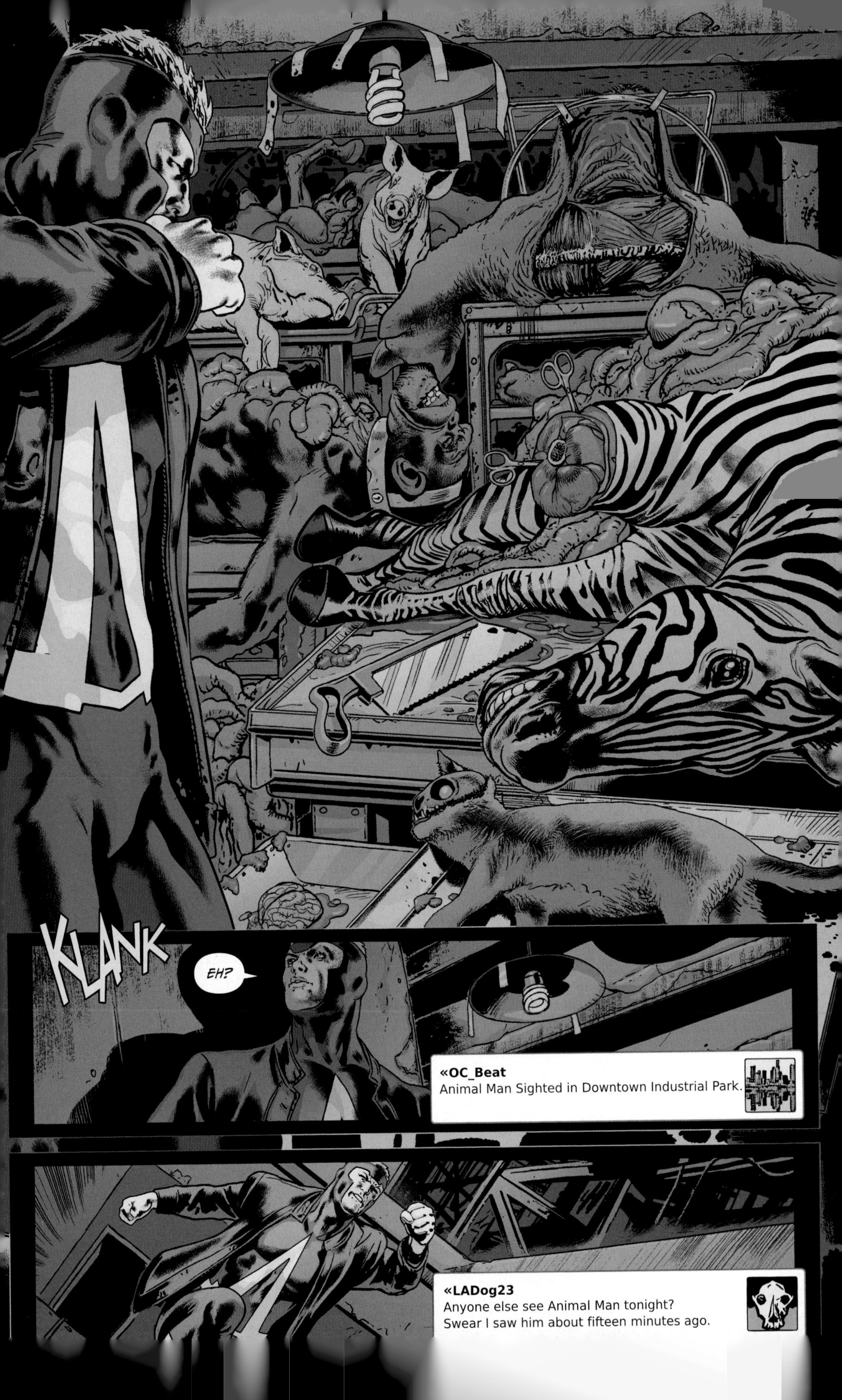
KLANK
EH?
«OC_Beat
Animal Man Sighted in Downtown Industrial Park.
«LADog23
Anyone else see Animal Man tonight?
Swear I saw him about fifteen minutes ago.

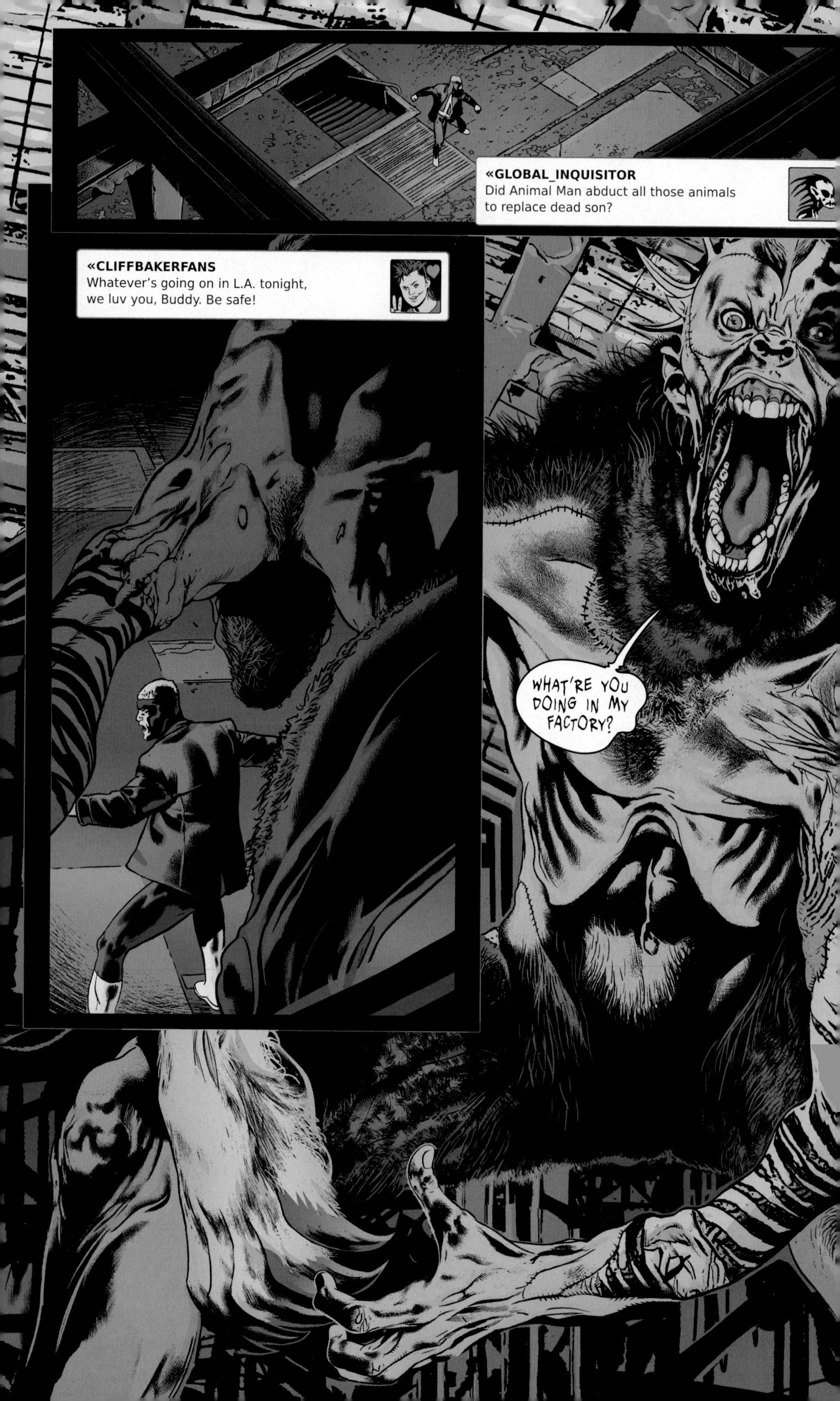
«GLOBAL_INQUISITOR
Did Animal Man abduct all those animals to replace dead son?
«CLIFFBAKERFANS
Whatever's going on in L.A. tonight, we luv you, Buddy. Be safe!
WHAT'RE YOU DOING IN MY FACTORY?

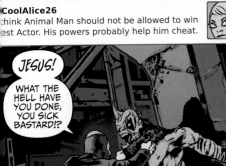

CoolAlice26
[t]hink Animal Man should not be allowed to win [B]est Actor. His powers probably help him cheat.

«OC_Beat
Police En Route Responding to Reports of Animal Man-Related Disturbance in Downtown L.A. OCB.dc/46382nb

JESUS!

WHAT THE HELL HAVE YOU DONE, YOU SICK BASTARD!?

«animalfan180
I can't believe all the haters out there. Buddy is the best. You guys suck. God Bless.

KRAK

«RUMORVULTURE
Breaking: Animal Man Back in Action in Downtown LA! RVult.dc/46382nb

UNGH!

«FILMBUFF52
Sources say tonight's "Animal Man Action" really just a movie of the week being filmed. FilmB.dc/3747hs

?!

«HEARD_IN_LA
Animal Man Sighting a Hoax? Accepting tips! Spread the word!

NO WAY. THERE IS NO WAY THIS GUY GETS AWAY WITH THIS!

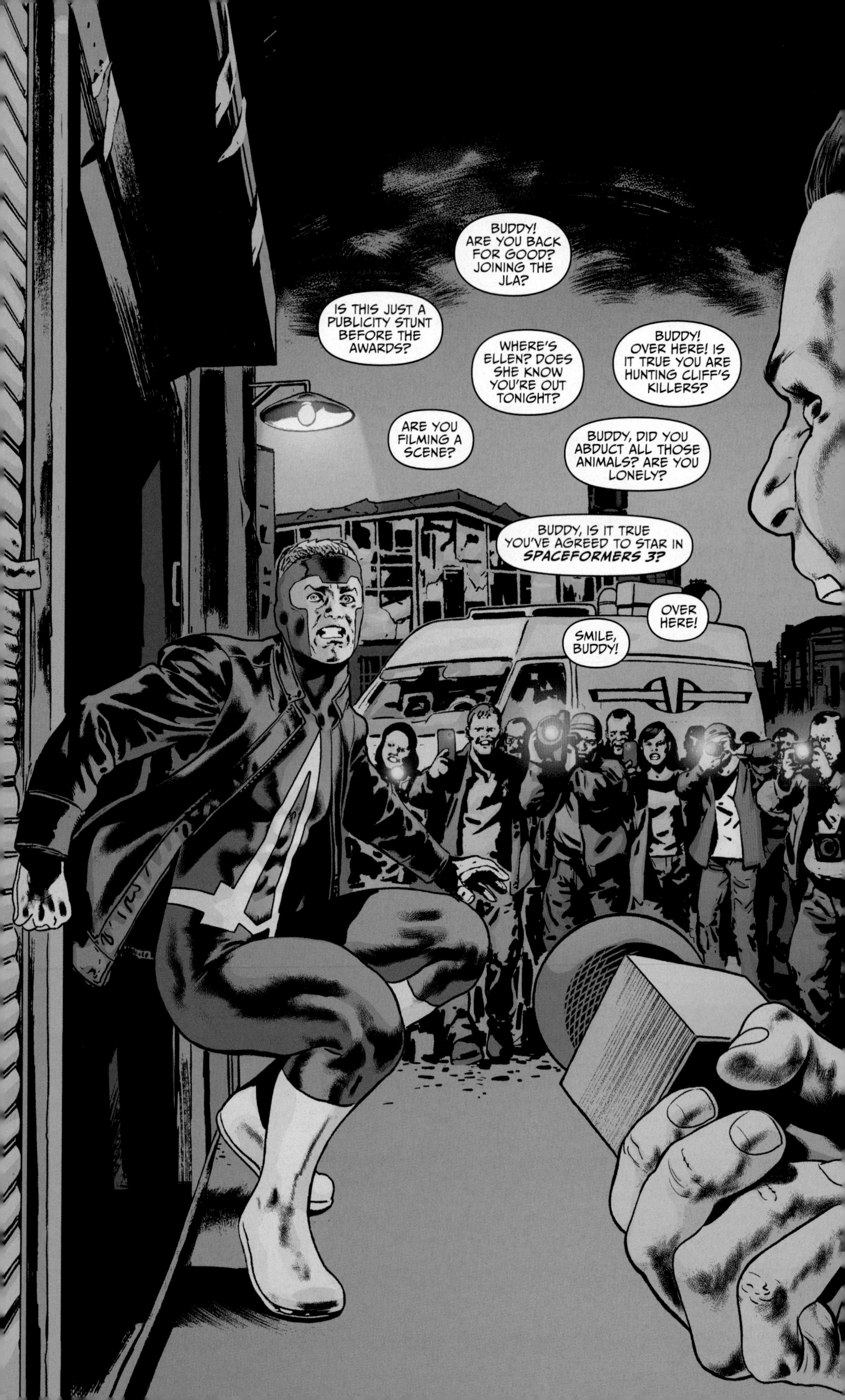
BUDDY! ARE YOU BACK FOR GOOD? JOINING THE JLA?
IS THIS JUST A PUBLICITY STUNT BEFORE THE AWARDS?
WHERE'S ELLEN? DOES SHE KNOW YOU'RE OUT TONIGHT?
BUDDY! OVER HERE! IS IT TRUE YOU ARE HUNTING CLIFF'S KILLERS?
ARE YOU FILMING A SCENE?
BUDDY, DID YOU ABDUCT ALL THOSE ANIMALS? ARE YOU LONELY?
BUDDY, IS IT TRUE YOU'VE AGREED TO STAR IN SPACEFORMERS 3?
OVER HERE!
SMILE, BUDDY!

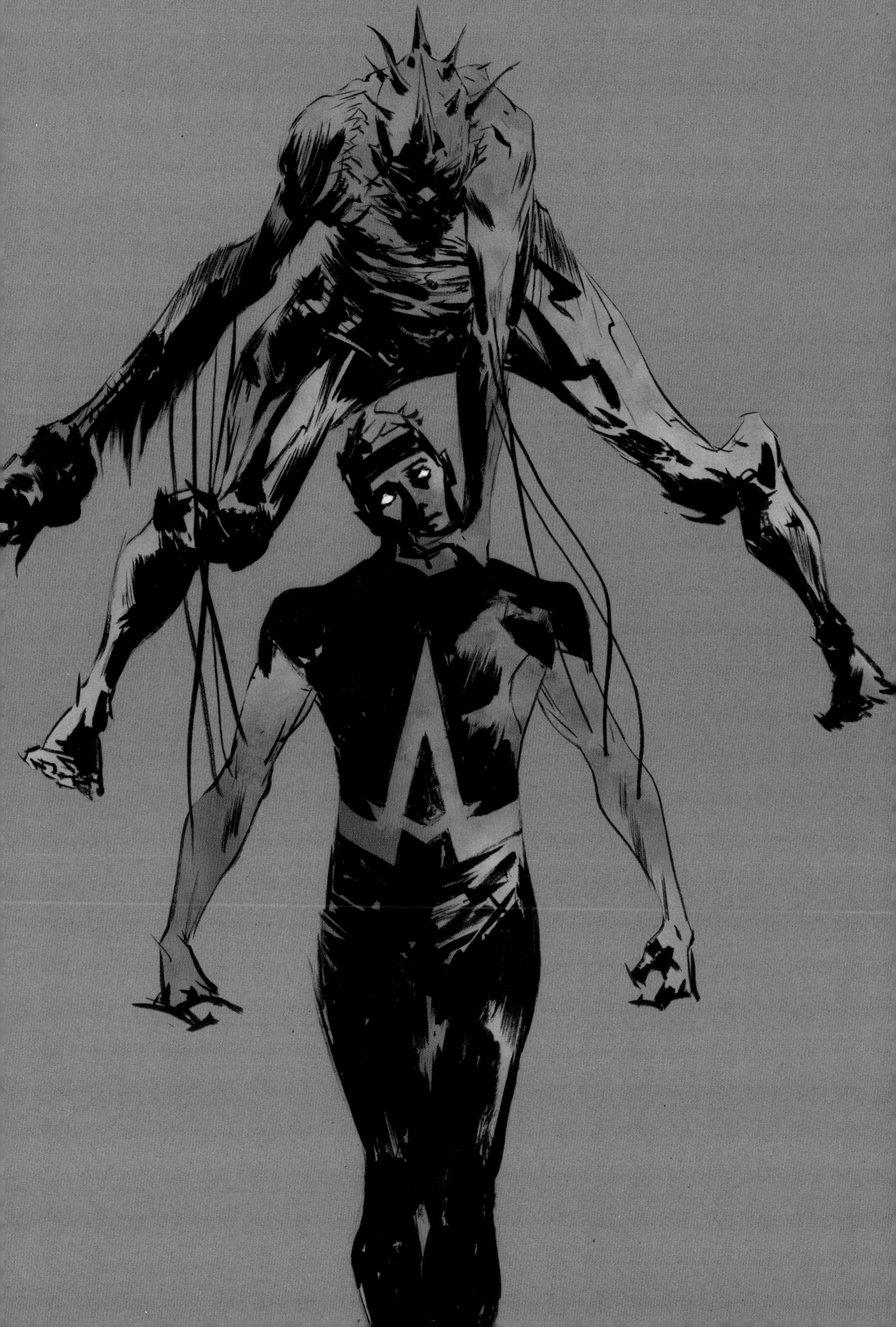

JEFF LEMIRE
writer

STEVE PUGH & FRANCIS PORTELA
artists

JAE LEE with JUNE CHUNG
cover artists

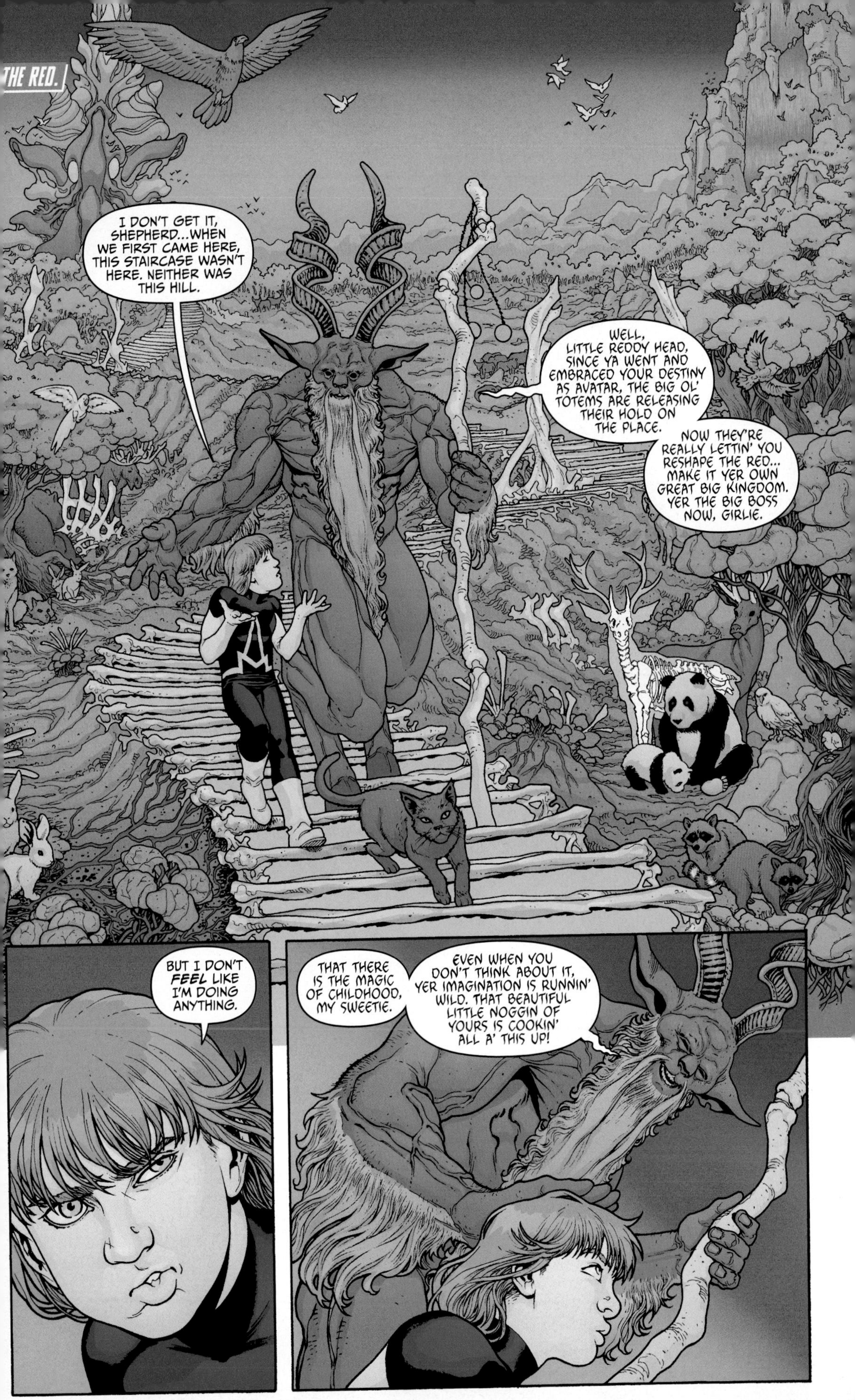
THE RED.
I DON'T GET IT, SHEPHERD...WHEN WE FIRST CAME HERE, THIS STAIRCASE WASN'T HERE. NEITHER WAS THIS HILL.
WELL, LITTLE REDDY HEAD, SINCE YA WENT AND EMBRACED YOUR DESTINY AS AVATAR, THE BIG OL' TOTEMS ARE RELEASING THEIR HOLD ON THE PLACE.
NOW THEY'RE REALLY LETTIN' YOU RESHAPE THE RED... MAKE IT YER OWN GREAT BIG KINGDOM. YER THE BIG BOSS NOW, GIRLIE.
BUT I DON'T FEEL LIKE I'M DOING ANYTHING.
THAT THERE IS THE MAGIC OF CHILDHOOD, MY SWEETIE.
EVEN WHEN YOU DON'T THINK ABOUT IT, YER IMAGINATION IS RUNNIN' WILD. THAT BEAUTIFUL LITTLE NOGGIN OF YOURS IS COOKIN' ALL A' THIS UP!

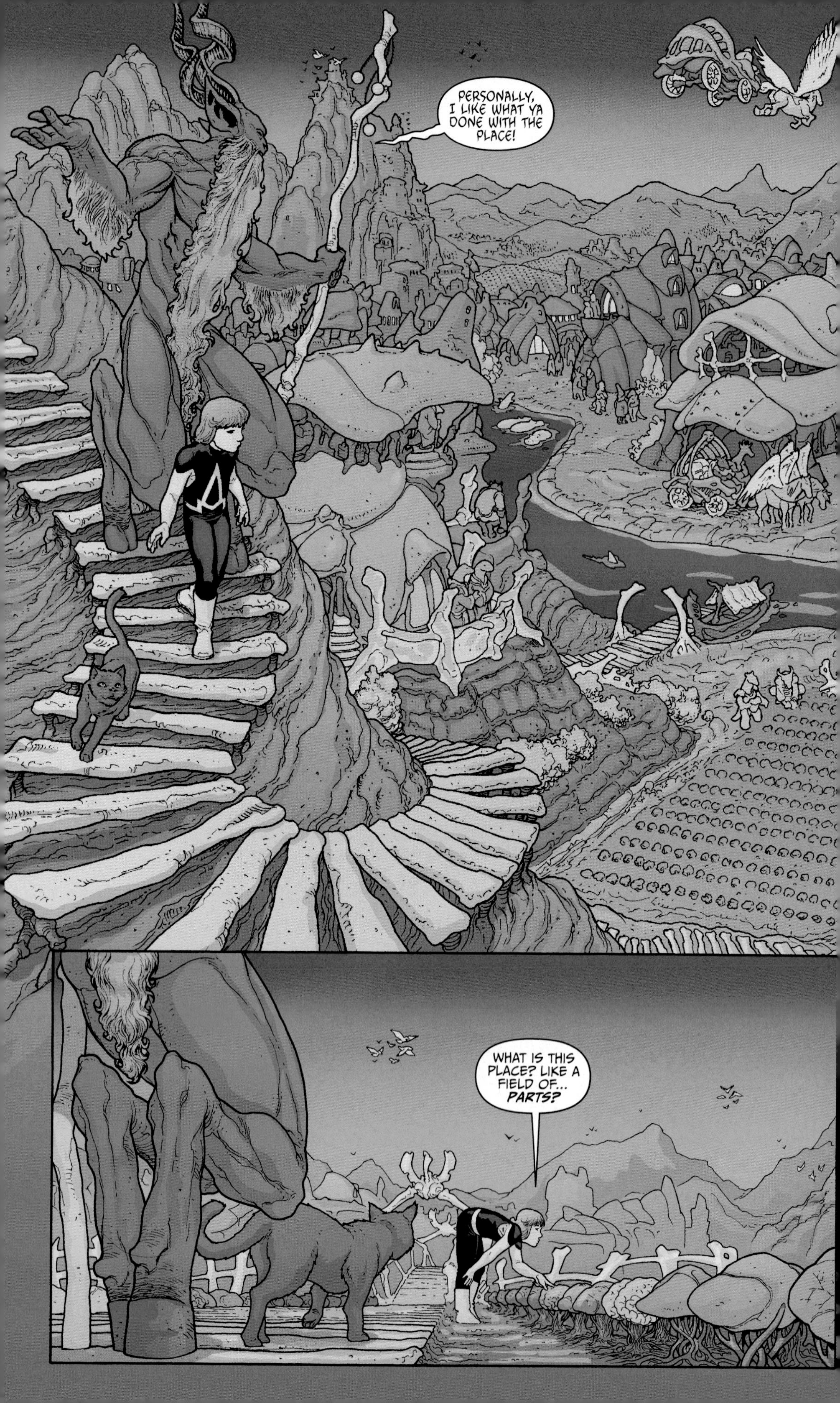
PERSONALLY, I LIKE WHAT YA DONE WITH THE PLACE!
WHAT IS THIS PLACE? LIKE A FIELD OF... *PARTS?*

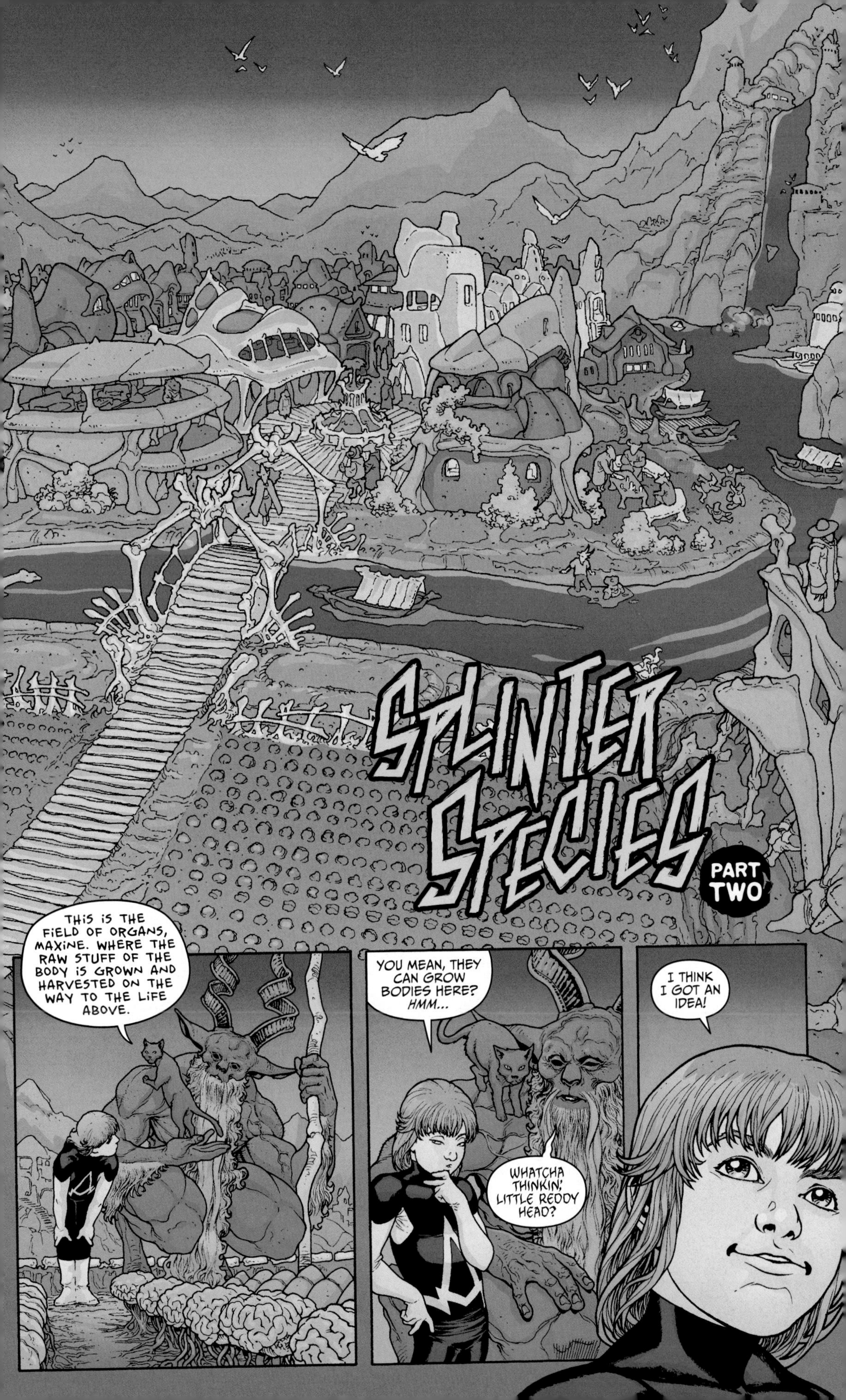
SPLINTER SPECIES
PART TWO
THIS IS THE FIELD OF ORGANS, MAXINE. WHERE THE RAW STUFF OF THE BODY IS GROWN AND HARVESTED ON THE WAY TO THE LIFE ABOVE.
YOU MEAN, THEY CAN GROW BODIES HERE? HMM...
WHATCHA THINKIN', LITTLE REDDY HEAD?
I THINK I GOT AN IDEA!

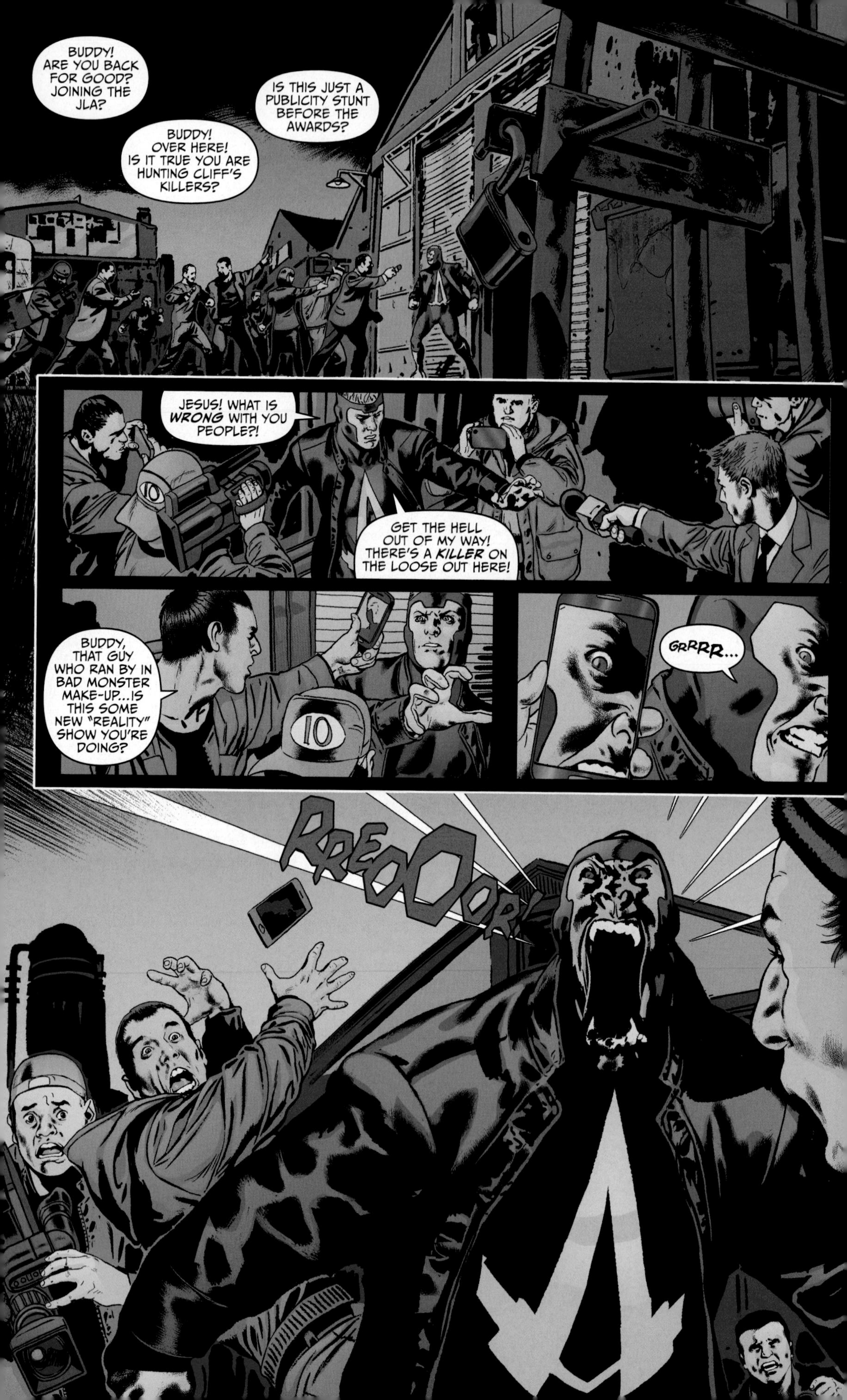
BUDDY!
ARE YOU BACK FOR GOOD? JOINING THE JLA?
BUDDY! OVER HERE! IS IT TRUE YOU ARE HUNTING CLIFF'S KILLERS?
IS THIS JUST A PUBLICITY STUNT BEFORE THE AWARDS?
JESUS! WHAT IS *WRONG* WITH YOU PEOPLE?!
GET THE HELL OUT OF MY WAY! THERE'S A *KILLER* ON THE LOOSE OUT HERE!
10
BUDDY, THAT GUY WHO RAN BY IN BAD MONSTER MAKE-UP...IS THIS SOME NEW "REALITY" SHOW YOU'RE DOING?
10
GRRRR...
RREOOOR!

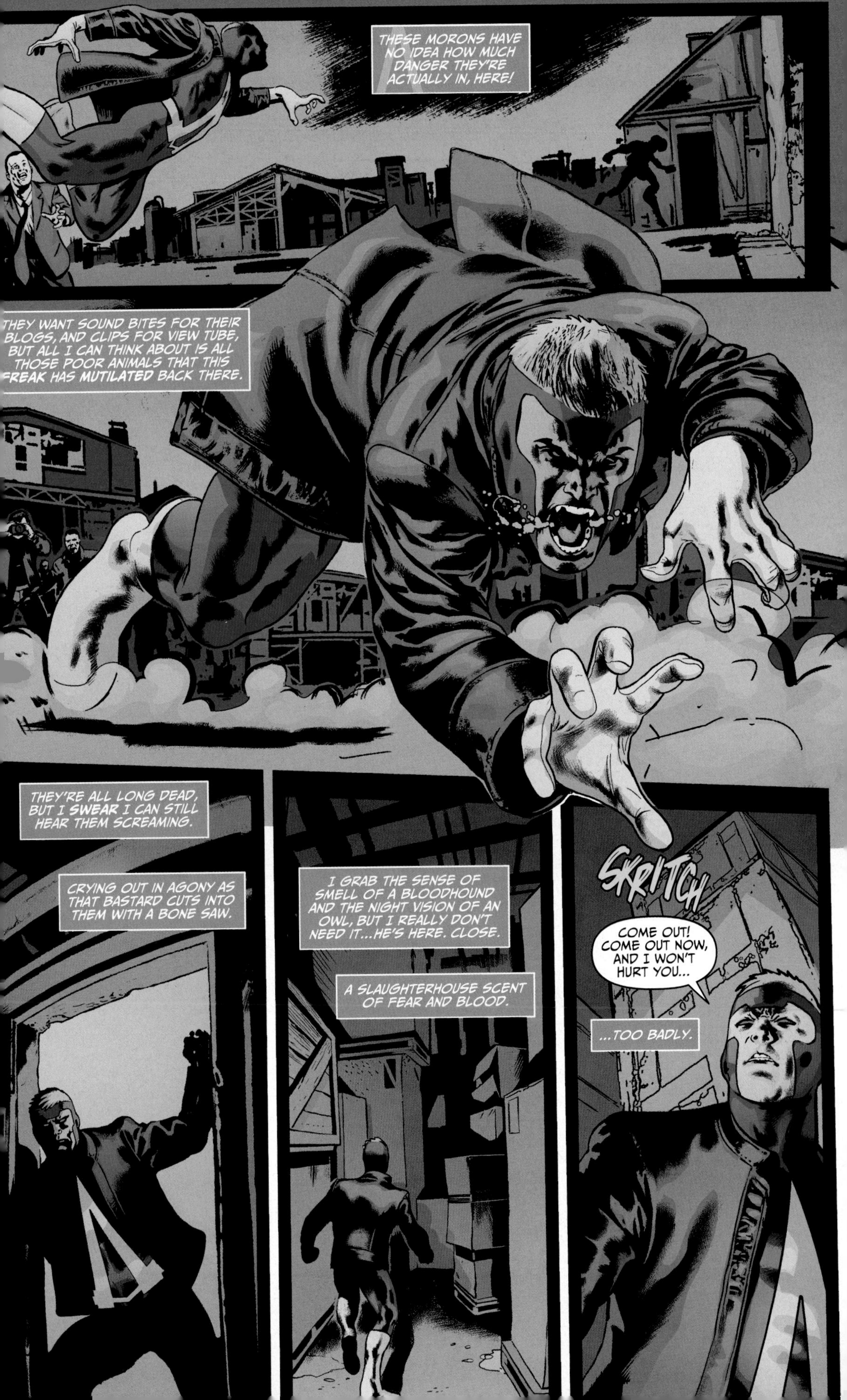
THESE MORONS HAVE NO IDEA HOW MUCH DANGER THEY'RE ACTUALLY IN, HERE!
THEY WANT SOUND BITES FOR THEIR BLOGS, AND CLIPS FOR VIEW TUBE, BUT ALL I CAN THINK ABOUT IS ALL THOSE POOR ANIMALS THAT THIS FREAK HAS MUTILATED BACK THERE.
THEY'RE ALL LONG DEAD, BUT I SWEAR I CAN STILL HEAR THEM SCREAMING.
CRYING OUT IN AGONY AS THAT BASTARD CUTS INTO THEM WITH A BONE SAW.
I GRAB THE SENSE OF SMELL OF A BLOODHOUND AND THE NIGHT VISION OF AN OWL, BUT I REALLY DON'T NEED IT...HE'S HERE. CLOSE.
A SLAUGHTERHOUSE SCENT OF FEAR AND BLOOD.
SKRITCH
COME OUT! COME OUT NOW, AND I WON'T HURT YOU...
...TOO BADLY.

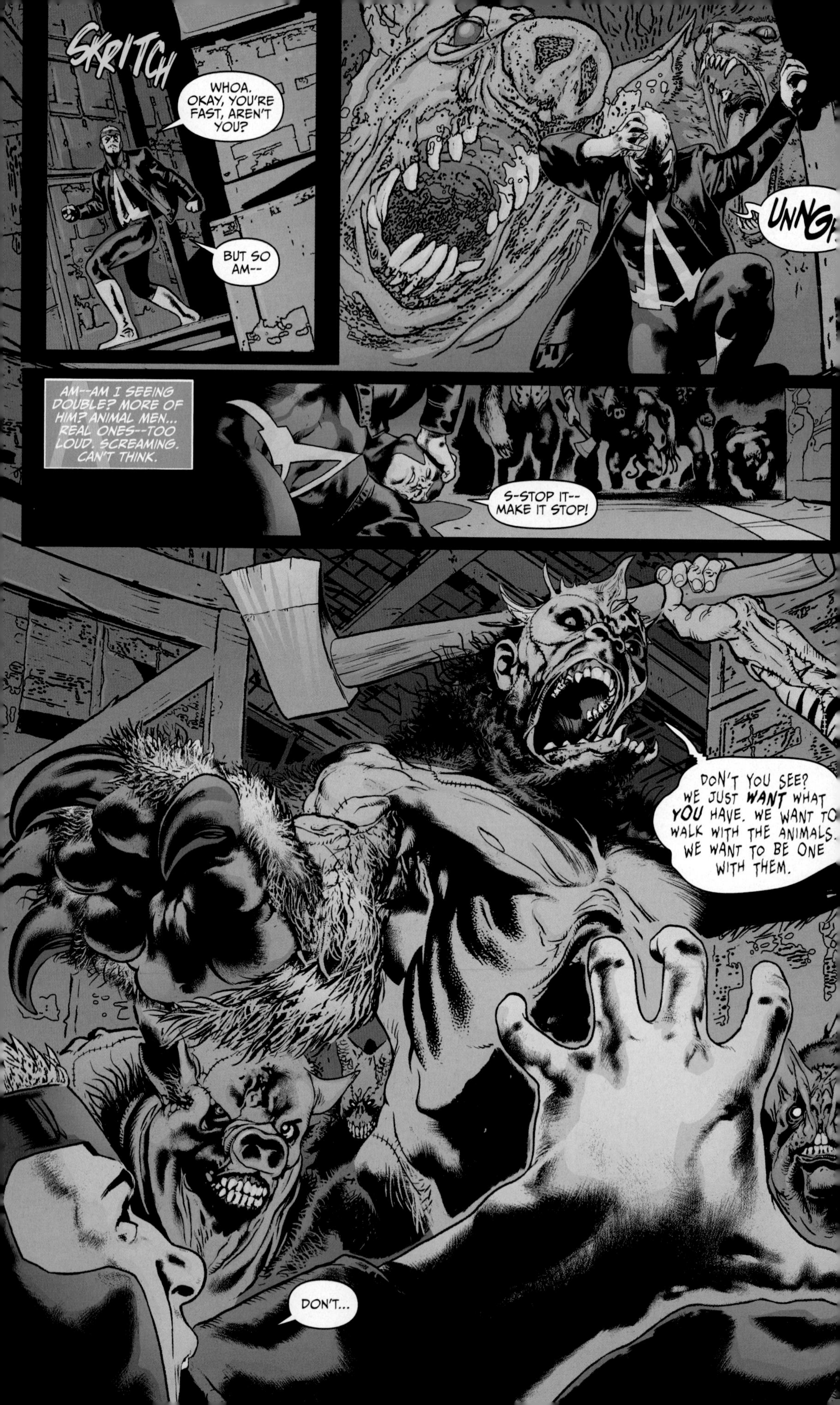
SKRITCH
WHOA. OKAY, YOU'RE FAST, AREN'T YOU?
BUT SO AM--
UNNGH
AM--AM I SEEING DOUBLE? MORE OF HIM? ANIMAL MEN... REAL ONES--TOO LOUD. SCREAMING. CAN'T THINK.
S-STOP IT-- MAKE IT STOP!
DON'T YOU SEE? WE JUST WANT WHAT YOU HAVE. WE WANT TO WALK WITH THE ANIMALS. WE WANT TO BE ONE WITH THEM.
DON'T...

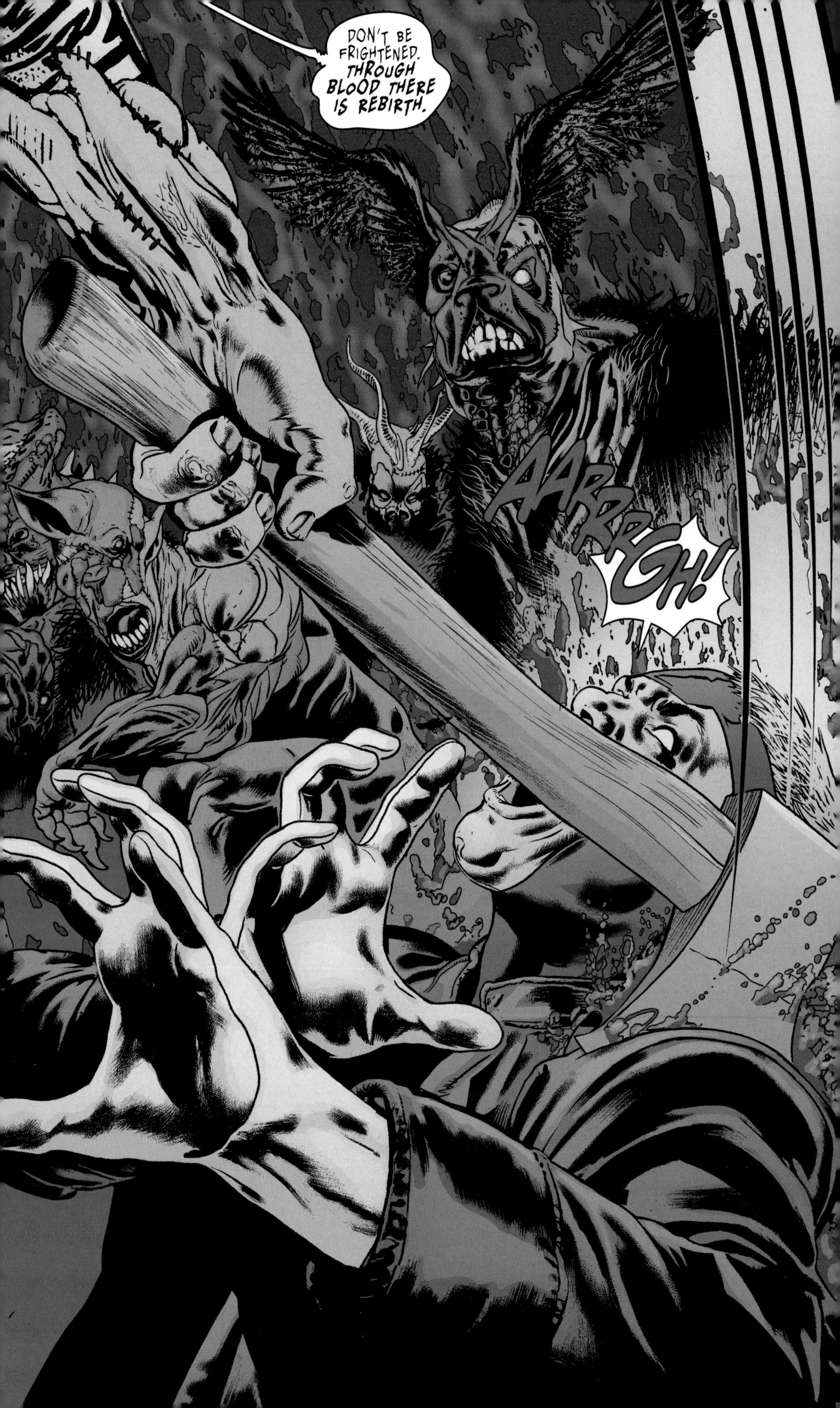
DON'T BE FRIGHTENED. THROUGH BLOOD THERE IS REBIRTH.
AARRRGH!!

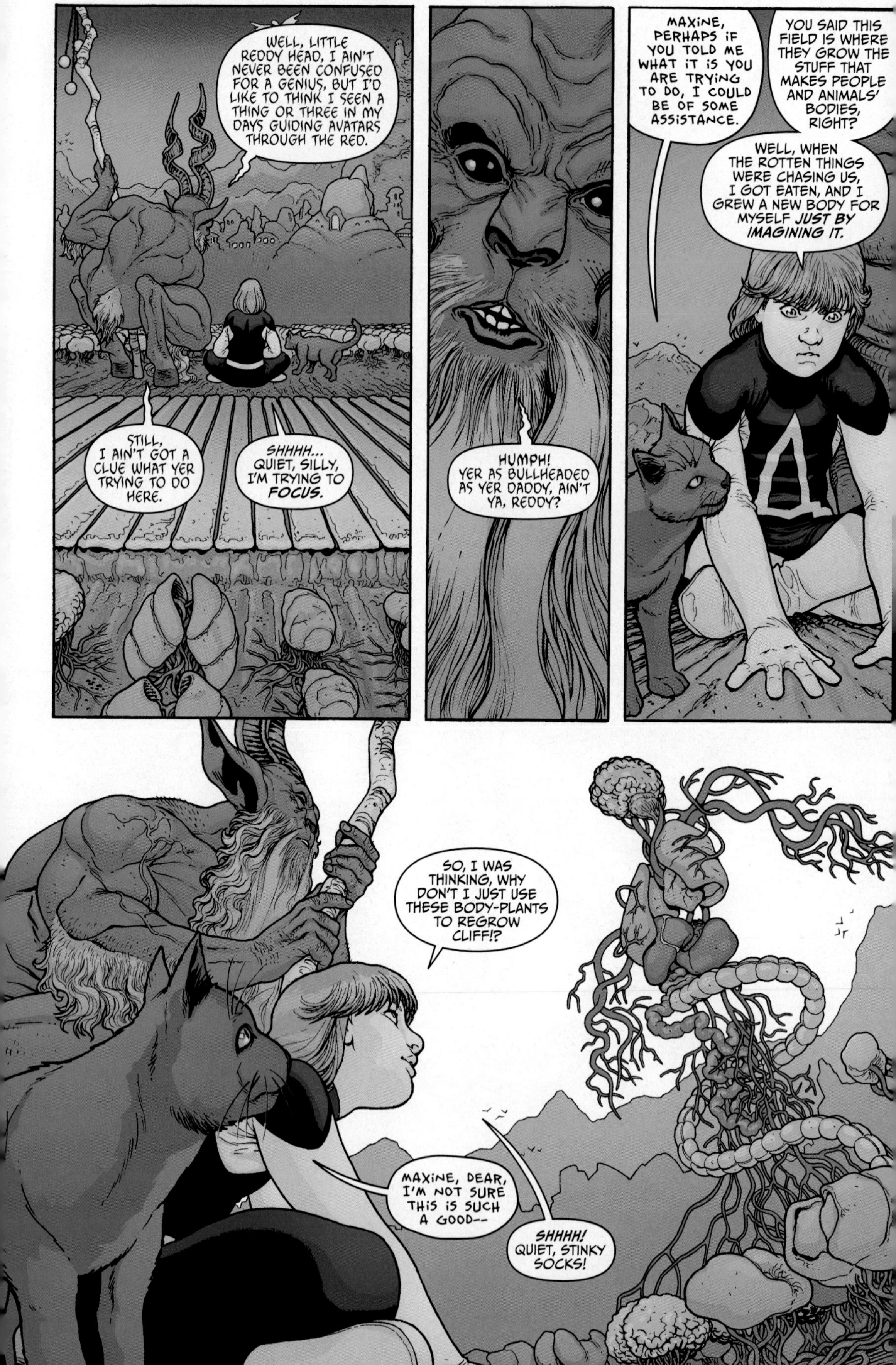
WELL, LITTLE REDDY HEAD, I AIN'T NEVER BEEN CONFUSED FOR A GENIUS, BUT I'D LIKE TO THINK I SEEN A THING OR THREE IN MY DAYS GUIDING AVATARS THROUGH THE RED.
STILL, I AIN'T GOT A CLUE WHAT YER TRYING TO DO HERE.
SHHHH... QUIET, SILLY, I'M TRYING TO FOCUS.
HUMPH! YER AS BULLHEADED AS YER DADDY, AIN'T YA, REDDY?
MAXINE, PERHAPS IF YOU TOLD ME WHAT IT IS YOU ARE TRYING TO DO, I COULD BE OF SOME ASSISTANCE.
YOU SAID THIS FIELD IS WHERE THEY GROW THE STUFF THAT MAKES PEOPLE AND ANIMALS' BODIES, RIGHT?
WELL, WHEN THE ROTTEN THINGS WERE CHASING US, I GOT EATEN, AND I GREW A NEW BODY FOR MYSELF JUST BY IMAGINING IT.
SO, I WAS THINKING, WHY DON'T I JUST USE THESE BODY-PLANTS TO REGROW CLIFF!?
MAXINE, DEAR, I'M NOT SURE THIS IS SUCH A GOOD--
SHHHH! QUIET, STINKY SOCKS!

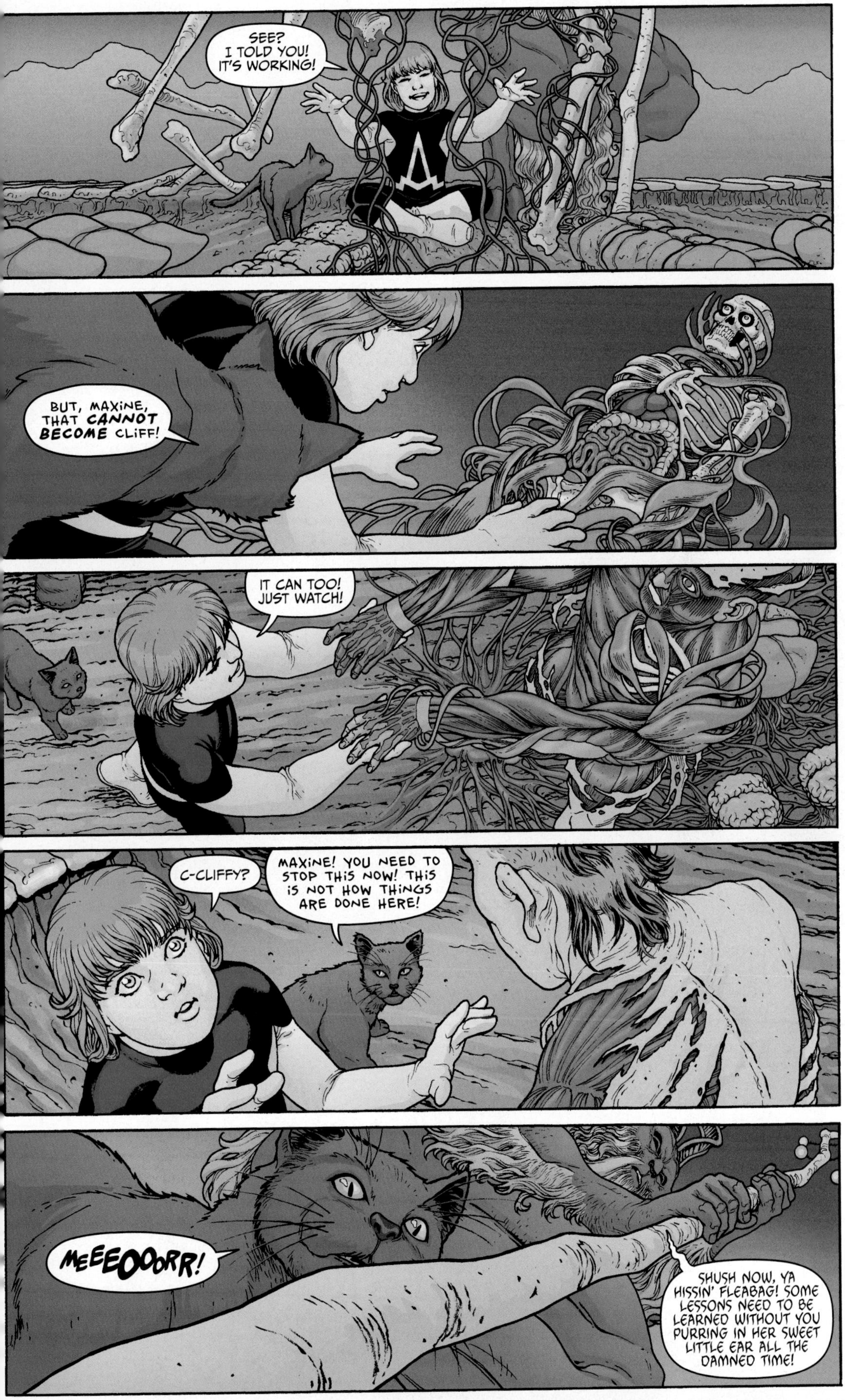
SEE? I TOLD YOU! IT'S WORKING!
BUT, MAXINE, THAT CANNOT BECOME CLIFF!
IT CAN TOO! JUST WATCH!
C-CLIFFY?
MAXINE! YOU NEED TO STOP THIS NOW! THIS IS NOT HOW THINGS ARE DONE HERE!
MEEEOOORR!
SHUSH NOW, YA HISSIN' FLEABAG! SOME LESSONS NEED TO BE LEARNED WITHOUT YOU PURRING IN HER SWEET LITTLE EAR ALL THE DAMNED TIME!

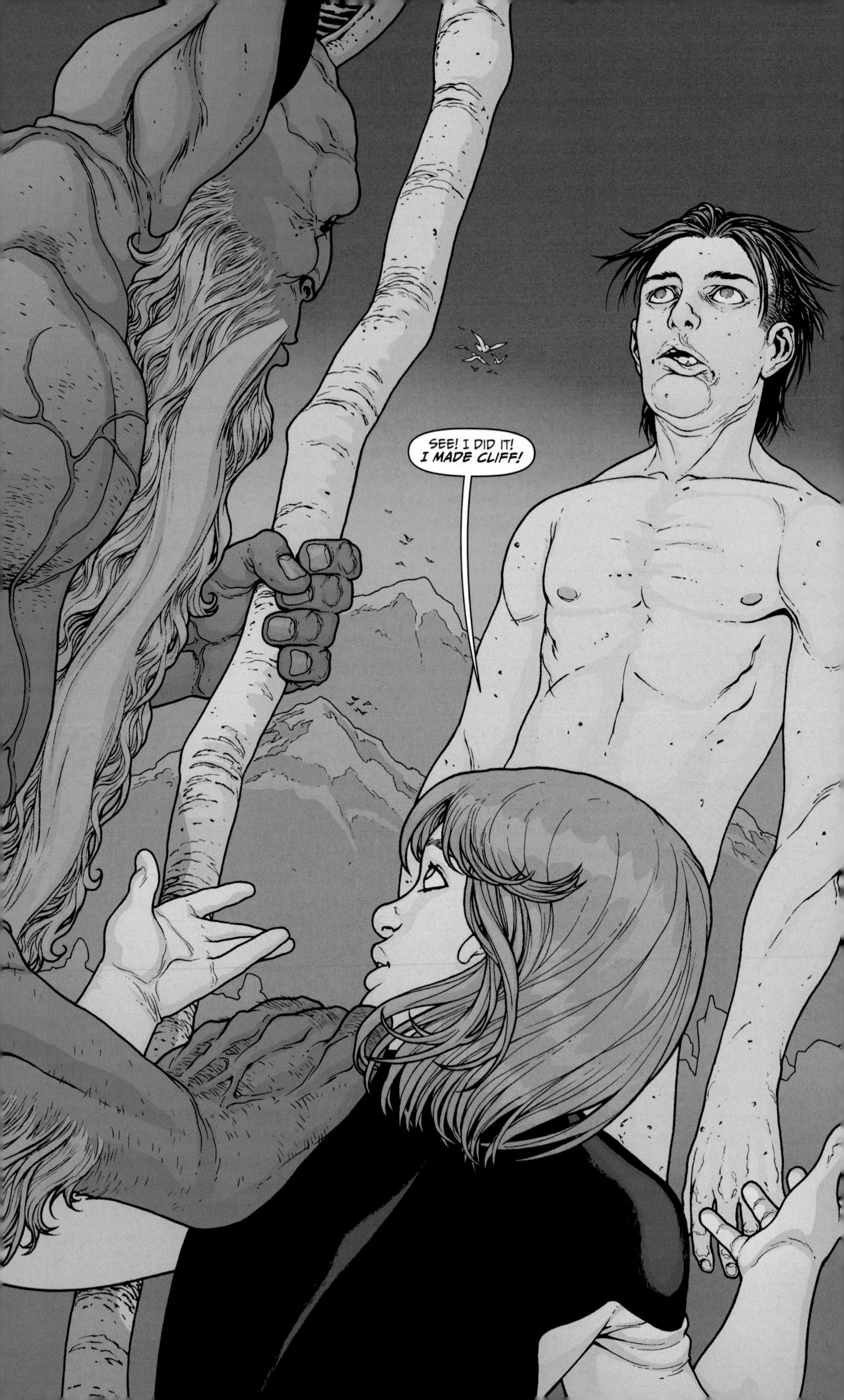
SEE! I DID IT!
I MADE CLIFF!

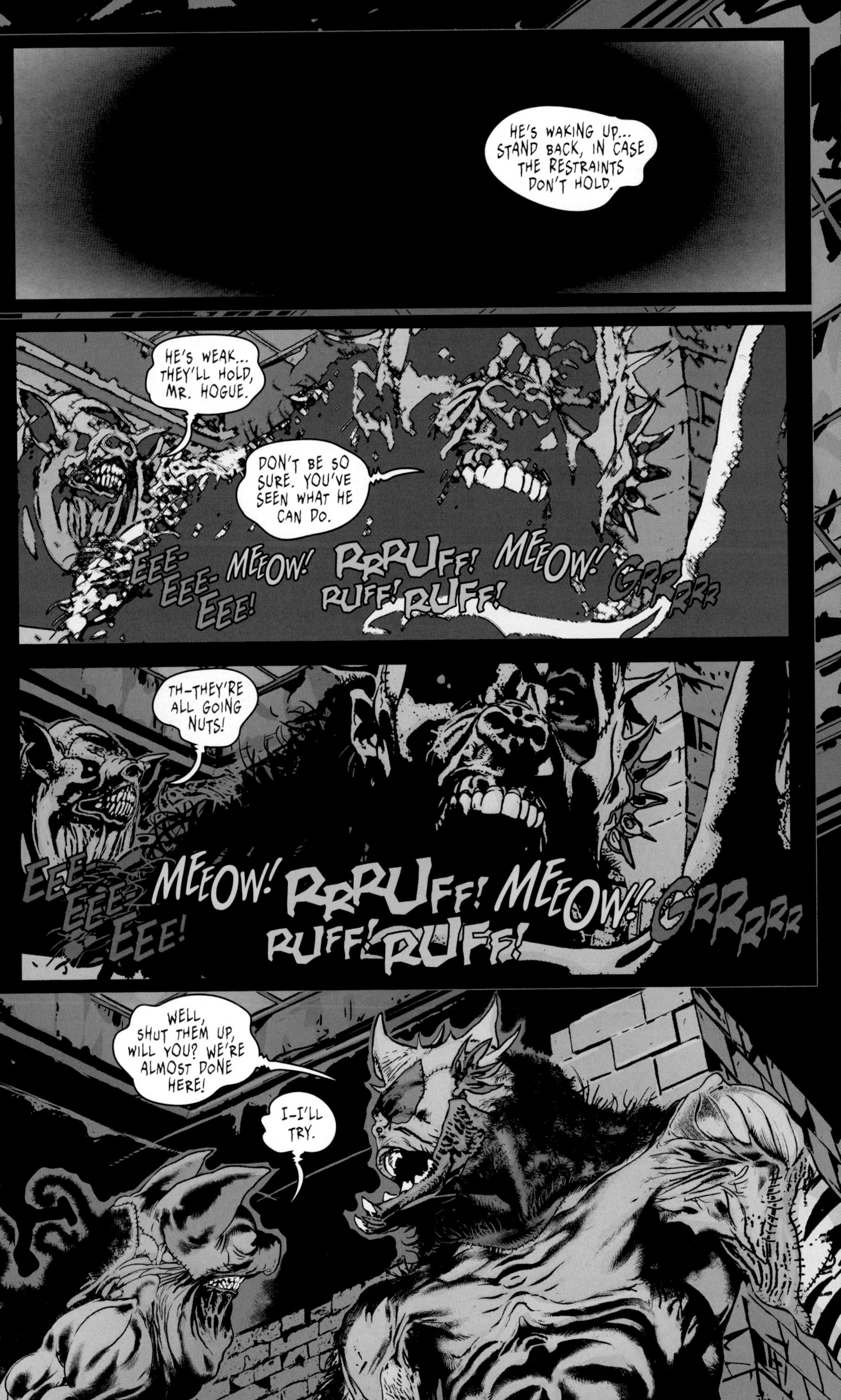
HE'S WAKING UP... STAND BACK, IN CASE THE RESTRAINTS DON'T HOLD.
HE'S WEAK... THEY'LL HOLD, MR. HOGUE.
DON'T BE SO SURE. YOU'VE SEEN WHAT HE CAN DO.
EEE-EEE-EEE! MEEOW! RRRUFF! RUFF! RUFF! MEEOW! GRRRRR
TH-THEY'RE ALL GOING NUTS!
EEE-EEE-EEE! MEEOW! RRRUFF! RUFF! RUFF! MEEOW! GRRRRR
WELL, SHUT THEM UP, WILL YOU? WE'RE ALMOST DONE HERE!
I-I'LL TRY.

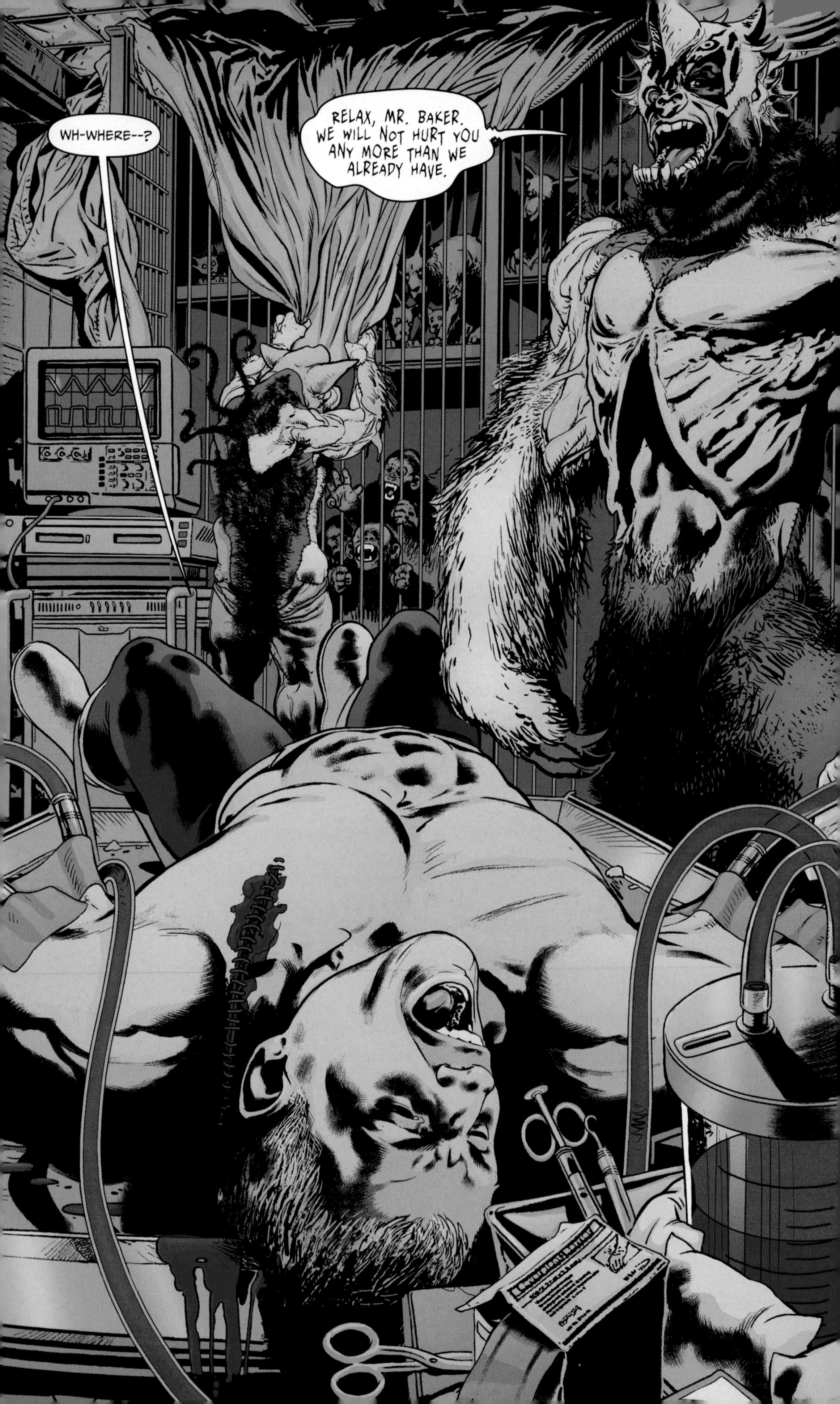
WH-WHERE--?
RELAX, MR. BAKER. WE WILL NOT HURT YOU ANY MORE THAN WE ALREADY HAVE.

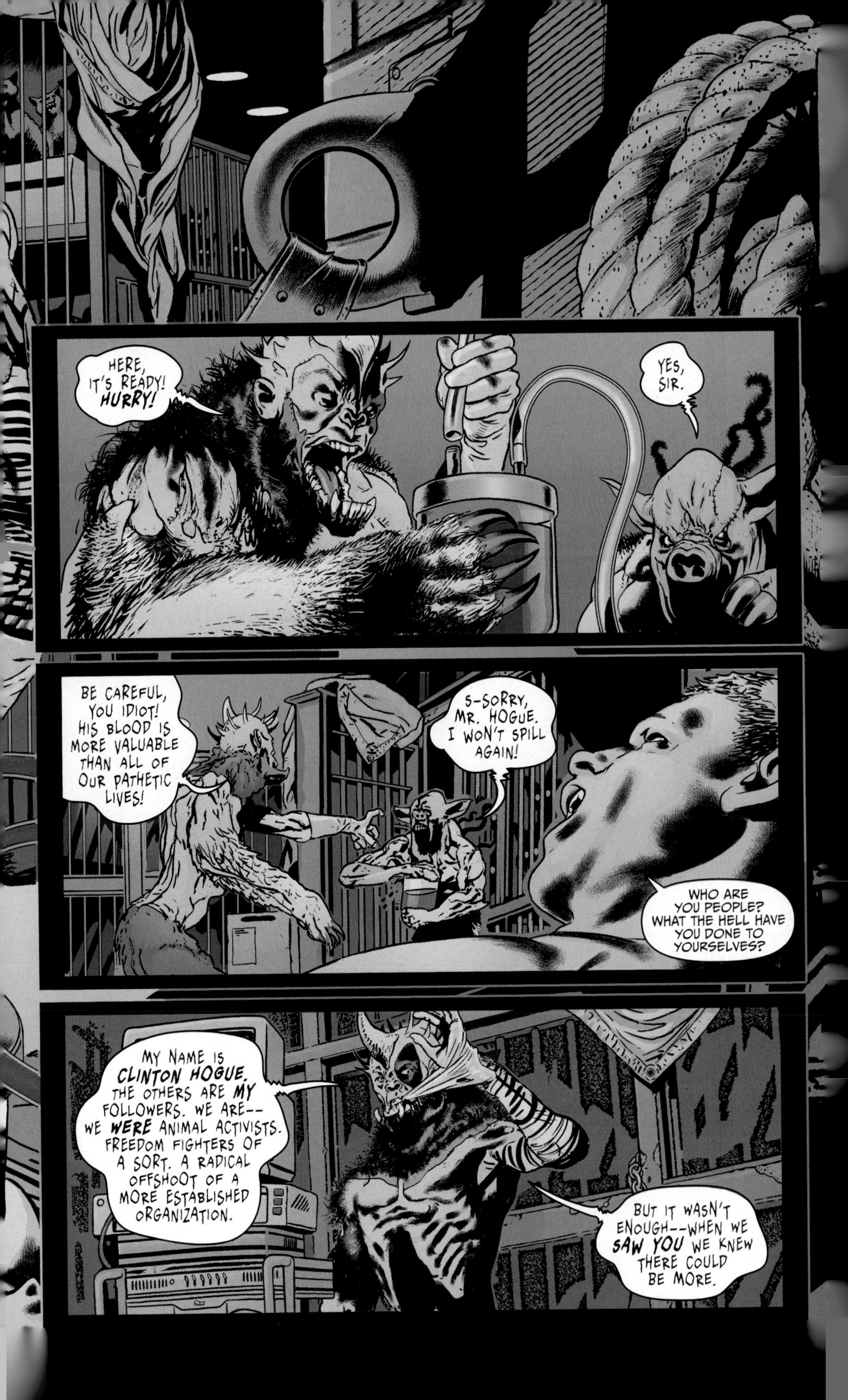
HERE, IT'S READY! HURRY!
YES, SIR.
BE CAREFUL, YOU IDIOT! HIS BLOOD IS MORE VALUABLE THAN ALL OF OUR PATHETIC LIVES!
S-SORRY, MR. HOGUE. I WON'T SPILL AGAIN!
WHO ARE YOU PEOPLE? WHAT THE HELL HAVE YOU DONE TO YOURSELVES?
MY NAME IS CLINTON HOGUE. THE OTHERS ARE MY FOLLOWERS. WE ARE-- WE WERE ANIMAL ACTIVISTS. FREEDOM FIGHTERS OF A SORT. A RADICAL OFFSHOOT OF A MORE ESTABLISHED ORGANIZATION.
BUT IT WASN'T ENOUGH--WHEN WE SAW YOU WE KNEW THERE COULD BE MORE.

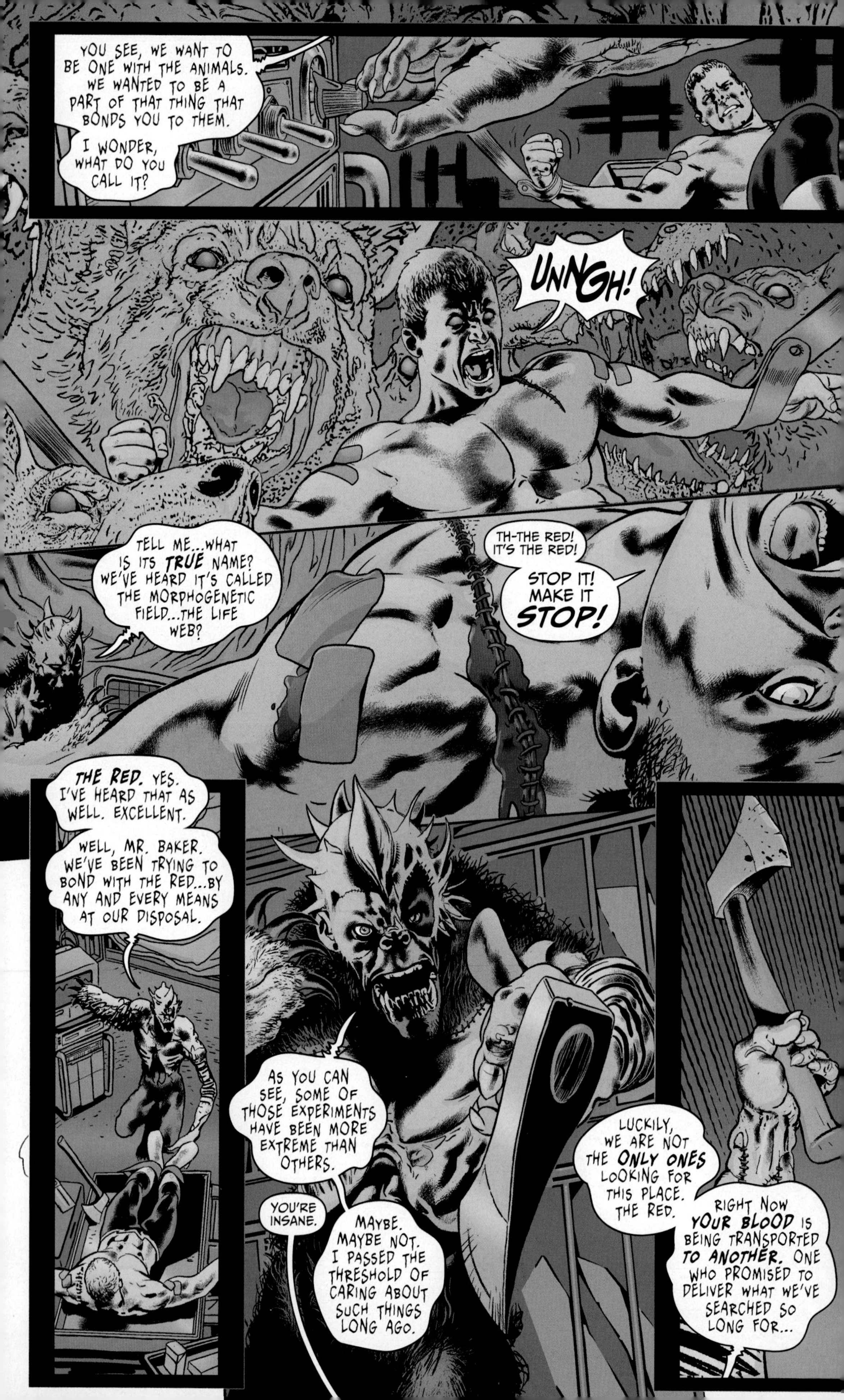
YOU SEE, WE WANT TO BE ONE WITH THE ANIMALS. WE WANTED TO BE A PART OF THAT THING THAT BONDS YOU TO THEM.
I WONDER, WHAT DO YOU CALL IT?
UNNGH!
TELL ME...WHAT IS ITS TRUE NAME? WE'VE HEARD IT'S CALLED THE MORPHOGENETIC FIELD...THE LIFE WEB?
TH-THE RED! IT'S THE RED!
STOP IT! MAKE IT STOP!
THE RED. YES. I'VE HEARD THAT AS WELL. EXCELLENT.
WELL, MR. BAKER. WE'VE BEEN TRYING TO BOND WITH THE RED...BY ANY AND EVERY MEANS AT OUR DISPOSAL.
AS YOU CAN SEE, SOME OF THOSE EXPERIMENTS HAVE BEEN MORE EXTREME THAN OTHERS.
YOU'RE INSANE.
MAYBE. MAYBE NOT. I PASSED THE THRESHOLD OF CARING ABOUT SUCH THINGS LONG AGO.
LUCKILY, WE ARE NOT THE ONLY ONES LOOKING FOR THIS PLACE. THE RED.
RIGHT NOW YOUR BLOOD IS BEING TRANSPORTED TO ANOTHER. ONE WHO PROMISED TO DELIVER WHAT WE'VE SEARCHED SO LONG FOR...

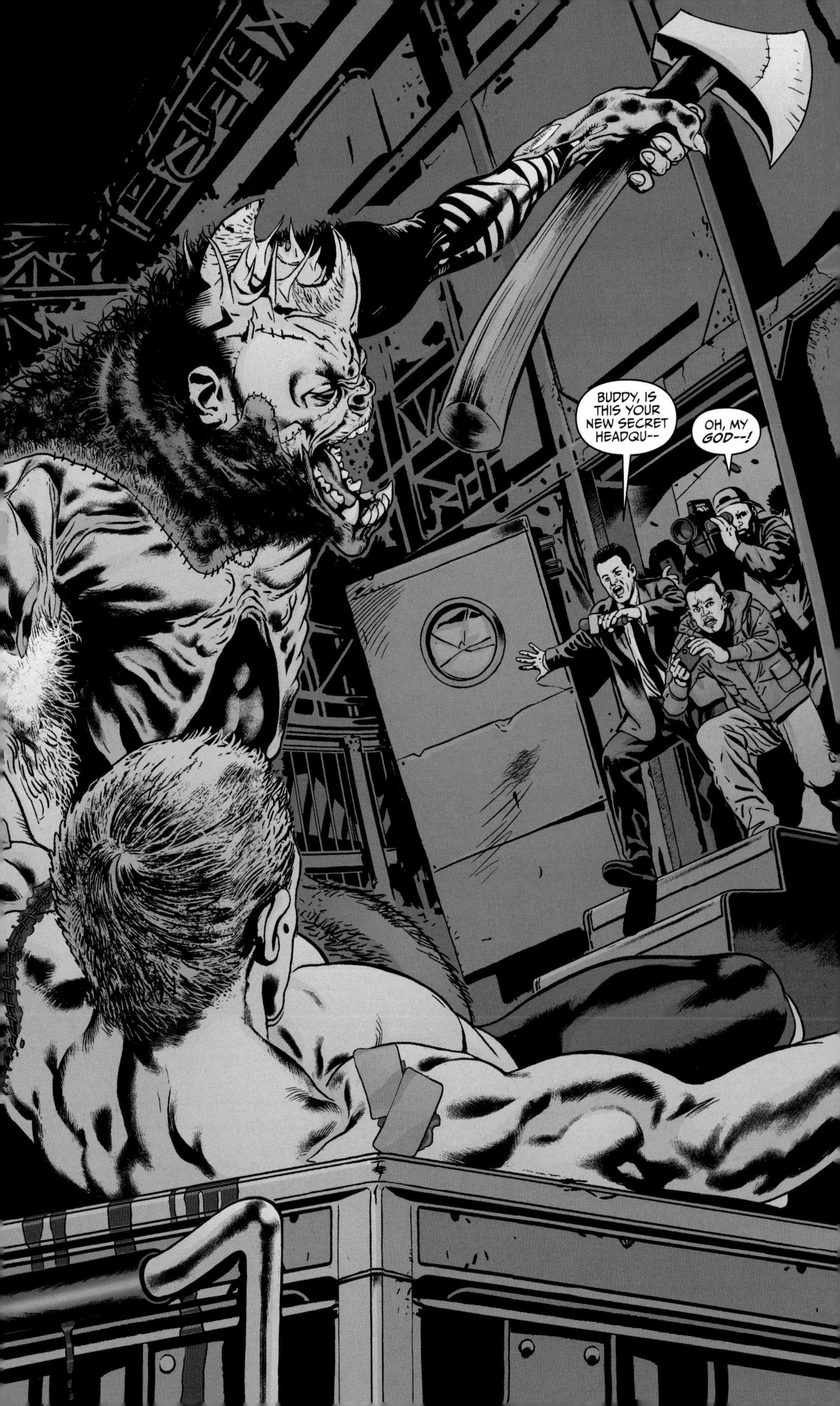
BUDDY, IS THIS YOUR NEW SECRET HEADQU--
OH, MY *GOD*--!

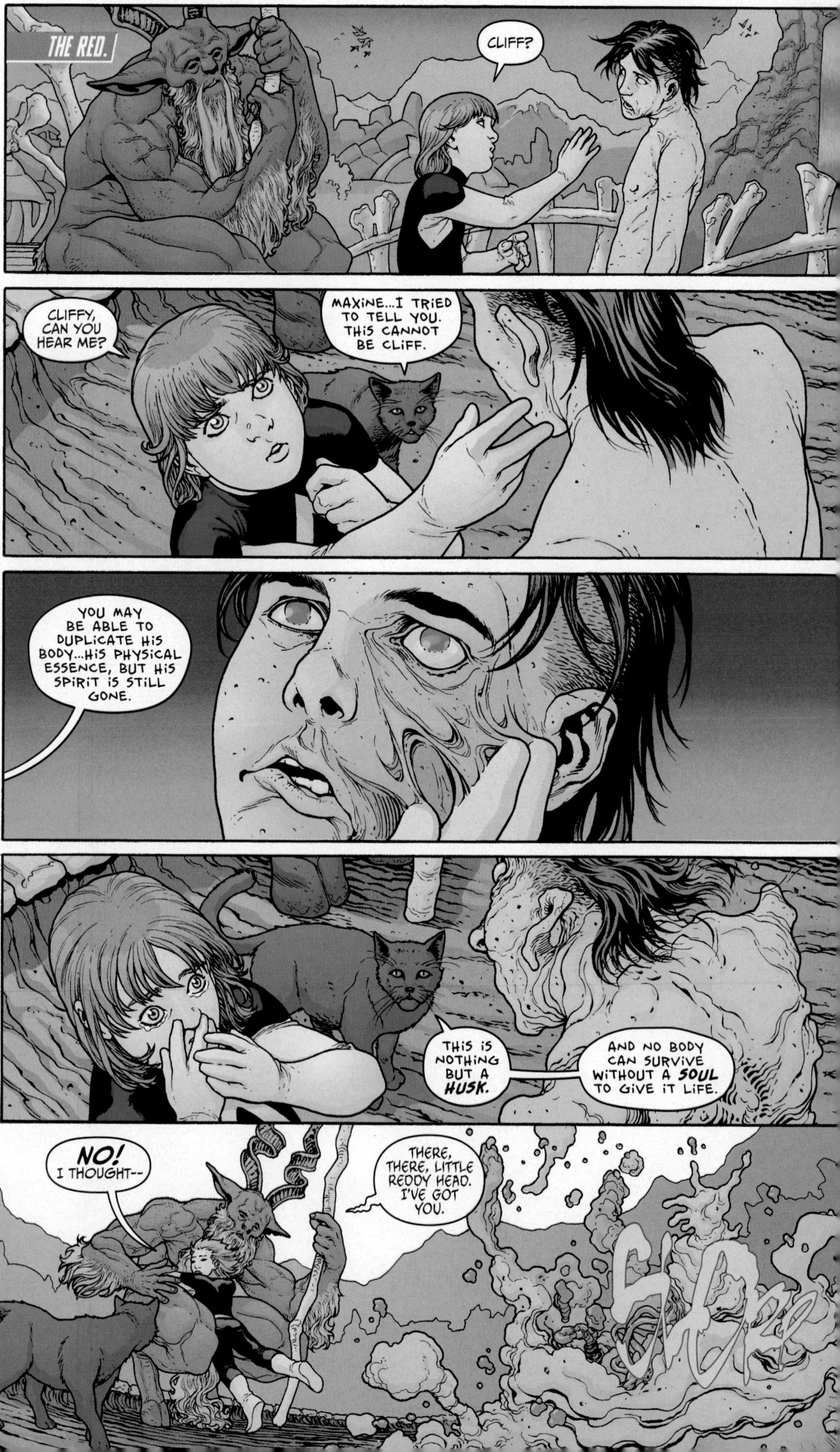
THE RED.
CLIFF?
CLIFFY, CAN YOU HEAR ME?
MAXINE...I TRIED TO TELL YOU. THIS CANNOT BE CLIFF.
YOU MAY BE ABLE TO DUPLICATE HIS BODY...HIS PHYSICAL ESSENCE, BUT HIS SPIRIT IS STILL GONE.
THIS IS NOTHING BUT A HUSK.
AND NO BODY CAN SURVIVE WITHOUT A SOUL TO GIVE IT LIFE.
NO! I THOUGHT--
THERE, THERE, LITTLE REDDY HEAD. I'VE GOT YOU.

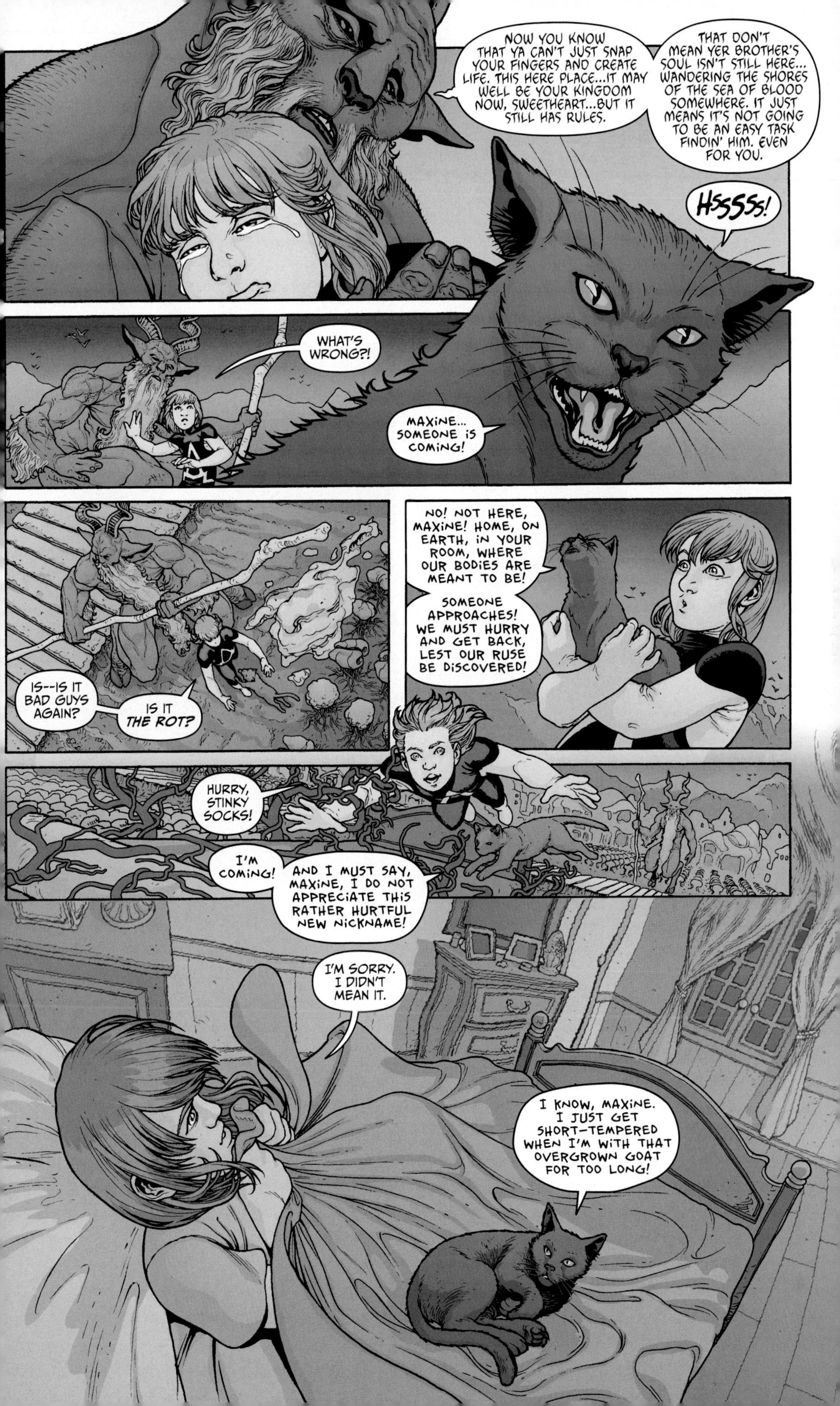
NOW YOU KNOW THAT YA CAN'T JUST SNAP YOUR FINGERS AND CREATE LIFE. THIS HERE PLACE...IT MAY WELL BE YOUR KINGDOM NOW, SWEETHEART...BUT IT STILL HAS RULES.
THAT DON'T MEAN YER BROTHER'S SOUL ISN'T STILL HERE... WANDERING THE SHORES OF THE SEA OF BLOOD SOMEWHERE. IT JUST MEANS IT'S NOT GOING TO BE AN EASY TASK FINDIN' HIM. EVEN FOR YOU.
HSSSSS!
WHAT'S WRONG?!
MAXINE... SOMEONE IS COMING!
IS--IS IT BAD GUYS AGAIN?
IS IT THE ROT?
NO! NOT HERE, MAXINE! HOME, ON EARTH, IN YOUR ROOM, WHERE OUR BODIES ARE MEANT TO BE!
SOMEONE APPROACHES! WE MUST HURRY AND GET BACK, LEST OUR RUSE BE DISCOVERED!
HURRY, STINKY SOCKS!
I'M COMING!
AND I MUST SAY, MAXINE, I DO NOT APPRECIATE THIS RATHER HURTFUL NEW NICKNAME!
I'M SORRY. I DIDN'T MEAN IT.
I KNOW, MAXINE. I JUST GET SHORT-TEMPERED WHEN I'M WITH THAT OVERGROWN GOAT FOR TOO LONG!

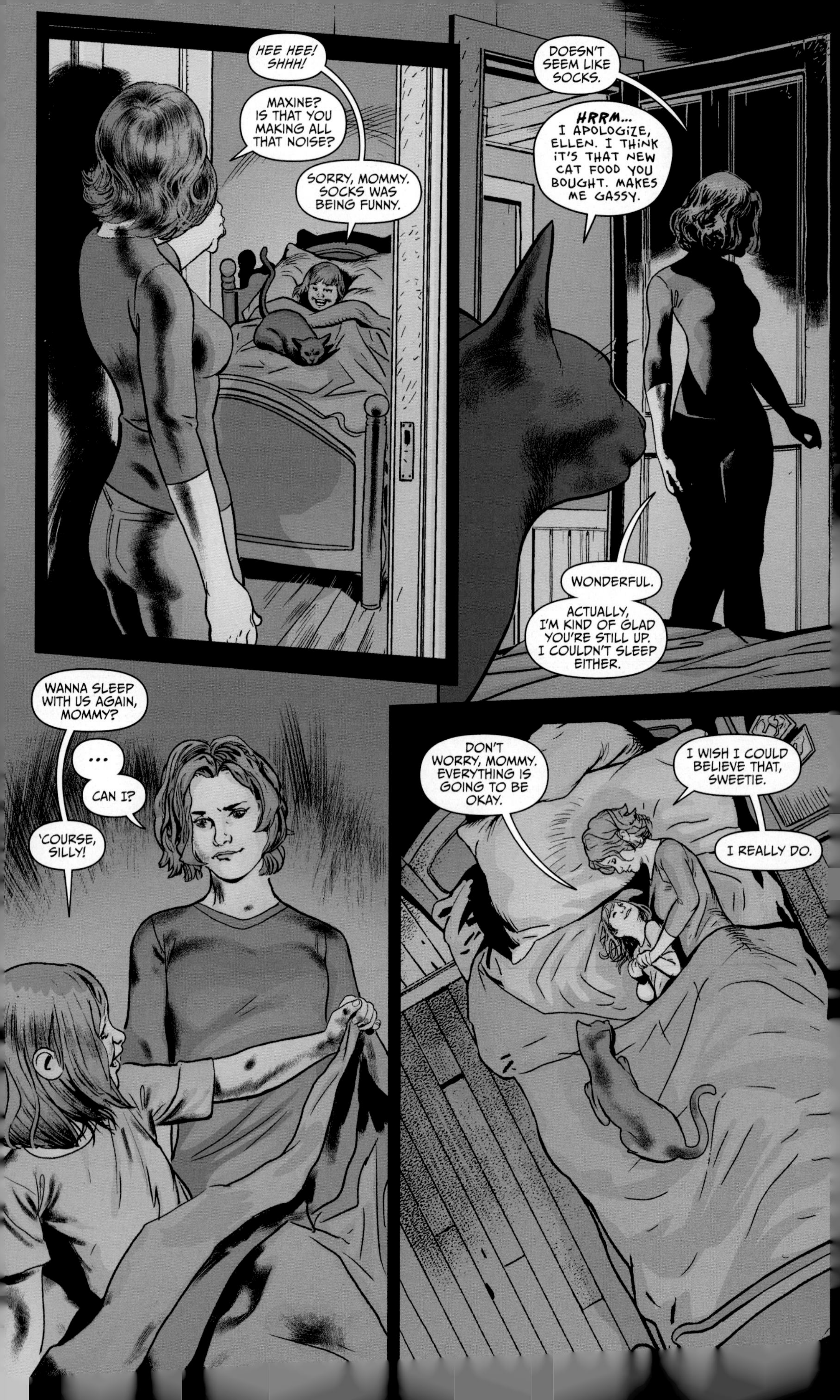
HEE HEE! SHHH!
MAXINE? IS THAT YOU MAKING ALL THAT NOISE?
SORRY, MOMMY. SOCKS WAS BEING FUNNY.
DOESN'T SEEM LIKE SOCKS.
HRRM... I APOLOGIZE, ELLEN. I THINK IT'S THAT NEW CAT FOOD YOU BOUGHT. MAKES ME GASSY.
WONDERFUL.
ACTUALLY, I'M KIND OF GLAD YOU'RE STILL UP. I COULDN'T SLEEP EITHER.
WANNA SLEEP WITH US AGAIN, MOMMY?
...
CAN I?
'COURSE, SILLY!
DON'T WORRY, MOMMY. EVERYTHING IS GOING TO BE OKAY.
I WISH I COULD BELIEVE THAT, SWEETIE.
I REALLY DO.

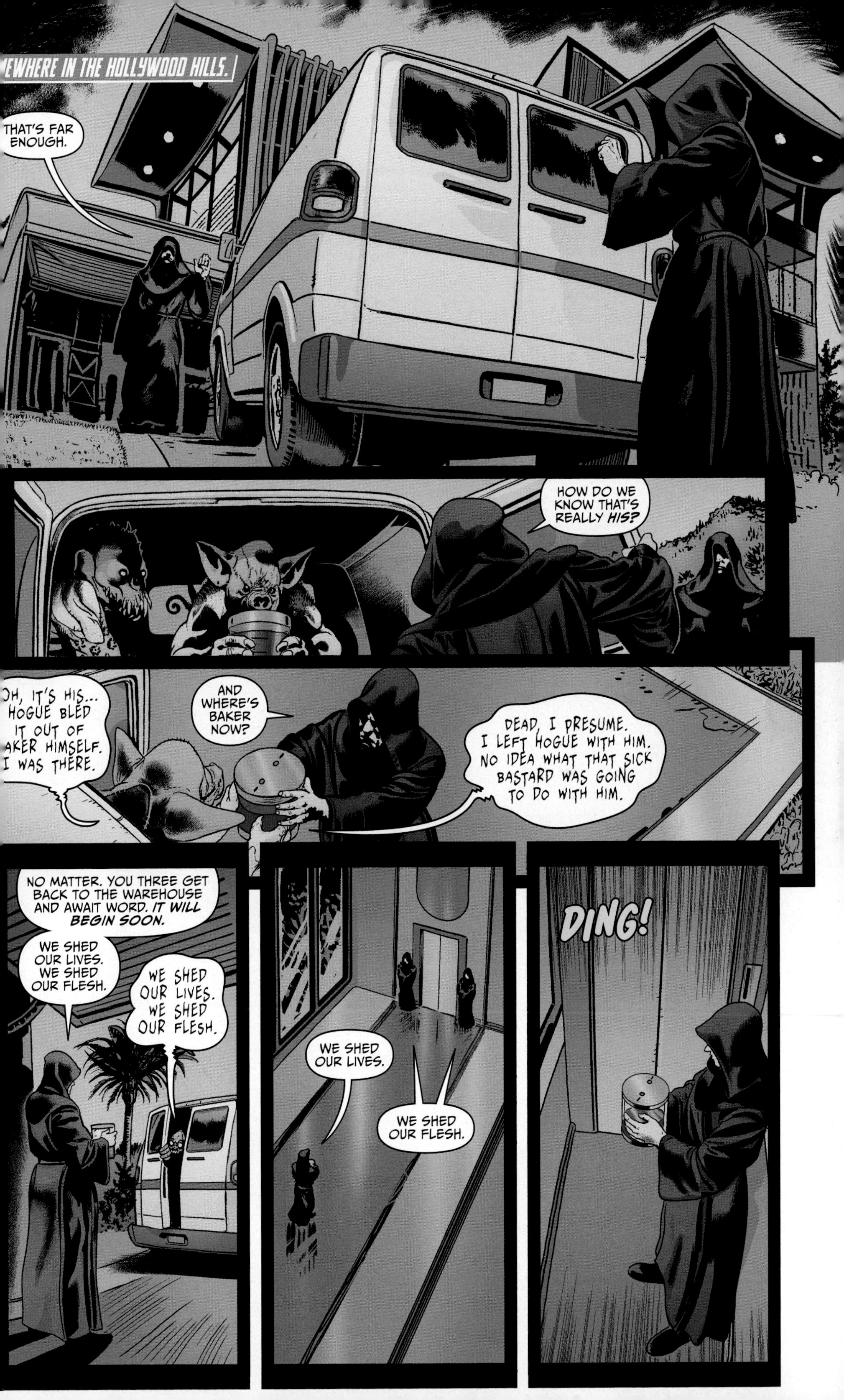
EWHERE IN THE HOLLYWOOD HILLS.
THAT'S FAR ENOUGH.
HOW DO WE KNOW THAT'S REALLY *HIS?*
OH, IT'S HIS... HOGUE BLED IT OUT OF AKER HIMSELF. I WAS THERE.
AND WHERE'S BAKER NOW?
DEAD, I PRESUME. I LEFT HOGUE WITH HIM. NO IDEA WHAT THAT SICK BASTARD WAS GOING TO DO WITH HIM.
NO MATTER. YOU THREE GET BACK TO THE WAREHOUSE AND AWAIT WORD. *IT WILL BEGIN SOON.*
WE SHED OUR LIVES. WE SHED OUR FLESH.
WE SHED OUR LIVES. WE SHED OUR FLESH.
WE SHED OUR LIVES.
WE SHED OUR FLESH.
DING!

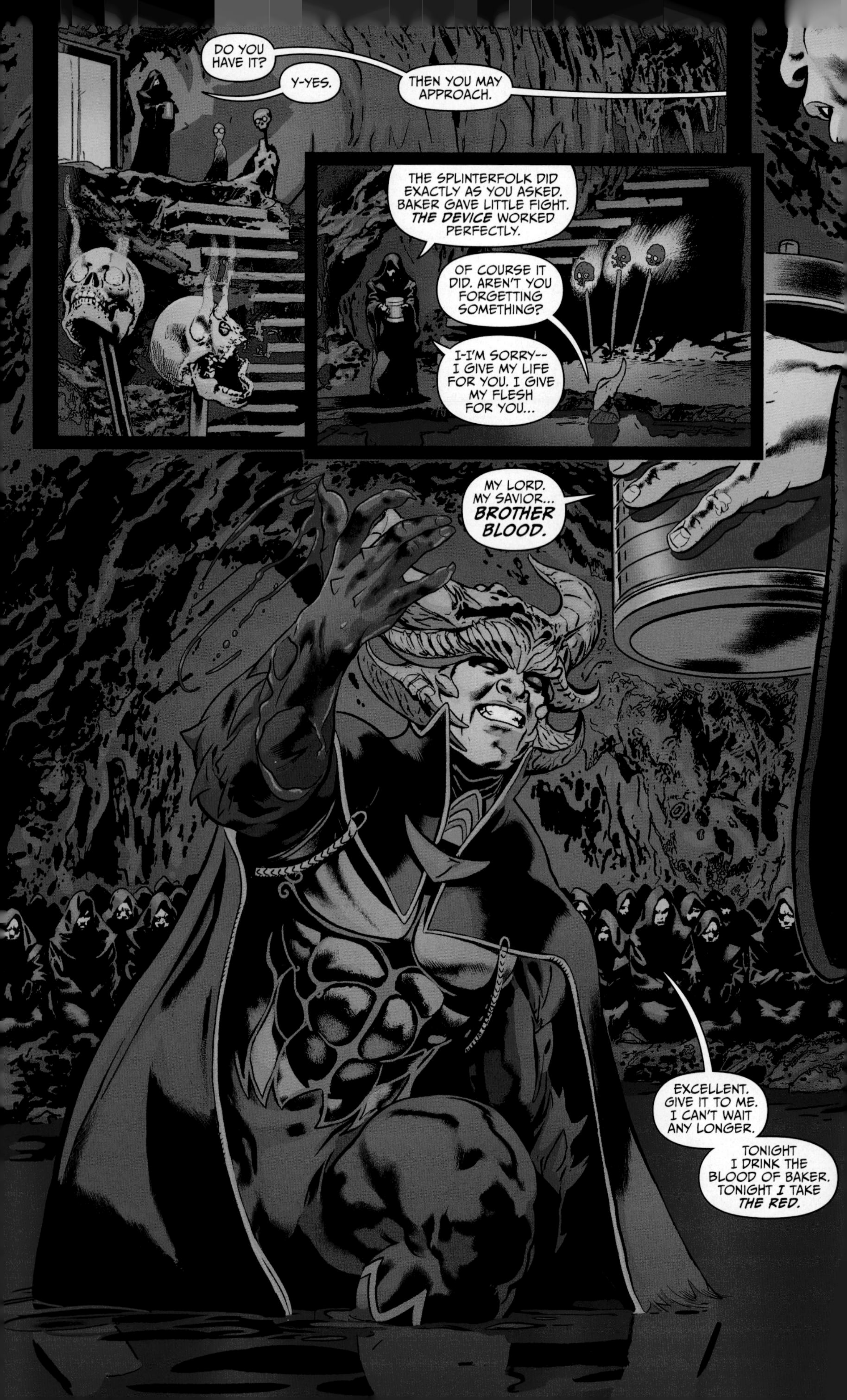
DO YOU HAVE IT?
Y-YES.
THEN YOU MAY APPROACH.
THE SPLINTERFOLK DID EXACTLY AS YOU ASKED. BAKER GAVE LITTLE FIGHT. THE DEVICE WORKED PERFECTLY.
OF COURSE IT DID. AREN'T YOU FORGETTING SOMETHING?
I-I'M SORRY-- I GIVE MY LIFE FOR YOU. I GIVE MY FLESH FOR YOU...
MY LORD. MY SAVIOR... BROTHER BLOOD.
EXCELLENT. GIVE IT TO ME. I CAN'T WAIT ANY LONGER.
TONIGHT I DRINK THE BLOOD OF BAKER. TONIGHT I TAKE THE RED.

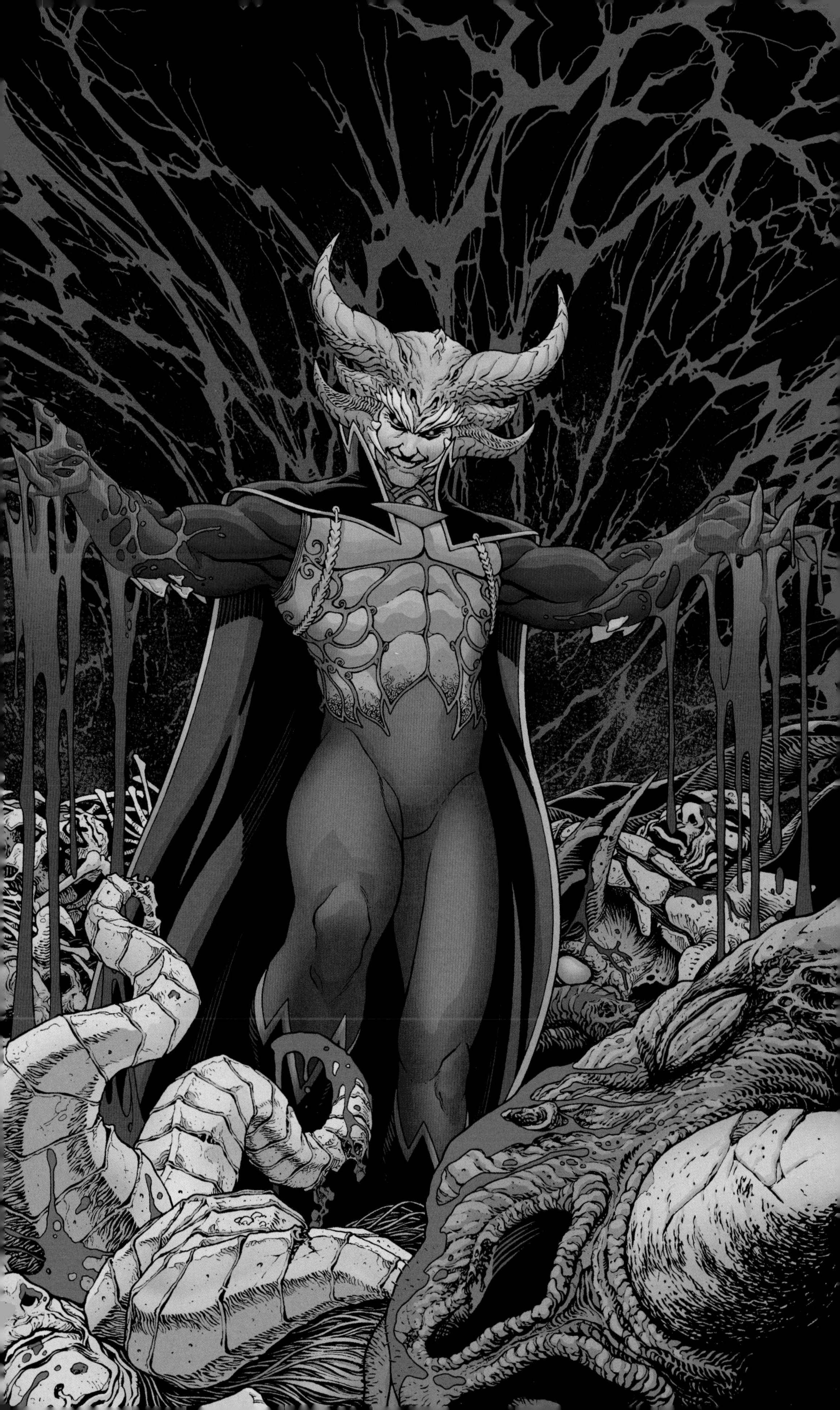

JEFF LEMIRE
writer

STEVE PUGH & FRANCIS PORTELA
artists

FRANCIS PORTELA with LOVERN KINDZIERSKI
cover artists

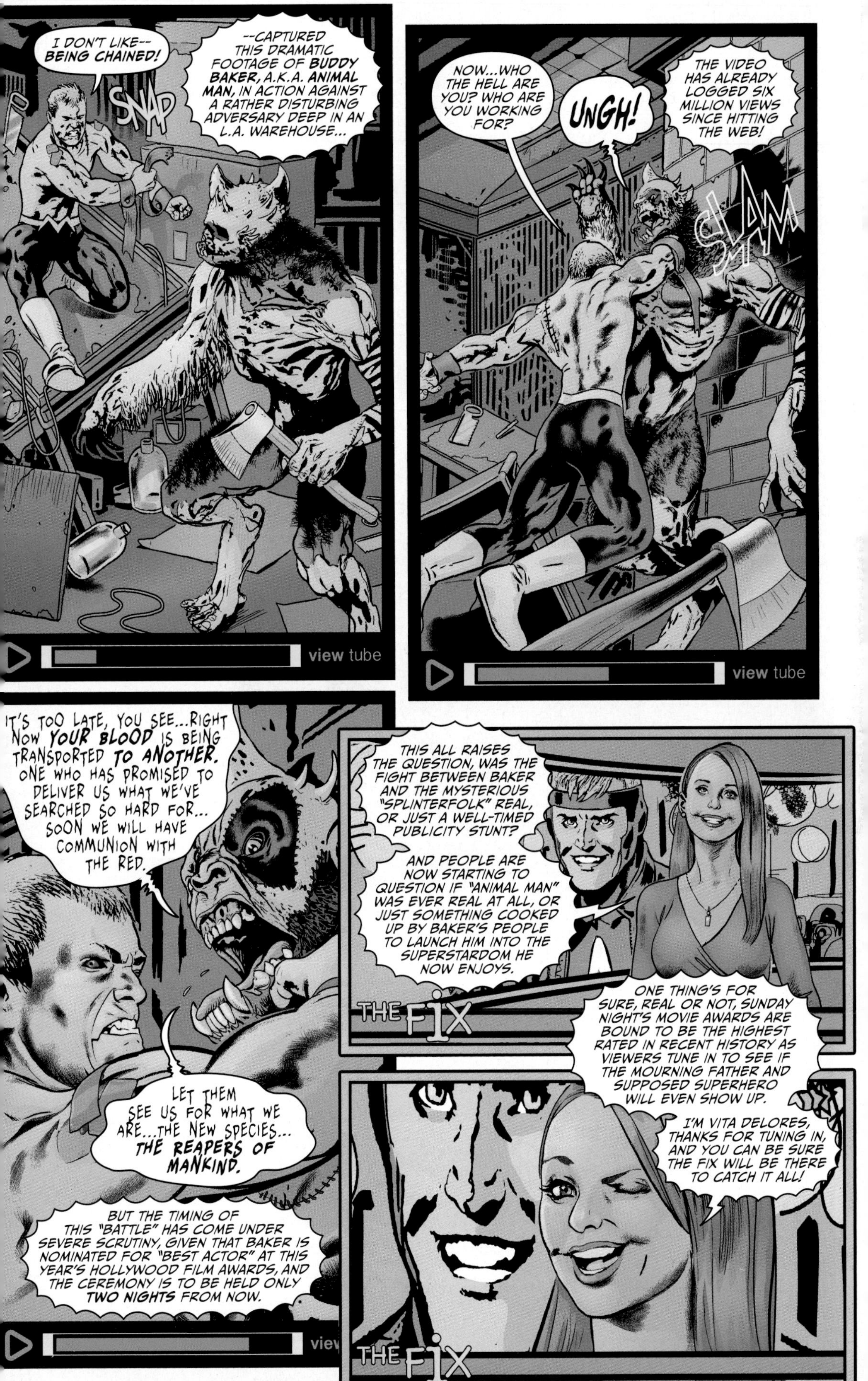
I DON'T LIKE-- BEING CHAINED!
SNAP
--CAPTURED THIS DRAMATIC FOOTAGE OF BUDDY BAKER, A.K.A. ANIMAL MAN, IN ACTION AGAINST A RATHER DISTURBING ADVERSARY DEEP IN AN L.A. WAREHOUSE...
view tube
NOW...WHO THE HELL ARE YOU? WHO ARE YOU WORKING FOR?
UNGH!
THE VIDEO HAS ALREADY LOGGED SIX MILLION VIEWS SINCE HITTING THE WEB!
SLAM
view tube
IT'S TOO LATE, YOU SEE...RIGHT NOW YOUR BLOOD IS BEING TRANSPORTED TO ANOTHER. ONE WHO HAS PROMISED TO DELIVER US WHAT WE'VE SEARCHED SO HARD FOR... SOON WE WILL HAVE COMMUNION WITH THE RED.
LET THEM SEE US FOR WHAT WE ARE...THE NEW SPECIES... THE REAPERS OF MANKIND.
BUT THE TIMING OF THIS "BATTLE" HAS COME UNDER SEVERE SCRUTINY, GIVEN THAT BAKER IS NOMINATED FOR "BEST ACTOR" AT THIS YEAR'S HOLLYWOOD FILM AWARDS, AND THE CEREMONY IS TO BE HELD ONLY TWO NIGHTS FROM NOW.
THIS ALL RAISES THE QUESTION, WAS THE FIGHT BETWEEN BAKER AND THE MYSTERIOUS "SPLINTERFOLK" REAL, OR JUST A WELL-TIMED PUBLICITY STUNT?
AND PEOPLE ARE NOW STARTING TO QUESTION IF "ANIMAL MAN" WAS EVER REAL AT ALL, OR JUST SOMETHING COOKED UP BY BAKER'S PEOPLE TO LAUNCH HIM INTO THE SUPERSTARDOM HE NOW ENJOYS.
THE FIX
ONE THING'S FOR SURE, REAL OR NOT, SUNDAY NIGHT'S MOVIE AWARDS ARE BOUND TO BE THE HIGHEST RATED IN RECENT HISTORY AS VIEWERS TUNE IN TO SEE IF THE MOURNING FATHER AND SUPPOSED SUPERHERO WILL EVEN SHOW UP.
I'M VITA DELORES, THANKS FOR TUNING IN, AND YOU CAN BE SURE THE FIX WILL BE THERE TO CATCH IT ALL!
THE FIX

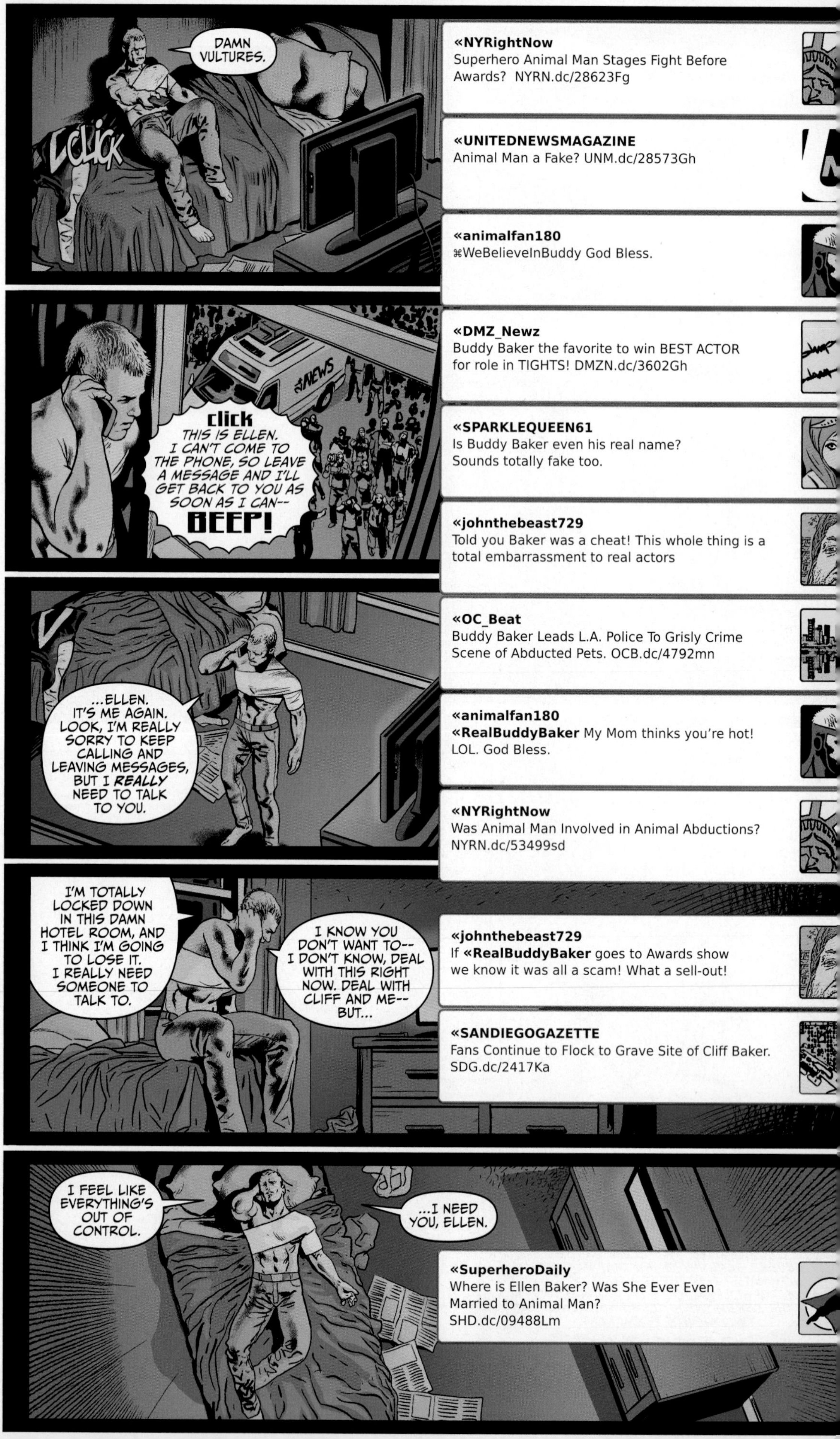

DAMN VULTURES.
CLICK
«NYRightNow
Superhero Animal Man Stages Fight Before Awards? NYRN.dc/28623Fg
«UNITEDNEWSMAGAZINE
Animal Man a Fake? UNM.dc/28573Gh
«animalfan180
⌘WeBelieveInBuddy God Bless.
click THIS IS ELLEN. I CAN'T COME TO THE PHONE, SO LEAVE A MESSAGE AND I'LL GET BACK TO YOU AS SOON AS I CAN-- BEEP!
NEWS
«DMZ_Newz
Buddy Baker the favorite to win BEST ACTOR for role in TIGHTS! DMZN.dc/3602Gh
«SPARKLEQUEEN61
Is Buddy Baker even his real name? Sounds totally fake too.
«johnthebeast729
Told you Baker was a cheat! This whole thing is a total embarrassment to real actors
...ELLEN. IT'S ME AGAIN. LOOK, I'M REALLY SORRY TO KEEP CALLING AND LEAVING MESSAGES, BUT I REALLY NEED TO TALK TO YOU.
«OC_Beat
Buddy Baker Leads L.A. Police To Grisly Crime Scene of Abducted Pets. OCB.dc/4792mn
«animalfan180
«RealBuddyBaker My Mom thinks you're hot! LOL. God Bless.
«NYRightNow
Was Animal Man Involved in Animal Abductions? NYRN.dc/53499sd
I'M TOTALLY LOCKED DOWN IN THIS DAMN HOTEL ROOM, AND I THINK I'M GOING TO LOSE IT. I REALLY NEED SOMEONE TO TALK TO.
I KNOW YOU DON'T WANT TO-- I DON'T KNOW, DEAL WITH THIS RIGHT NOW. DEAL WITH CLIFF AND ME-- BUT...
«johnthebeast729
If «RealBuddyBaker goes to Awards show we know it was all a scam! What a sell-out!
«SANDIEGOGAZETTE
Fans Continue to Flock to Grave Site of Cliff Baker. SDG.dc/2417Ka
I FEEL LIKE EVERYTHING'S OUT OF CONTROL.
...I NEED YOU, ELLEN.
«SuperheroDaily
Where is Ellen Baker? Was She Ever Even Married to Animal Man? SHD.dc/09488Lm

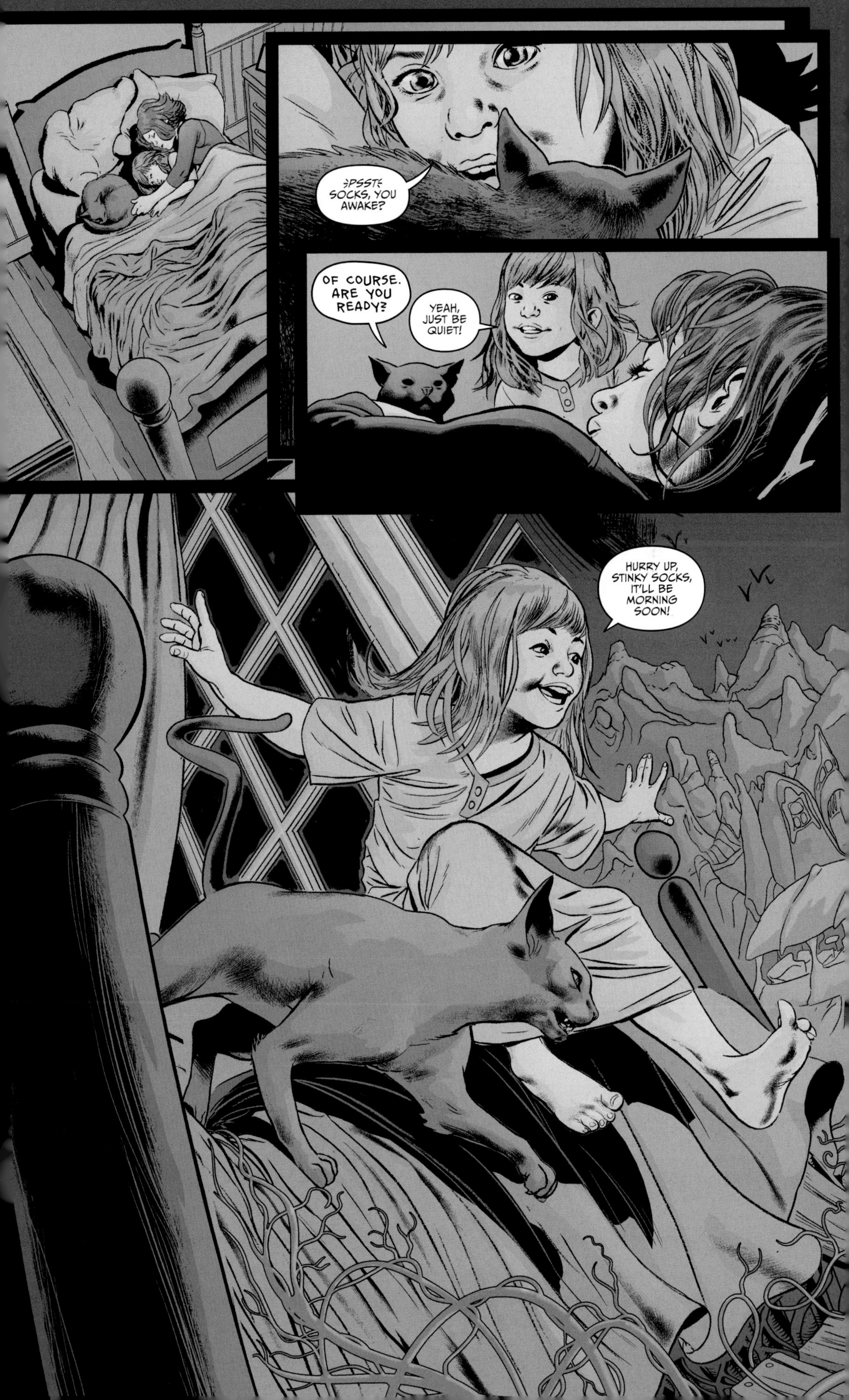

PSST. SOCKS, YOU AWAKE?
OF COURSE. ARE YOU READY?
YEAH, JUST BE QUIET!
HURRY UP, STINKY SOCKS, IT'LL BE MORNING SOON!

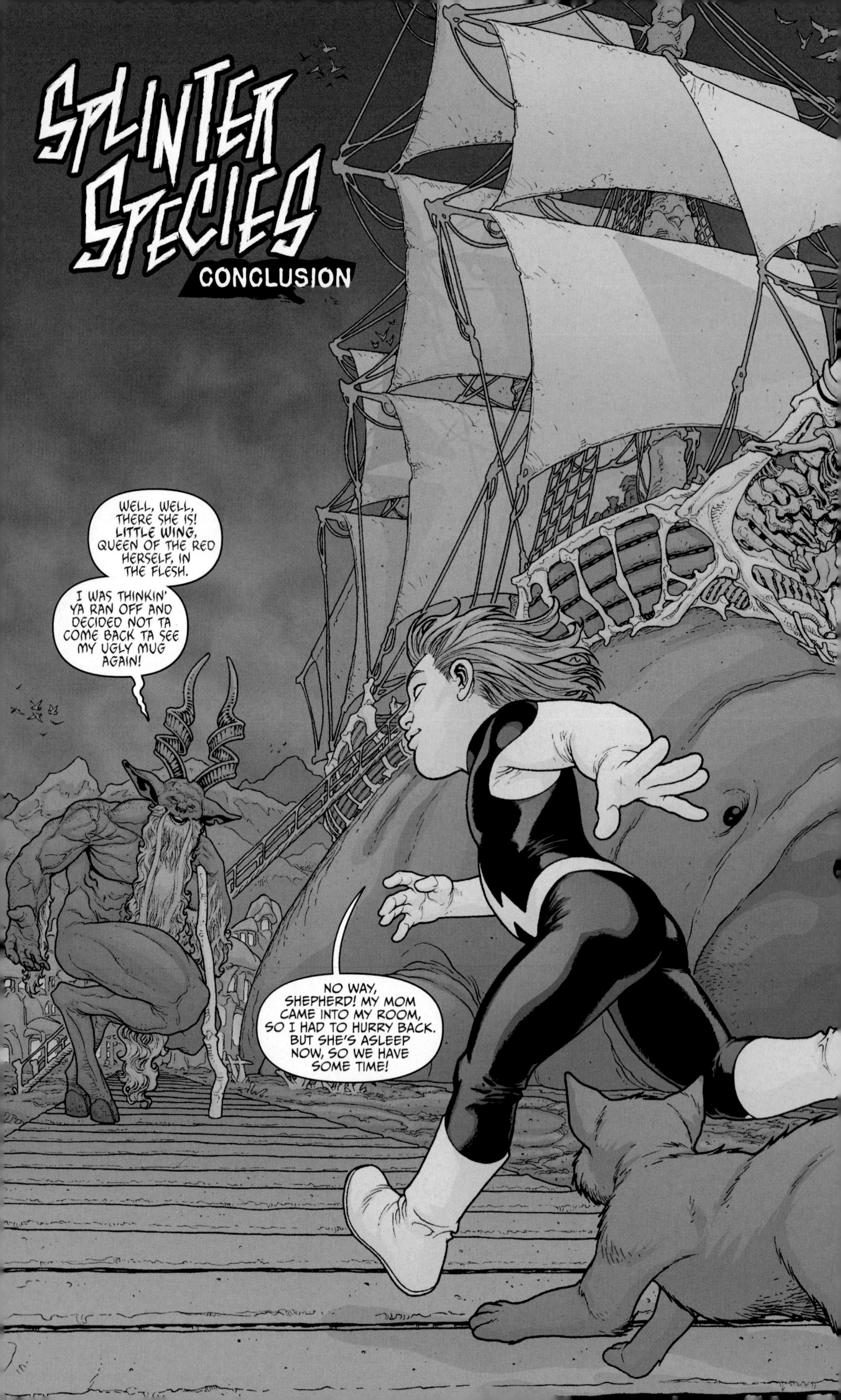
SPLINTER SPECIES
CONCLUSION
WELL, WELL, THERE SHE IS! LITTLE WING, QUEEN OF THE RED HERSELF, IN THE FLESH.
I WAS THINKIN' YA RAN OFF AND DECIDED NOT TA COME BACK TA SEE MY UGLY MUG AGAIN!
NO WAY, SHEPHERD! MY MOM CAME INTO MY ROOM, SO I HAD TO HURRY BACK. BUT SHE'S ASLEEP NOW, SO WE HAVE SOME TIME!

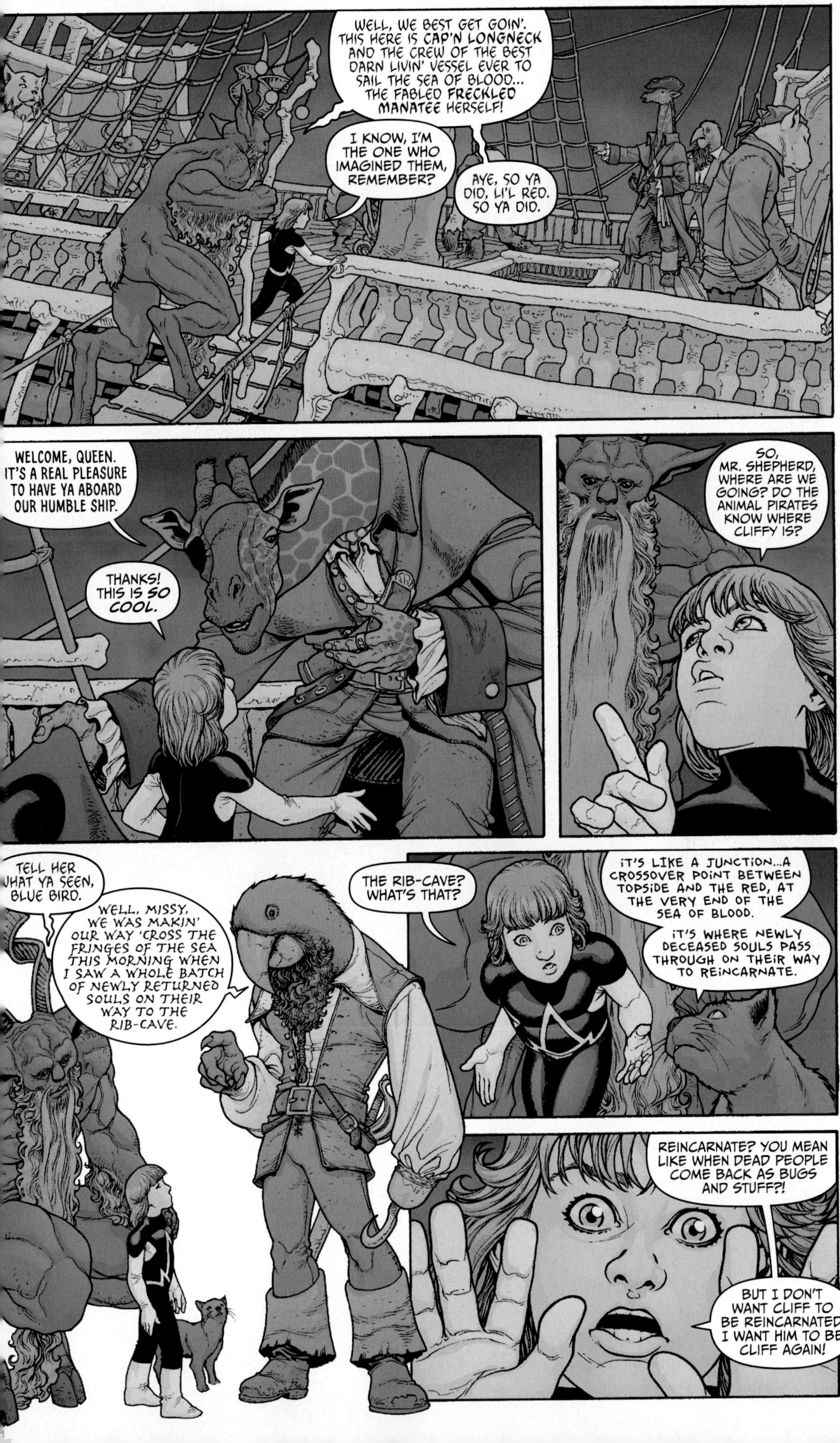
WELL, WE BEST GET GOIN'. THIS HERE IS CAP'N LONGNECK AND THE CREW OF THE BEST DARN LIVIN' VESSEL EVER TO SAIL THE SEA OF BLOOD... THE FABLED FRECKLED MANATEE HERSELF!
I KNOW, I'M THE ONE WHO IMAGINED THEM, REMEMBER?
AYE, SO YA DID, LI'L RED. SO YA DID.
WELCOME, QUEEN. IT'S A REAL PLEASURE TO HAVE YA ABOARD OUR HUMBLE SHIP.
THANKS! THIS IS SO COOL.
SO, MR. SHEPHERD, WHERE ARE WE GOING? DO THE ANIMAL PIRATES KNOW WHERE CLIFFY IS?
TELL HER WHAT YA SEEN, BLUE BIRD.
WELL, MISSY, WE WAS MAKIN' OUR WAY 'CROSS THE FRINGES OF THE SEA THIS MORNING WHEN I SAW A WHOLE BATCH OF NEWLY RETURNED SOULS ON THEIR WAY TO THE RIB-CAVE.
THE RIB-CAVE? WHAT'S THAT?
IT'S LIKE A JUNCTION...A CROSSOVER POINT BETWEEN TOPSIDE AND THE RED, AT THE VERY END OF THE SEA OF BLOOD.
IT'S WHERE NEWLY DECEASED SOULS PASS THROUGH ON THEIR WAY TO REINCARNATE.
REINCARNATE? YOU MEAN LIKE WHEN DEAD PEOPLE COME BACK AS BUGS AND STUFF?!
BUT I DON'T WANT CLIFF TO BE REINCARNATED, I WANT HIM TO BE CLIFF AGAIN!

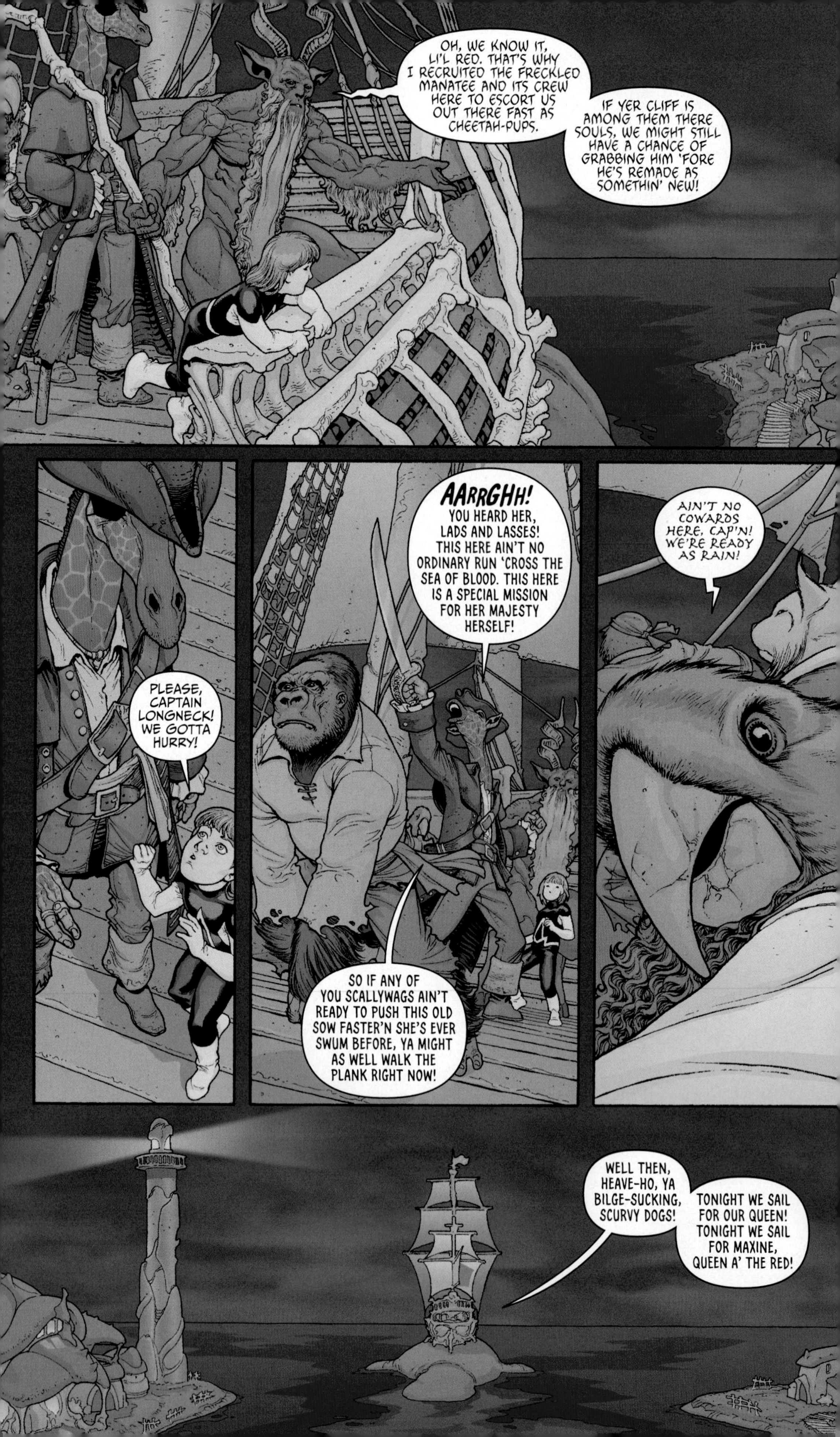
OH, WE KNOW IT, LI'L RED. THAT'S WHY I RECRUITED THE FRECKLED MANATEE AND ITS CREW HERE TO ESCORT US OUT THERE FAST AS CHEETAH-PUPS.
IF YER CLIFF IS AMONG THEM THERE SOULS, WE MIGHT STILL HAVE A CHANCE OF GRABBING HIM 'FORE HE'S REMADE AS SOMETHIN' NEW!
PLEASE, CAPTAIN LONGNECK! WE GOTTA HURRY!
AARRGHH!
YOU HEARD HER, LADS AND LASSES! THIS HERE AIN'T NO ORDINARY RUN 'CROSS THE SEA OF BLOOD. THIS HERE IS A SPECIAL MISSION FOR HER MAJESTY HERSELF!
SO IF ANY OF YOU SCALLYWAGS AIN'T READY TO PUSH THIS OLD SOW FASTER'N SHE'S EVER SWUM BEFORE, YA MIGHT AS WELL WALK THE PLANK RIGHT NOW!
AIN'T NO COWARDS HERE, CAP'N! WE'RE READY AS RAIN!
WELL THEN, HEAVE-HO, YA BILGE-SUCKING, SCURVY DOGS!
TONIGHT WE SAIL FOR OUR QUEEN! TONIGHT WE SAIL FOR MAXINE, QUEEN A' THE RED!

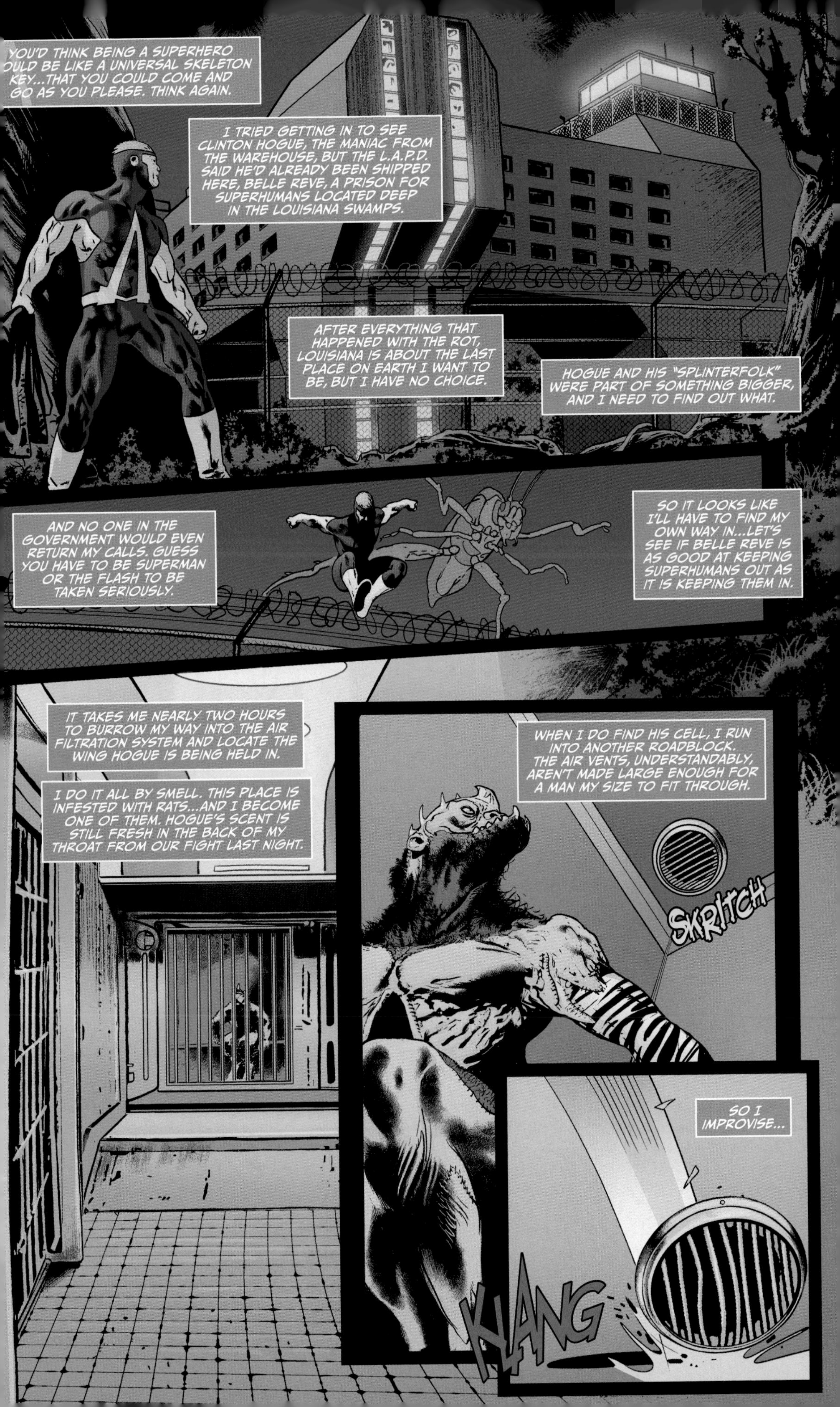

YOU'D THINK BEING A SUPERHERO OULD BE LIKE A UNIVERSAL SKELETON KEY...THAT YOU COULD COME AND GO AS YOU PLEASE. THINK AGAIN.
I TRIED GETTING IN TO SEE CLINTON HOGUE, THE MANIAC FROM THE WAREHOUSE, BUT THE L.A.P.D. SAID HE'D ALREADY BEEN SHIPPED HERE, BELLE REVE, A PRISON FOR SUPERHUMANS LOCATED DEEP IN THE LOUISIANA SWAMPS.
AFTER EVERYTHING THAT HAPPENED WITH THE ROT, LOUISIANA IS ABOUT THE LAST PLACE ON EARTH I WANT TO BE, BUT I HAVE NO CHOICE.
HOGUE AND HIS "SPLINTERFOLK" WERE PART OF SOMETHING BIGGER, AND I NEED TO FIND OUT WHAT.
AND NO ONE IN THE GOVERNMENT WOULD EVEN RETURN MY CALLS. GUESS YOU HAVE TO BE SUPERMAN OR THE FLASH TO BE TAKEN SERIOUSLY.
SO IT LOOKS LIKE I'LL HAVE TO FIND MY OWN WAY IN...LET'S SEE IF BELLE REVE IS AS GOOD AT KEEPING SUPERHUMANS OUT AS IT IS KEEPING THEM IN.
IT TAKES ME NEARLY TWO HOURS TO BURROW MY WAY INTO THE AIR FILTRATION SYSTEM AND LOCATE THE WING HOGUE IS BEING HELD IN.
I DO IT ALL BY SMELL. THIS PLACE IS INFESTED WITH RATS...AND I BECOME ONE OF THEM. HOGUE'S SCENT IS STILL FRESH IN THE BACK OF MY THROAT FROM OUR FIGHT LAST NIGHT.
WHEN I DO FIND HIS CELL, I RUN INTO ANOTHER ROADBLOCK. THE AIR VENTS, UNDERSTANDABLY, AREN'T MADE LARGE ENOUGH FOR A MAN MY SIZE TO FIT THROUGH.
SKRITCH
SO I IMPROVISE...
KLANG

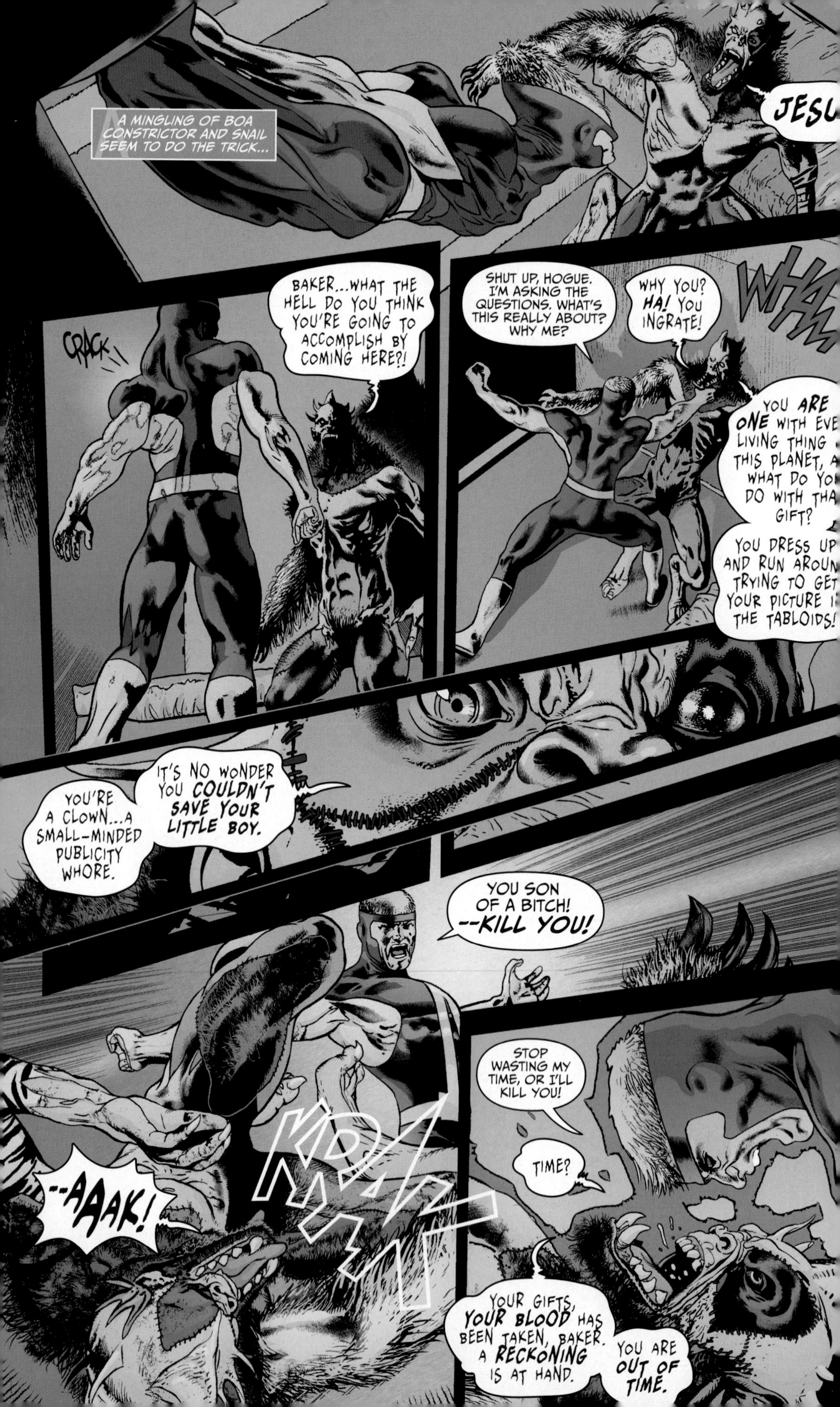
A MINGLING OF BOA CONSTRICTOR AND SNAIL SEEM TO DO THE TRICK...
JESU
CRACK
BAKER...WHAT THE HELL DO YOU THINK YOU'RE GOING TO ACCOMPLISH BY COMING HERE?!
SHUT UP, HOGUE. I'M ASKING THE QUESTIONS. WHAT'S THIS REALLY ABOUT? WHY ME?
WHY YOU? HA! YOU INGRATE!
WHAM
YOU ARE ONE WITH EVE LIVING THING THIS PLANET, A WHAT DO YO DO WITH THA GIFT?
YOU DRESS UP AND RUN AROUN TRYING TO GET YOUR PICTURE I THE TABLOIDS!
YOU'RE A CLOWN...A SMALL-MINDED PUBLICITY WHORE.
IT'S NO WONDER YOU COULDN'T SAVE YOUR LITTLE BOY.
YOU SON OF A BITCH! --KILL YOU!
--AAAK!
STOP WASTING MY TIME, OR I'LL KILL YOU!
TIME?
YOUR GIFTS, YOUR BLOOD HAS BEEN TAKEN, BAKER. A RECKONING IS AT HAND.
YOU ARE OUT OF TIME.

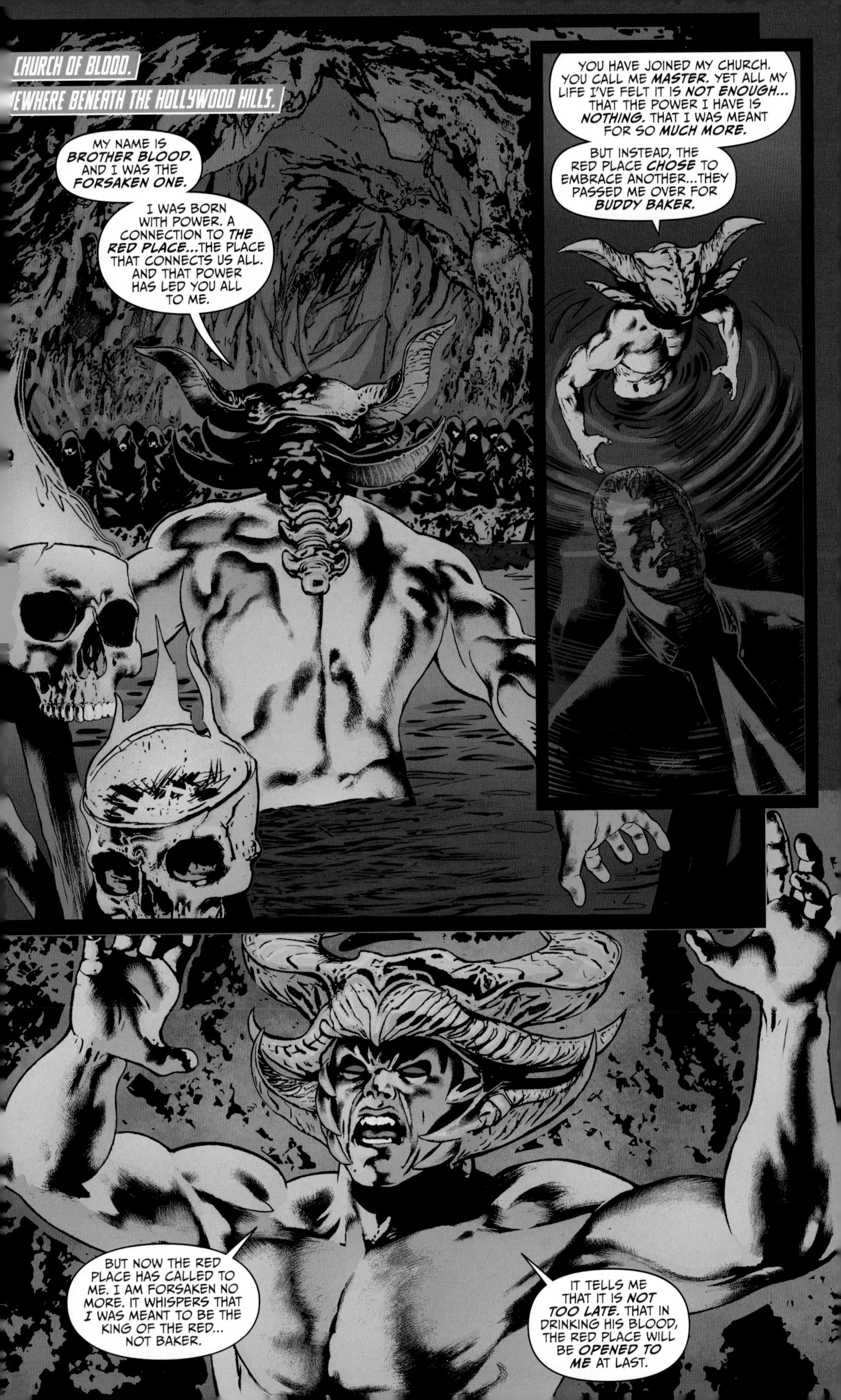
CHURCH OF BLOOD.
EWHERE BENEATH THE HOLLYWOOD HILLS.
MY NAME IS BROTHER BLOOD. AND I WAS THE FORSAKEN ONE.
I WAS BORN WITH POWER. A CONNECTION TO THE RED PLACE...THE PLACE THAT CONNECTS US ALL. AND THAT POWER HAS LED YOU ALL TO ME.
YOU HAVE JOINED MY CHURCH. YOU CALL ME MASTER. YET ALL MY LIFE I'VE FELT IT IS NOT ENOUGH... THAT THE POWER I HAVE IS NOTHING. THAT I WAS MEANT FOR SO MUCH MORE.
BUT INSTEAD, THE RED PLACE CHOSE TO EMBRACE ANOTHER...THEY PASSED ME OVER FOR BUDDY BAKER.
BUT NOW THE RED PLACE HAS CALLED TO ME. I AM FORSAKEN NO MORE. IT WHISPERS THAT I WAS MEANT TO BE THE KING OF THE RED... NOT BAKER.
IT TELLS ME THAT IT IS NOT TOO LATE. THAT IN DRINKING HIS BLOOD, THE RED PLACE WILL BE OPENED TO ME AT LAST.

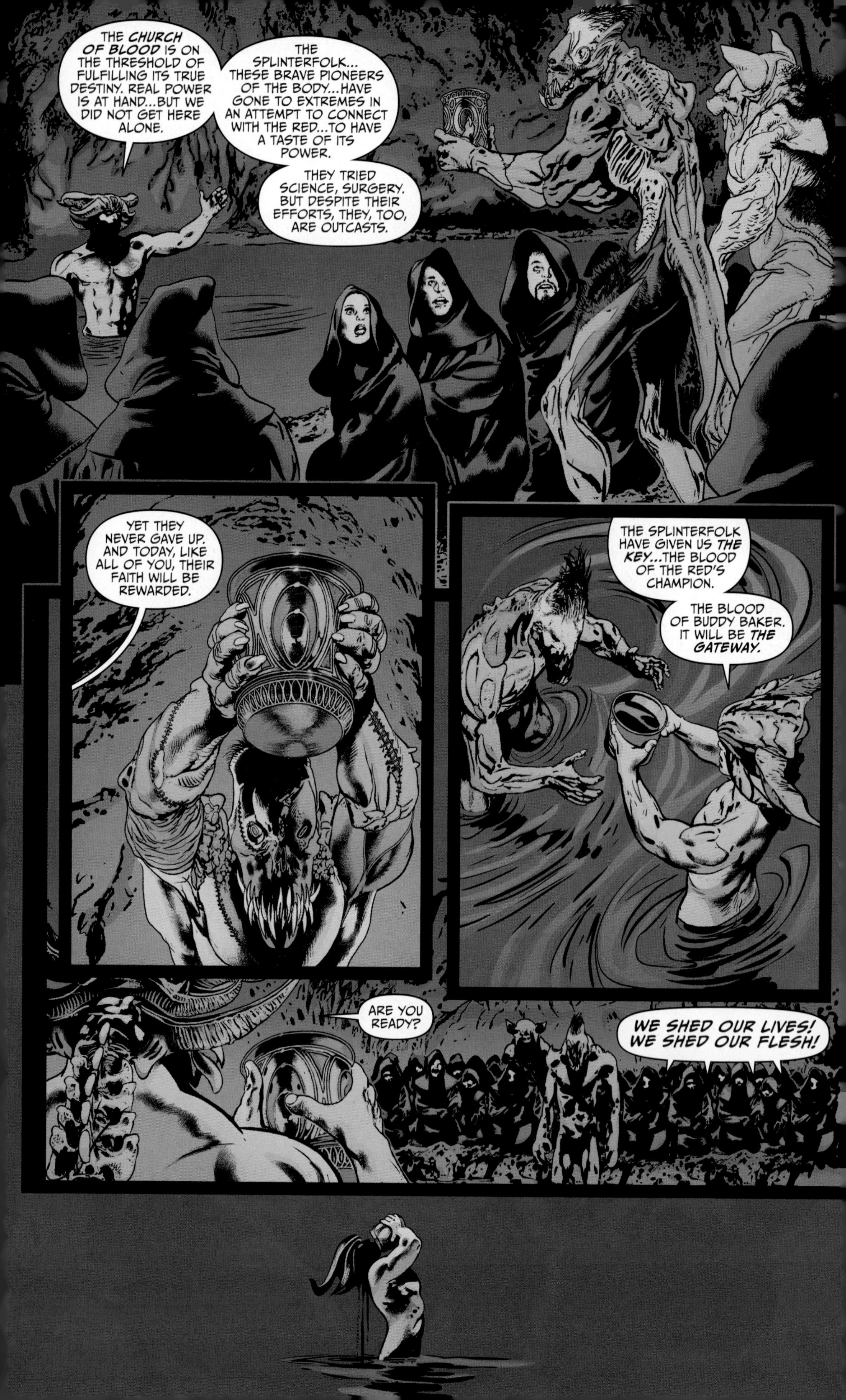
THE CHURCH OF BLOOD IS ON THE THRESHOLD OF FULFILLING ITS TRUE DESTINY. REAL POWER IS AT HAND...BUT WE DID NOT GET HERE ALONE.
THE SPLINTERFOLK... THESE BRAVE PIONEERS OF THE BODY...HAVE GONE TO EXTREMES IN AN ATTEMPT TO CONNECT WITH THE RED...TO HAVE A TASTE OF ITS POWER.
THEY TRIED SCIENCE, SURGERY. BUT DESPITE THEIR EFFORTS, THEY, TOO, ARE OUTCASTS.
YET THEY NEVER GAVE UP. AND TODAY, LIKE ALL OF YOU, THEIR FAITH WILL BE REWARDED.
THE SPLINTERFOLK HAVE GIVEN US THE KEY...THE BLOOD OF THE RED'S CHAMPION.
THE BLOOD OF BUDDY BAKER. IT WILL BE THE GATEWAY.
ARE YOU READY?
WE SHED OUR LIVES! WE SHED OUR FLESH!

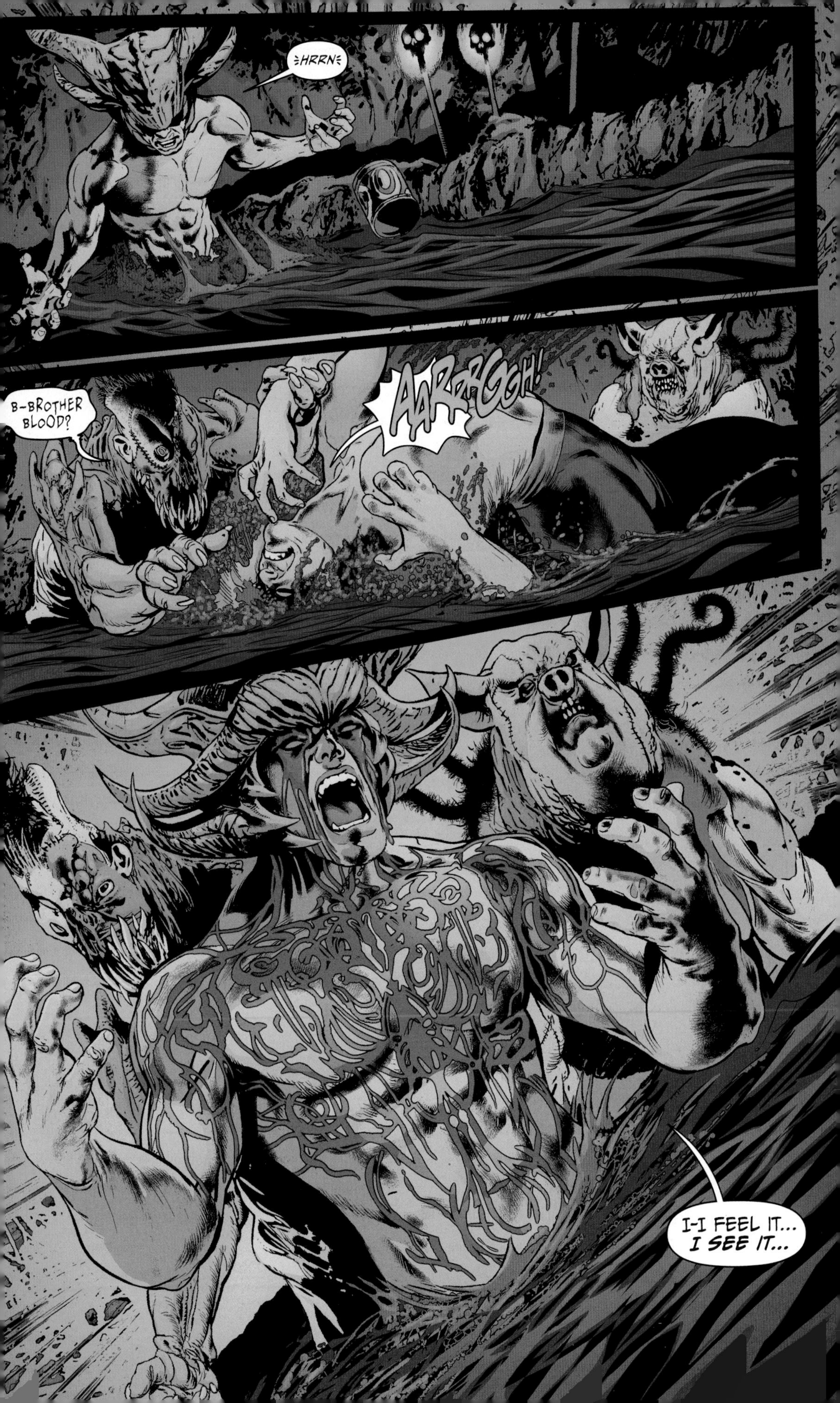
HRRN
B-BROTHER BLOOD?
AARRRGGH!
I-I FEEL IT... I SEE IT...

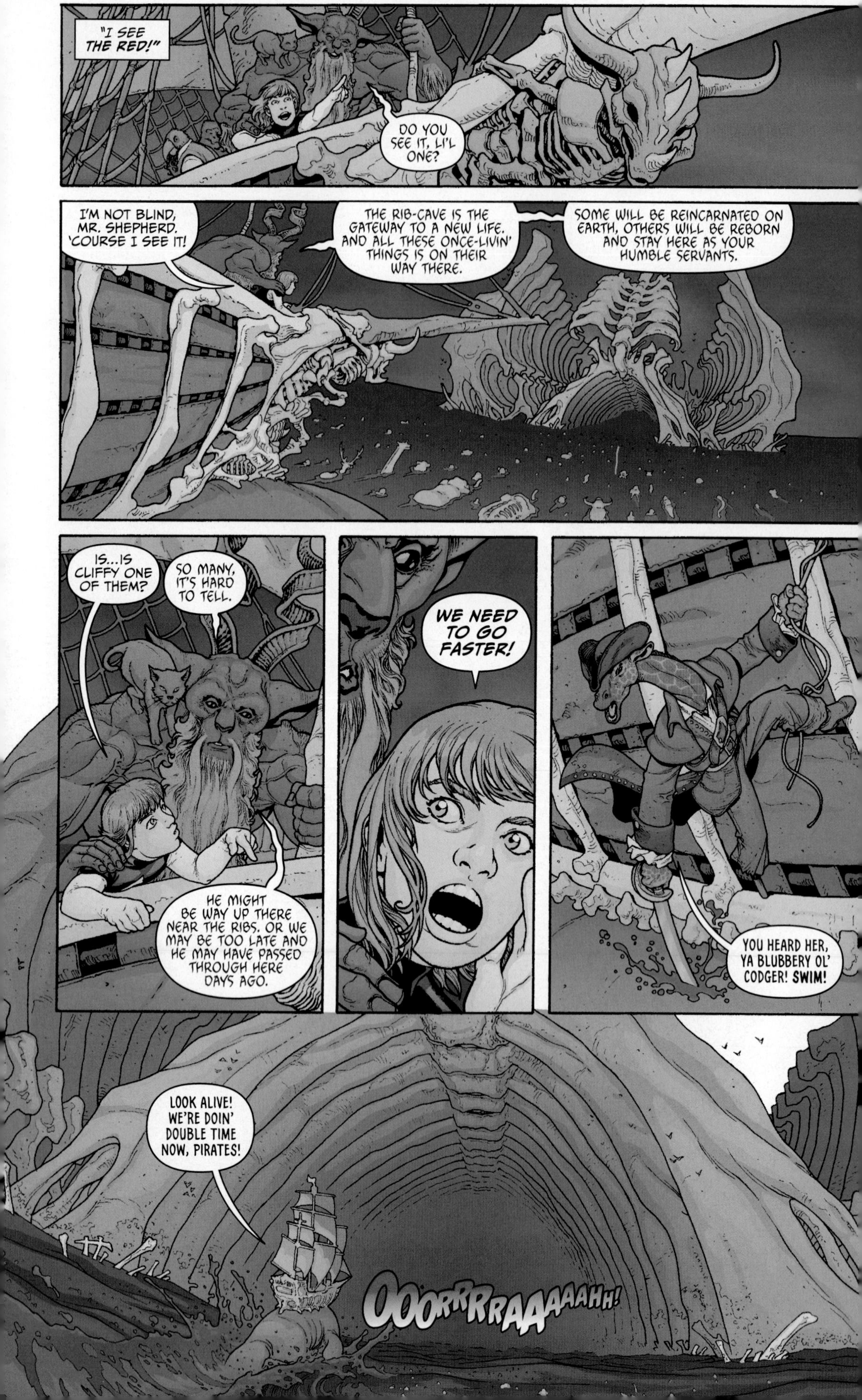
"I SEE THE RED!"
DO YOU SEE IT, LI'L ONE?
I'M NOT BLIND, MR. SHEPHERD. 'COURSE I SEE IT!
THE RIB-CAVE IS THE GATEWAY TO A NEW LIFE. AND ALL THESE ONCE-LIVIN' THINGS IS ON THEIR WAY THERE.
SOME WILL BE REINCARNATED ON EARTH, OTHERS WILL BE REBORN AND STAY HERE AS YOUR HUMBLE SERVANTS.
IS...IS CLIFFY ONE OF THEM?
SO MANY, IT'S HARD TO TELL.
HE MIGHT BE WAY UP THERE NEAR THE RIBS. OR WE MAY BE TOO LATE AND HE MAY HAVE PASSED THROUGH HERE DAYS AGO.
WE NEED TO GO FASTER!
YOU HEARD HER, YA BLUBBERY OL' CODGER! SWIM!
LOOK ALIVE! WE'RE DOIN' DOUBLE TIME NOW, PIRATES!
OOORRRRAAAAAAHH!

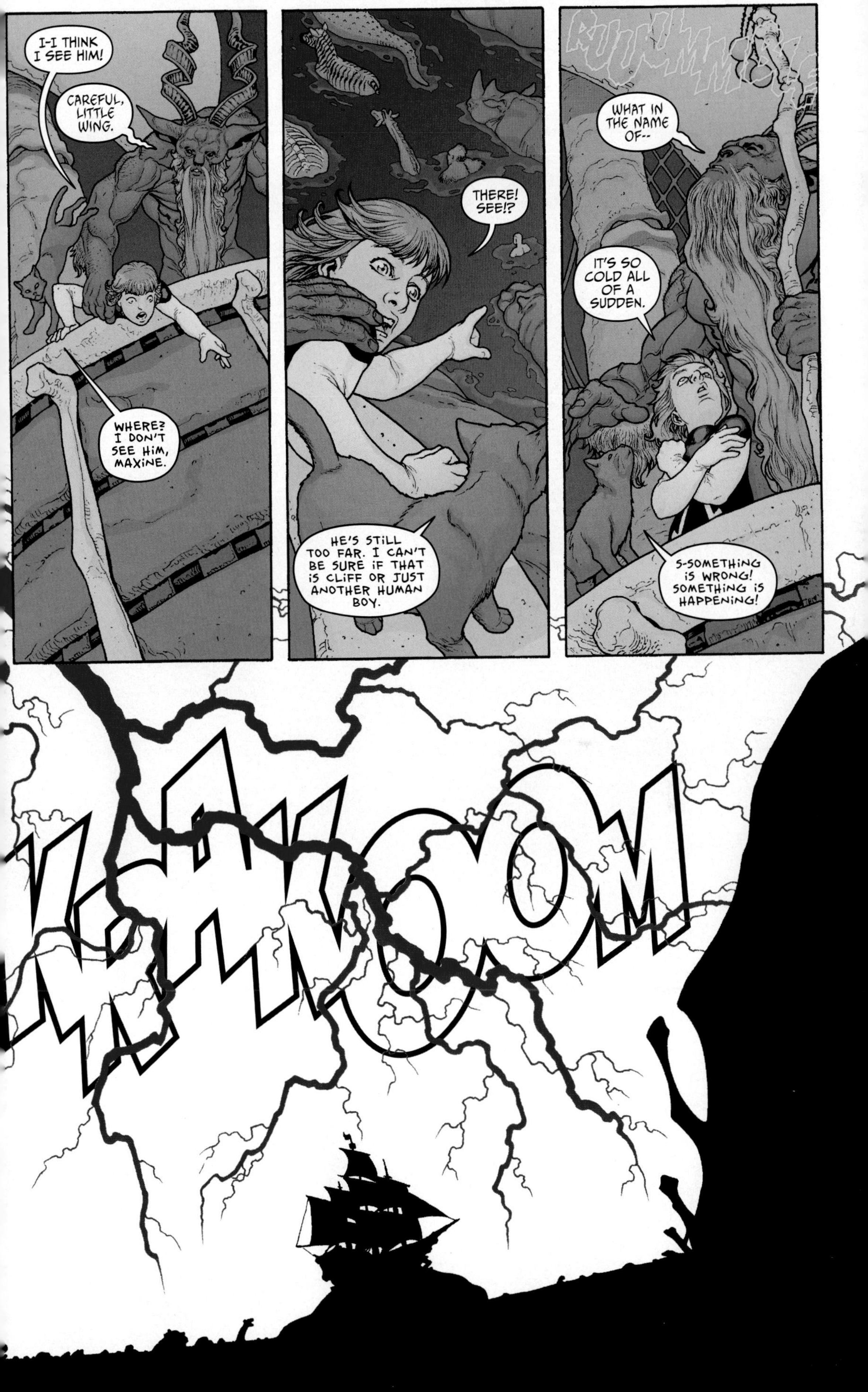
I-I THINK I SEE HIM!
CAREFUL, LITTLE WING.
WHERE? I DON'T SEE HIM, MAXINE.
THERE! SEE!?
HE'S STILL TOO FAR. I CAN'T BE SURE IF THAT IS CLIFF OR JUST ANOTHER HUMAN BOY.
WHAT IN THE NAME OF--
IT'S SO COLD ALL OF A SUDDEN.
S-SOMETHING IS WRONG! SOMETHING IS HAPPENING!
KAWOOM

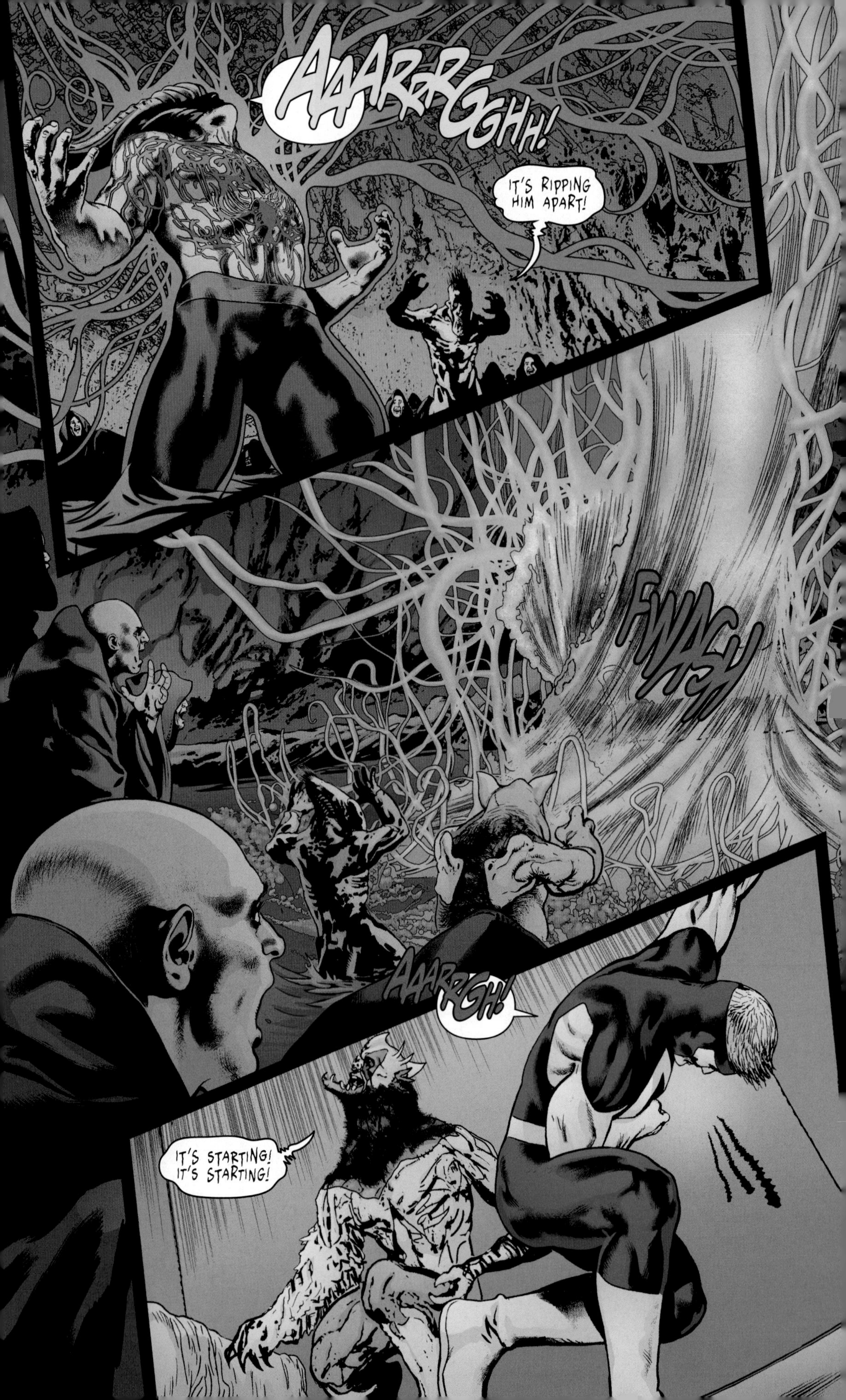
AAARRRGGHH!
IT'S RIPPING HIM APART!
FWASH
AAARRGH!
IT'S STARTING! IT'S STARTING!

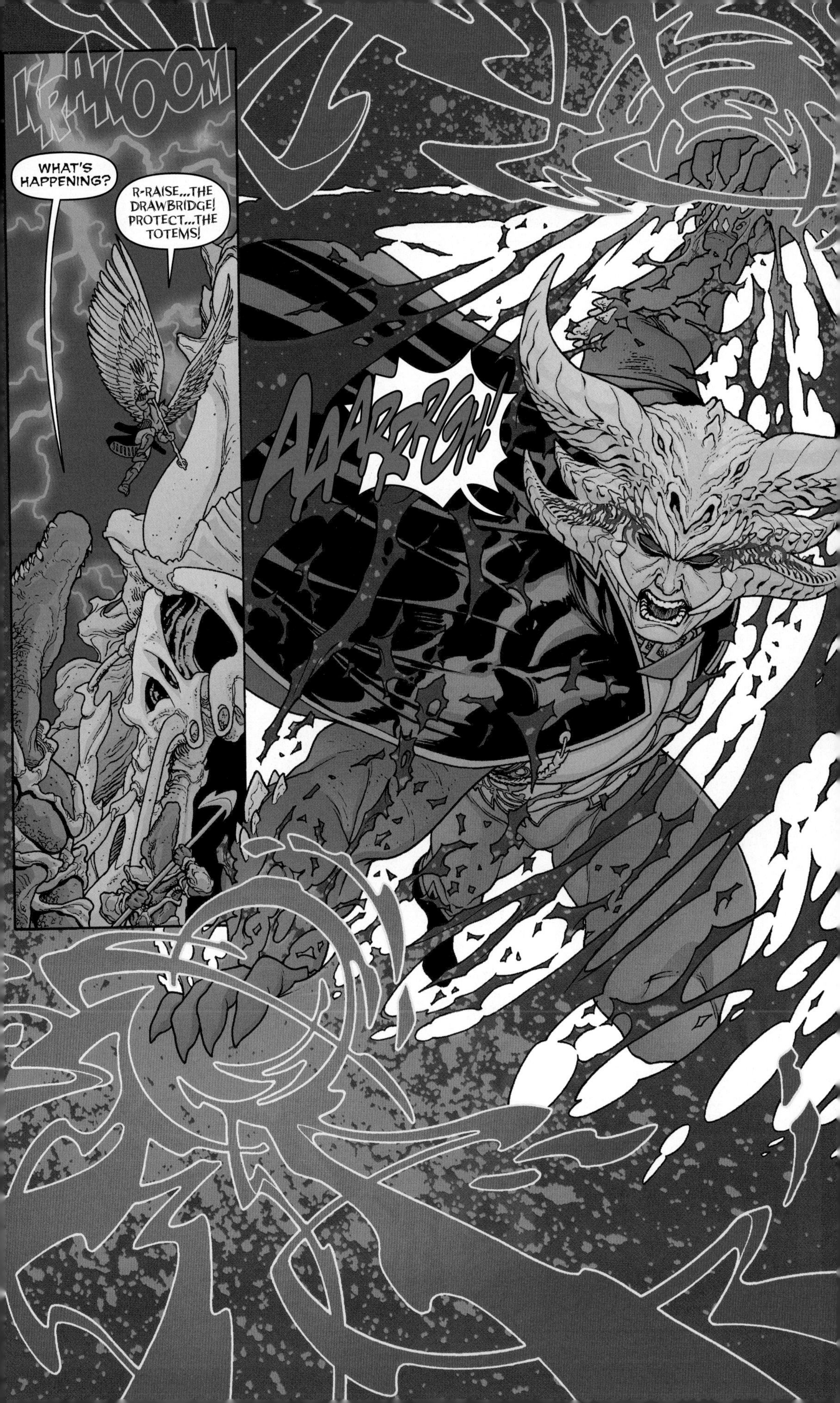
KRAKKOOM
WHAT'S HAPPENING?
R-RAISE...THE DRAWBRIDGE! PROTECT...THE TOTEMS!
AAARRRGH!

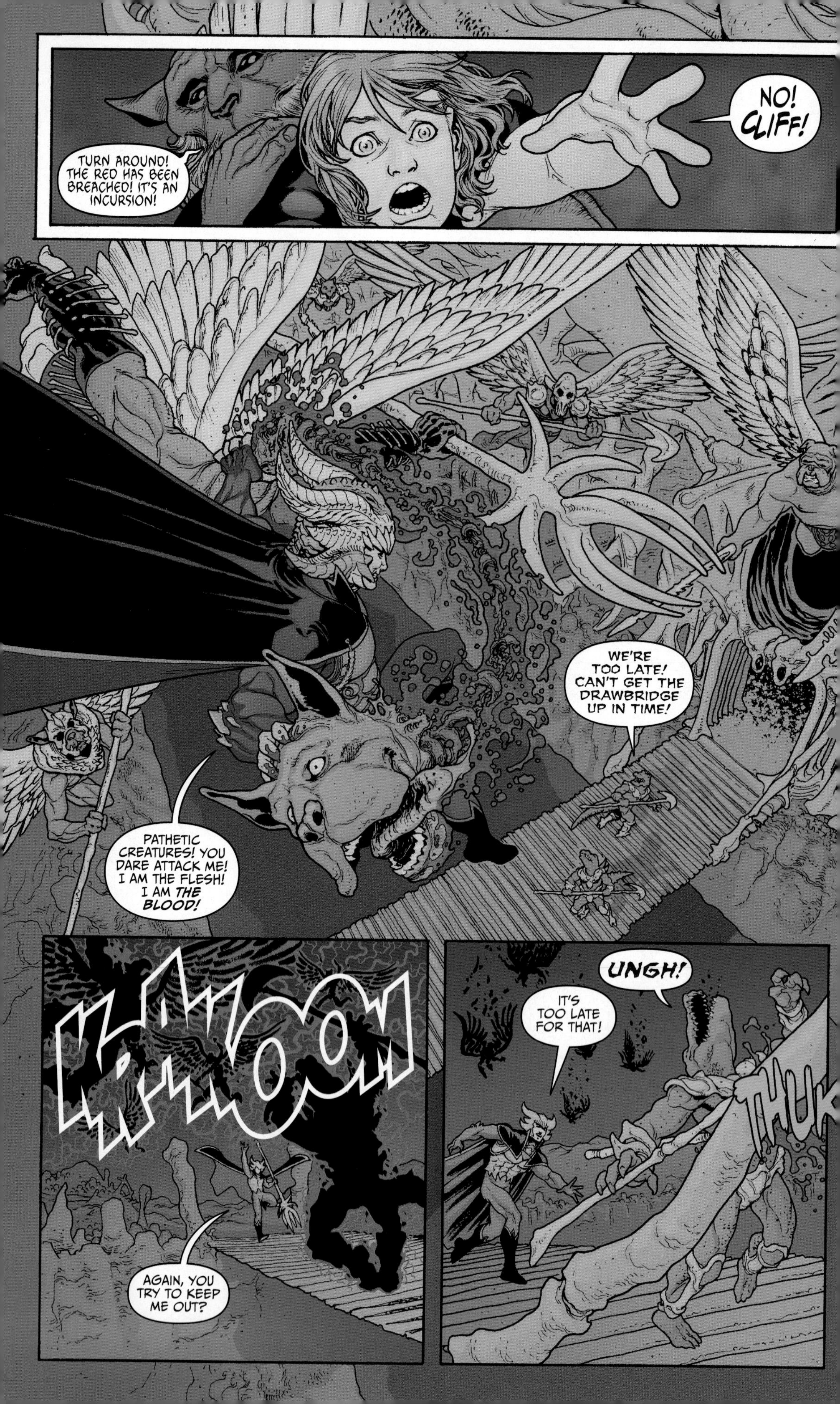
TURN AROUND! THE RED HAS BEEN BREACHED! IT'S AN INCURSION!
NO! CLIFF!
WE'RE TOO LATE! CAN'T GET THE DRAWBRIDGE UP IN TIME!
PATHETIC CREATURES! YOU DARE ATTACK ME! I AM THE FLESH! I AM *THE BLOOD!*
KAHOOOM
AGAIN, YOU TRY TO KEEP ME OUT?
UNGH!
IT'S TOO LATE FOR THAT!
THUK

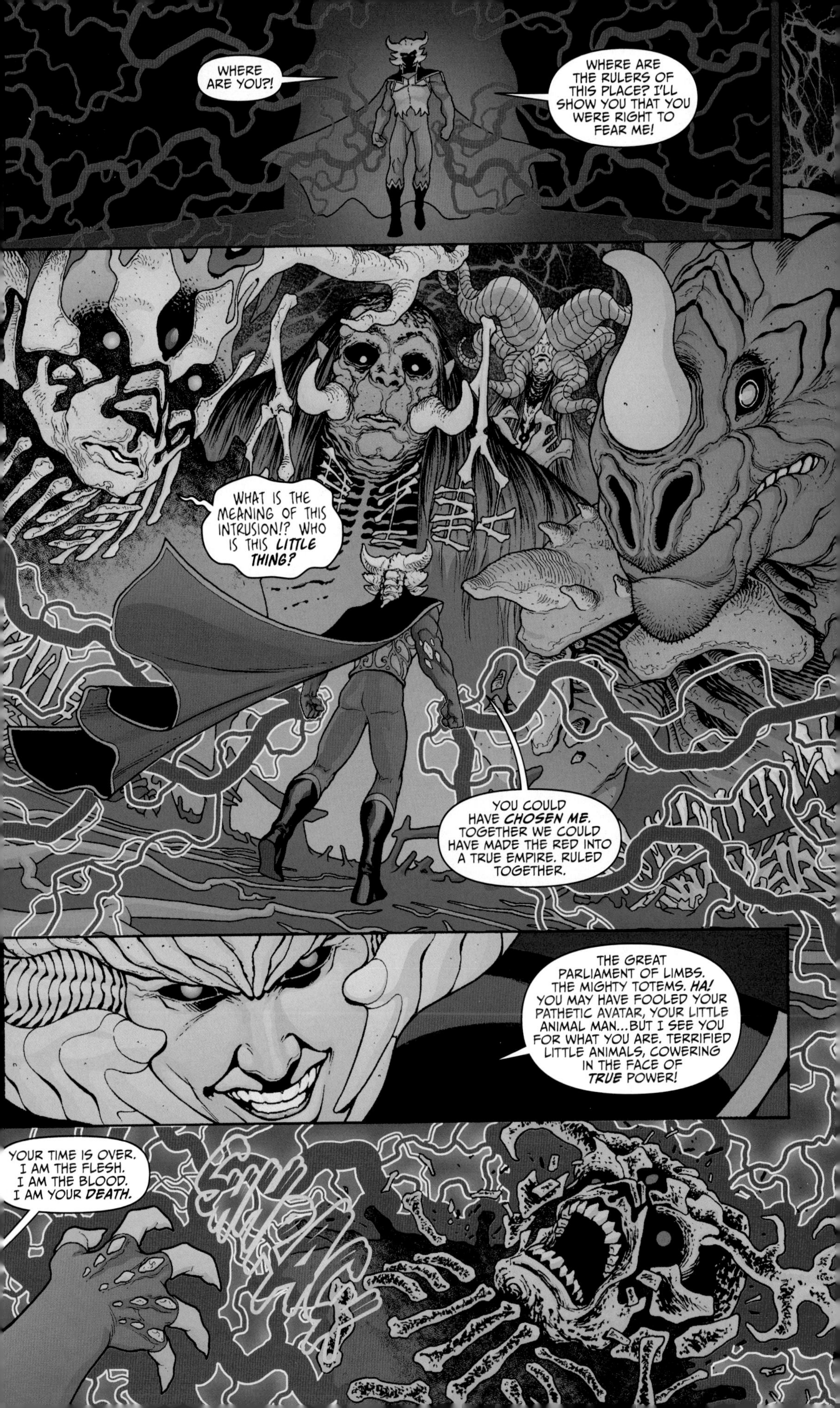
WHERE ARE YOU?!
WHERE ARE THE RULERS OF THIS PLACE? I'LL SHOW YOU THAT YOU WERE RIGHT TO FEAR ME!
WHAT IS THE MEANING OF THIS INTRUSION!? WHO IS THIS LITTLE THING?
YOU COULD HAVE CHOSEN ME. TOGETHER WE COULD HAVE MADE THE RED INTO A TRUE EMPIRE. RULED TOGETHER.
THE GREAT PARLIAMENT OF LIMBS. THE MIGHTY TOTEMS. HA! YOU MAY HAVE FOOLED YOUR PATHETIC AVATAR, YOUR LITTLE ANIMAL MAN...BUT I SEE YOU FOR WHAT YOU ARE. TERRIFIED LITTLE ANIMALS, COWERING IN THE FACE OF TRUE POWER!
YOUR TIME IS OVER. I AM THE FLESH. I AM THE BLOOD. I AM YOUR DEATH.

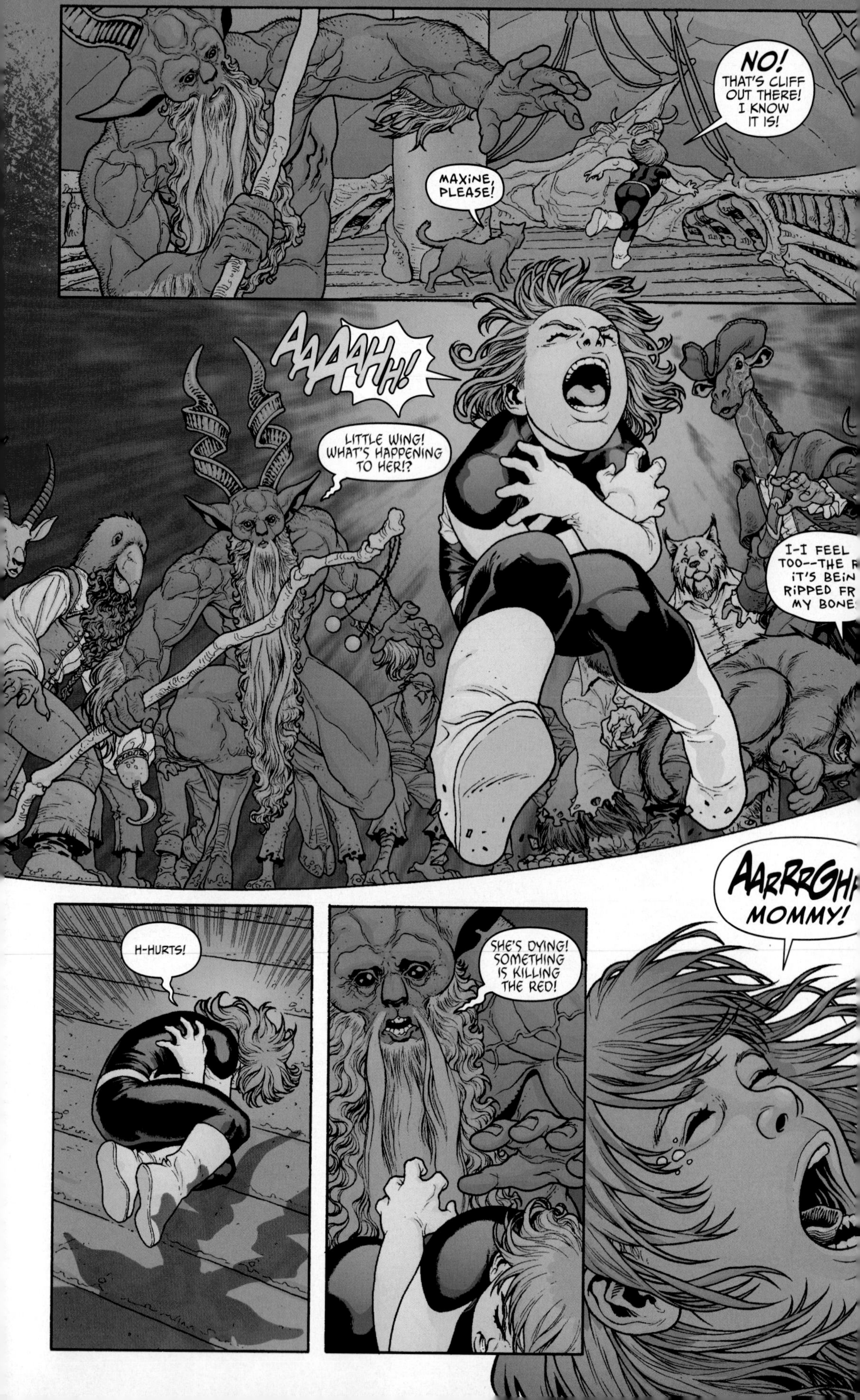
NO! THAT'S CLIFF OUT THERE! I KNOW IT IS!
MAXINE, PLEASE!
AAAAHH!
LITTLE WING! WHAT'S HAPPENING TO HER!?
I-I FEEL TOO--THE R IT'S BEIN RIPPED FR MY BONE
AARRRGH MOMMY!
H-HURTS!
SHE'S DYING! SOMETHING IS KILLING THE RED!

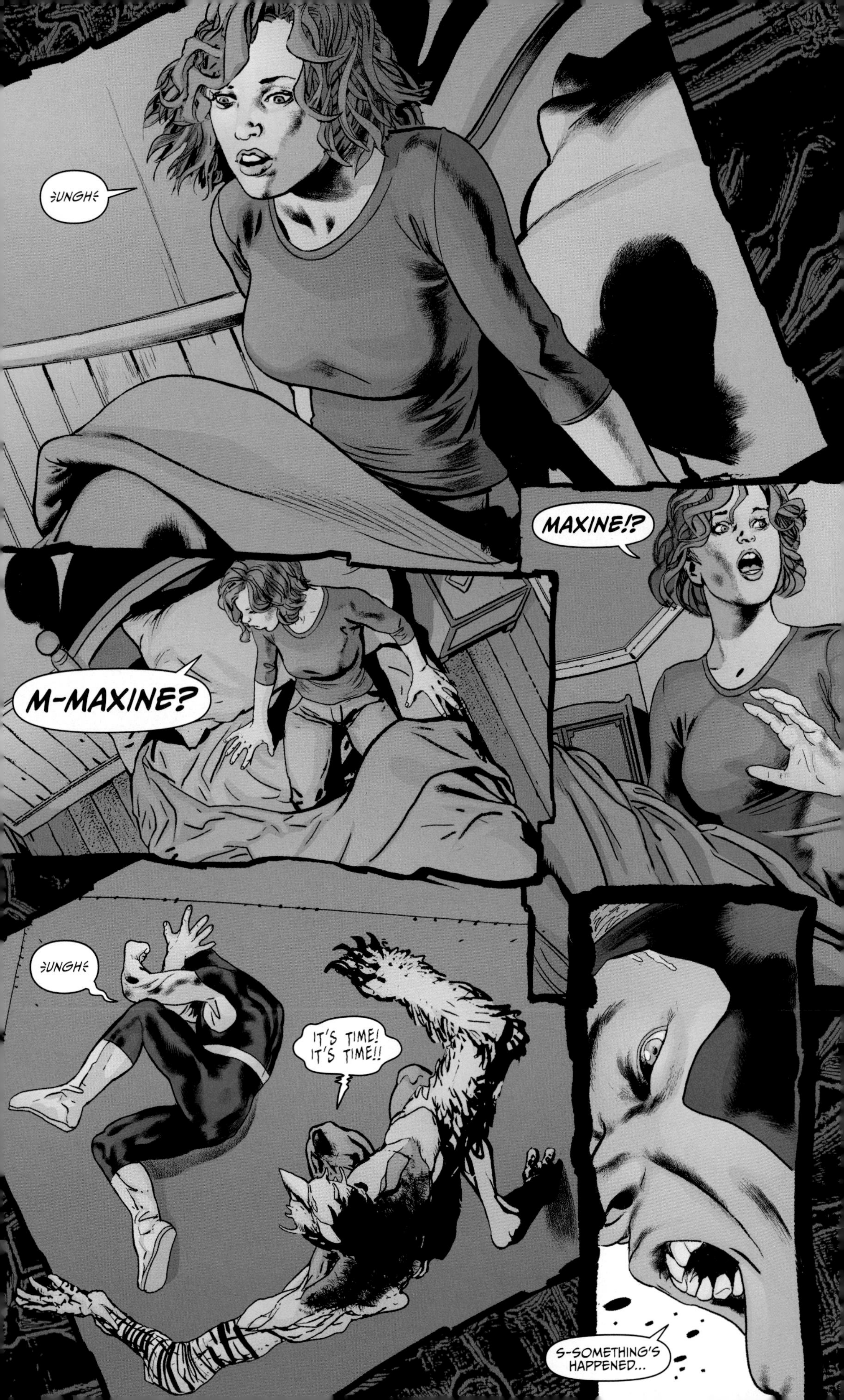
UNGH
MAXINE!?
M-MAXINE?
UNGH
IT'S TIME! IT'S TIME!!
S-SOMETHING'S HAPPENED...

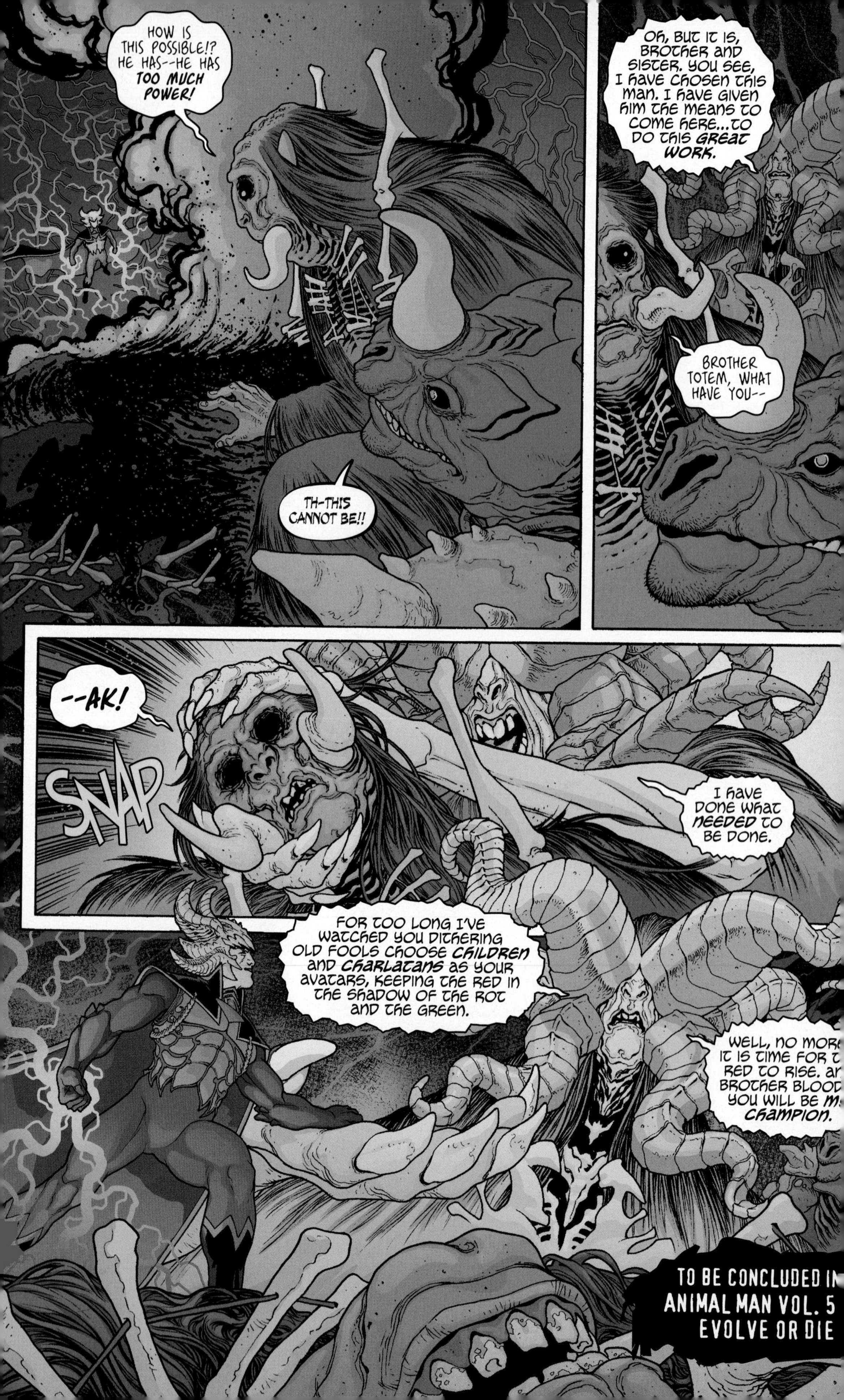
HOW IS THIS POSSIBLE!? HE HAS--HE HAS TOO MUCH POWER!
TH-THIS CANNOT BE!!
OH, BUT IT IS, BROTHER AND SISTER. YOU SEE, I HAVE CHOSEN THIS MAN. I HAVE GIVEN HIM THE MEANS TO COME HERE...TO DO THIS GREAT WORK.
BROTHER TOTEM, WHAT HAVE YOU--
--AK!
SNAP
I HAVE DONE WHAT NEEDED TO BE DONE.
FOR TOO LONG I'VE WATCHED YOU DITHERING OLD FOOLS CHOOSE CHILDREN AND CHARLATANS AS YOUR AVATARS, KEEPING THE RED IN THE SHADOW OF THE ROT AND THE GREEN.
WELL, NO MOR IT IS TIME FOR T RED TO RISE. A BROTHER BLOOD YOU WILL BE M CHAMPION.
TO BE CONCLUDED IN
ANIMAL MAN VOL. 5
EVOLVE OR DIE

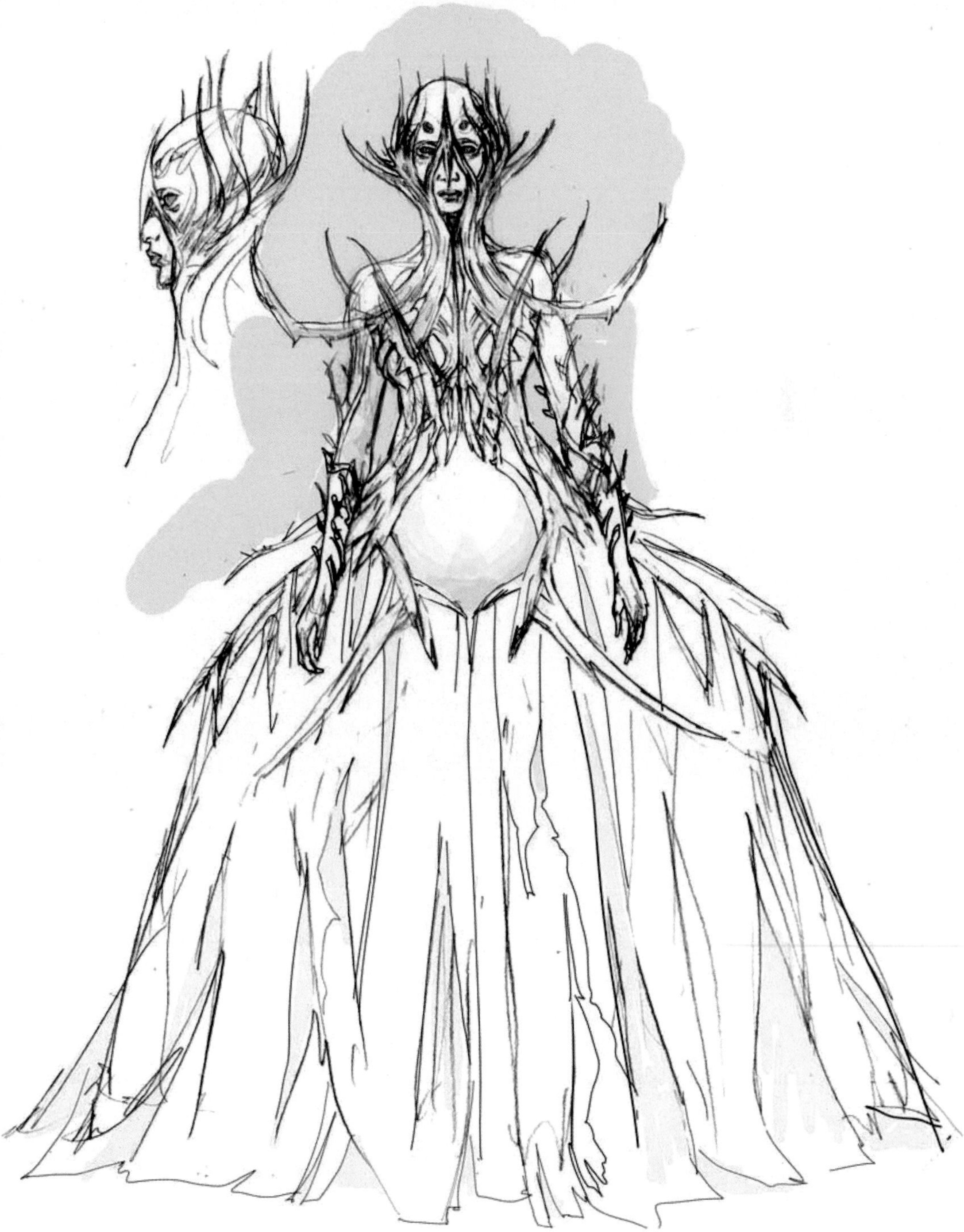

Design by Travel Foreman

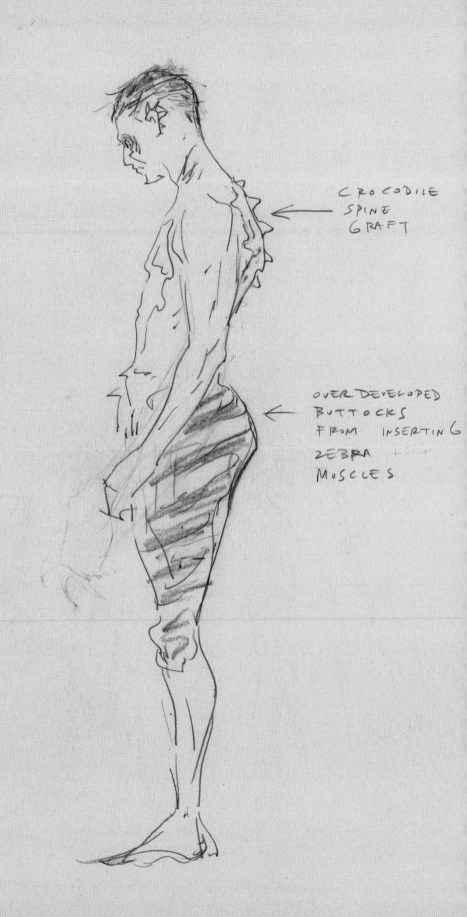

CROCODILE
SPINE
GRAFT

OVER DEVELOPED
BUTTOCKS
FROM INSERTING
ZEBRA
MUSCLES

esign by Jae Lee

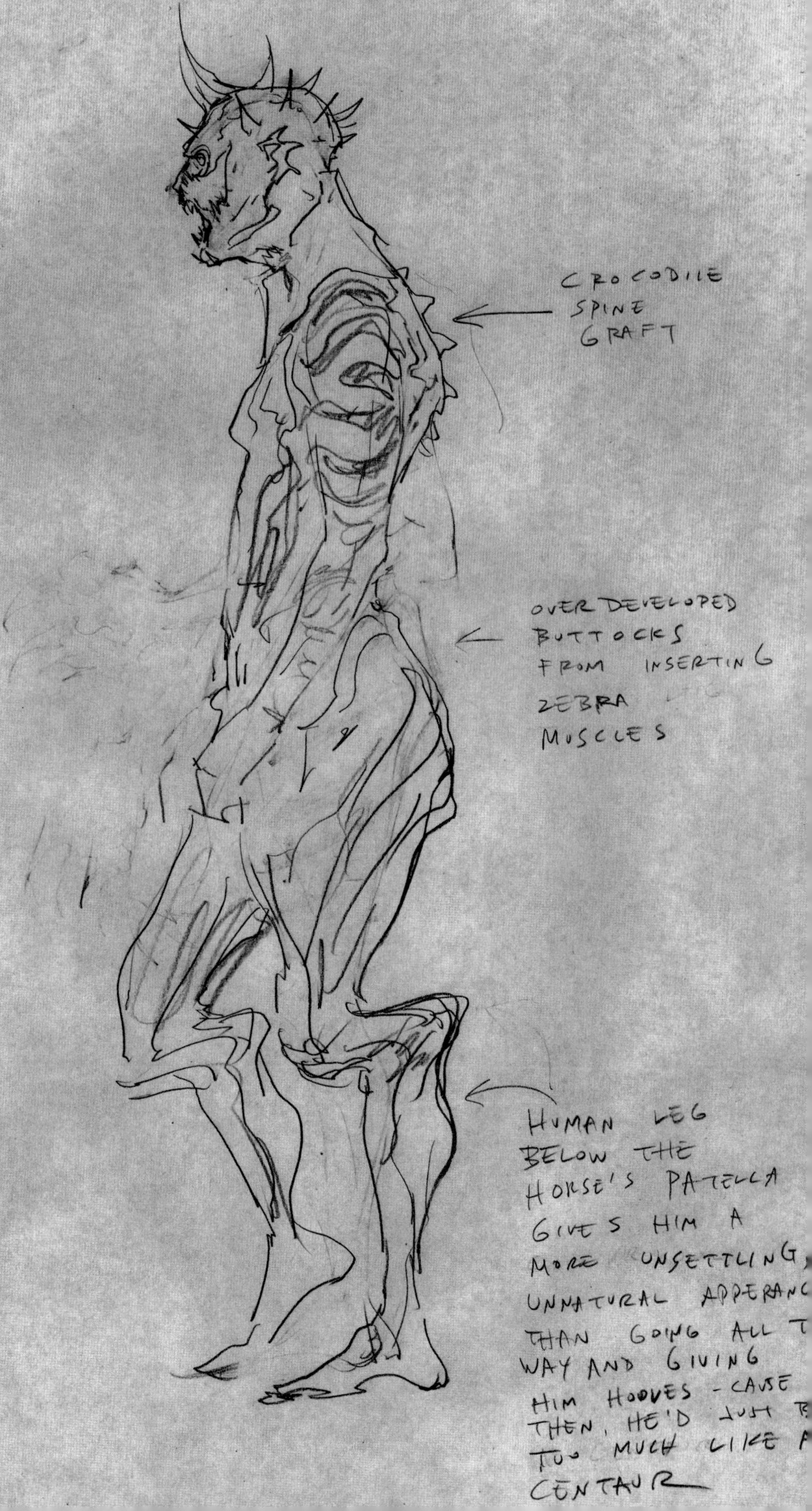
CROCODILE
SPINE
GRAFT
OVER DEVELOPED
BUTTOCKS
FROM INSERTING
ZEBRA
MUSCLES
HUMAN LEG
BELOW THE
HORSE'S PATELLA
GIVES HIM A
MORE UNSETTLING,
UNNATURAL APPERANC
THAN GOING ALL T
WAY AND GIVING
HIM HOOVES - CAUSE
THEN, HE'D JUST
TOO MUCH LIKE A
CENTAUR

Design by Jae Lee

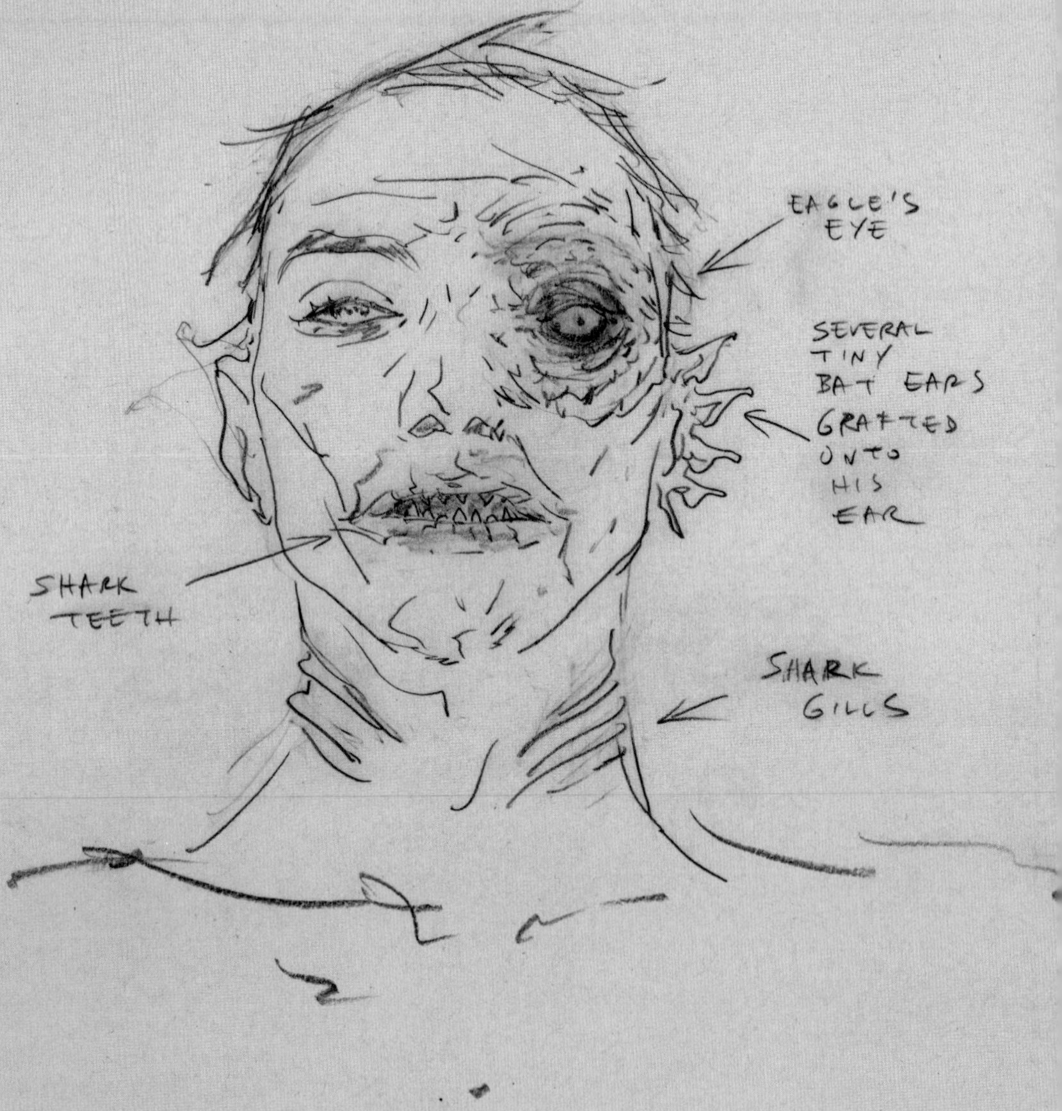
EAGLE'S
EYE
SEVERAL
TINY
BAT EARS
GRAFTED
ONTO
HIS
EAR
SHARK
TEETH
SHARK
GILLS

Design by Jae Lee

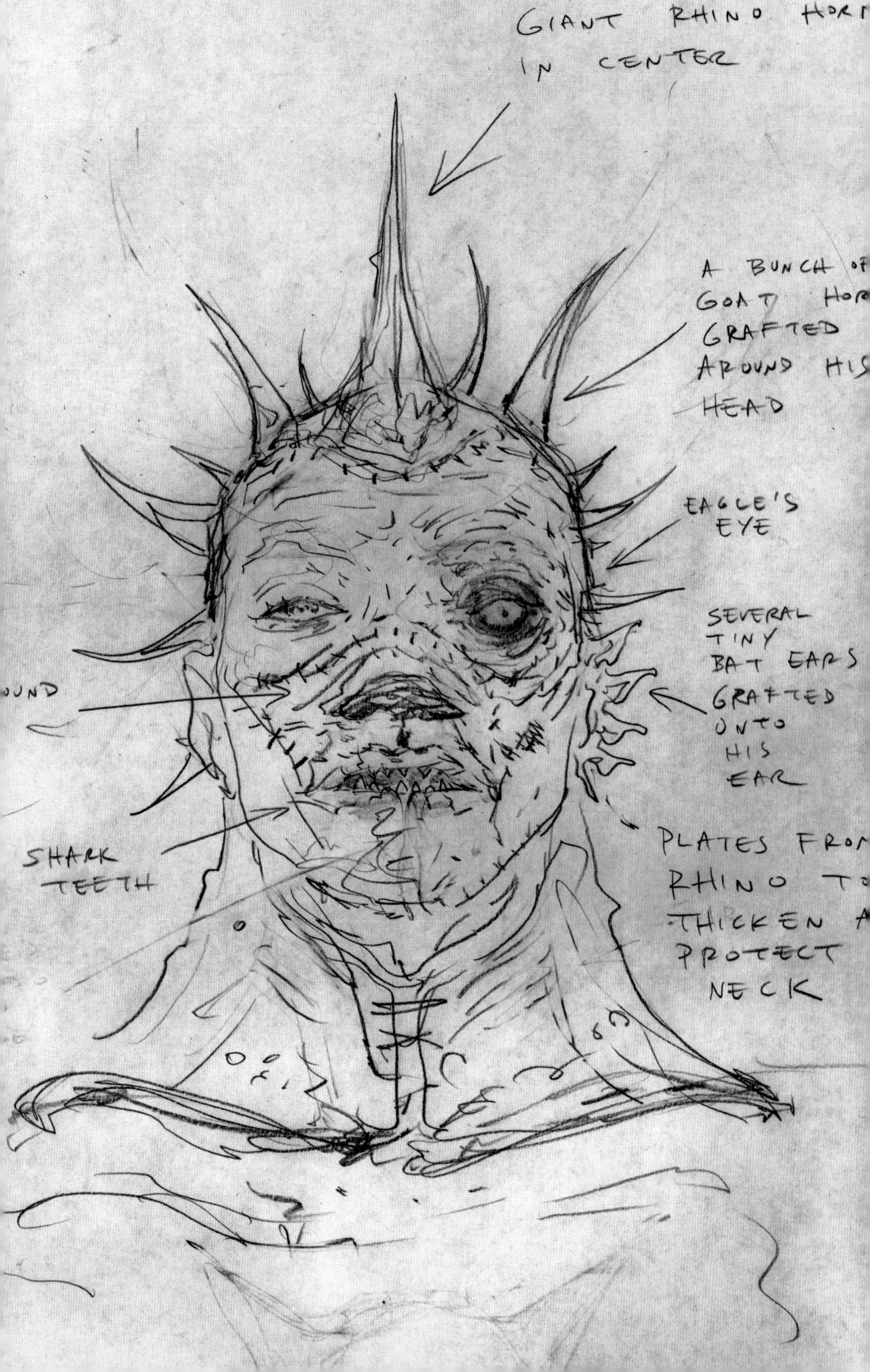

GIANT RHINO HOR
IN CENTER
A BUNCH OF
GOAT HOR
GRAFTED
AROUND HIS
HEAD
EAGLE'S
EYE
SEVERAL
TINY
BAT EARS
GRAFTED
ONTO
HIS
EAR
OUND
SHARK
TEETH
PLATES FROM
RHINO TO
THICKEN A
PROTECT
NECK

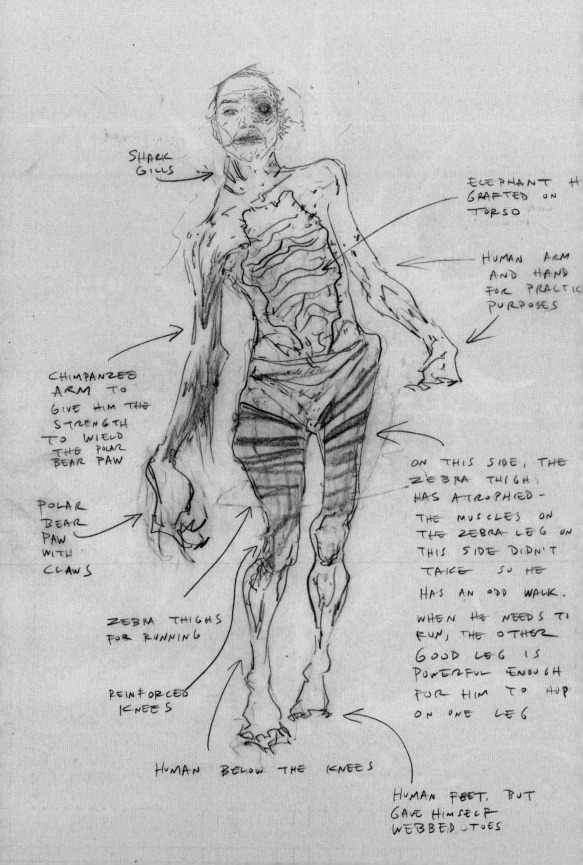

Design by Jae Lee

SHARK GILLS

ELEPHANT H GRAFTED ON TORSO

HUMAN ARM AND HAND FOR PRACTIC PURPOSES

CHIMPANZEE ARM TO GIVE HIM THE STRENGTH TO WIELD THE POLAR BEAR PAW

POLAR BEAR PAW WITH CLAWS

ON THIS SIDE, THE ZEBRA THIGH HAS ATROPHIED - THE MUSCLES ON THE ZEBRA LEG ON THIS SIDE DIDN'T TAKE SO HE HAS AN ODD WALK. WHEN HE NEEDS TO RUN, THE OTHER GOOD LEG IS POWERFUL ENOUGH FOR HIM TO HOP ON ONE LEG

ZEBRA THIGHS FOR RUNNING

REINFORCED KNEES

HUMAN BELOW THE KNEES

HUMAN FEET, BUT GAVE HIMSELF WEBBED TOES

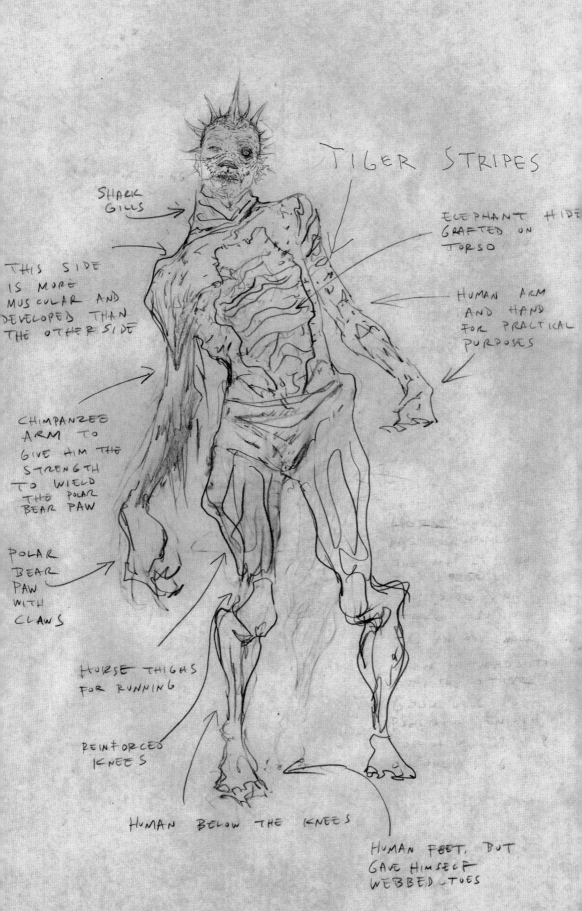

TIGER STRIPES

SHARK GILLS

ELEPHANT HIDE GRAFTED ON TORSO

THIS SIDE IS MORE MUSCULAR AND DEVELOPED THAN THE OTHER SIDE

HUMAN ARM AND HAND FOR PRACTICAL PURPOSES

CHIMPANZEE ARM TO GIVE HIM THE STRENGTH TO WIELD THE POLAR BEAR PAW

POLAR BEAR PAW WITH CLAWS

HORSE THIGHS FOR RUNNING

REINFORCED KNEES

HUMAN BELOW THE KNEES

HUMAN FEET, BUT GAVE HIMSELF WEBBED TOES

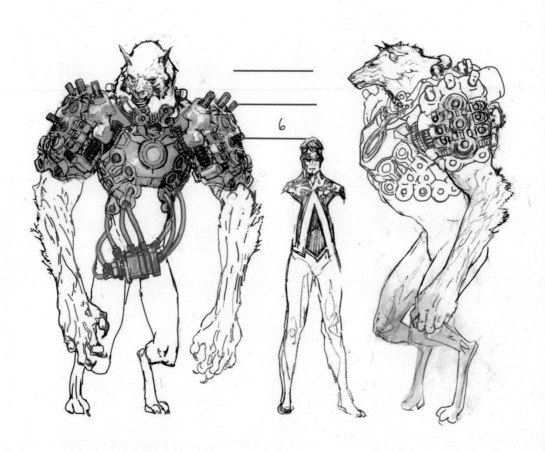

6

Design by Travel Foreman

"If you don't love it from the very first page, you're not human."
—MTV GEEK

"ANIMAL MAN has the sensational Jeff Lemire at the helm."
—ENTERTAINMENT WEEKLY

START AT THE BEGINNING!

ANIMAL MAN VOLUME 1: THE HUNT

JUSTICE LEAGUE DARK VOLUME 1: IN THE DARK

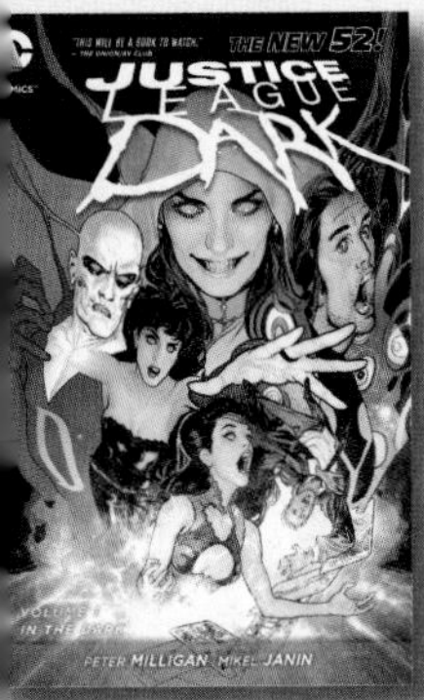
THE NEW 52!
JUSTICE LEAGUE DARK
PETER MILLIGAN MIKEL JANIN

RESURRECTION MAN VOLUME 1: DEAD AGAIN

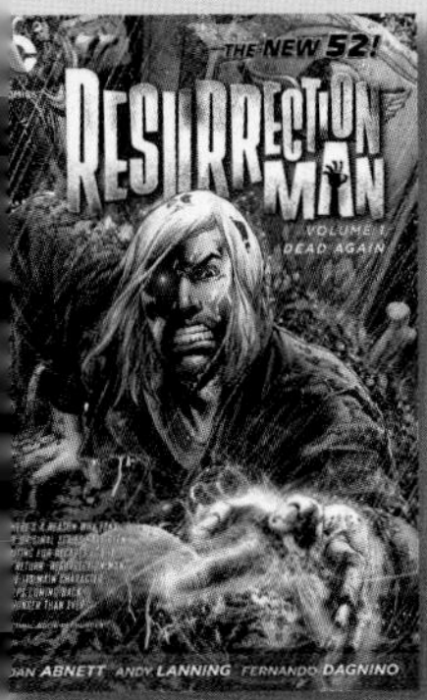
THE NEW 52!
RESURRECTION MAN
VOLUME 1 DEAD AGAIN
ANDY LANNING FERNANDO DAGNINO

FRANKENSTEIN AGENT OF S.H.A.D.E. VOLUME 1: WAR OF THE MONSTERS

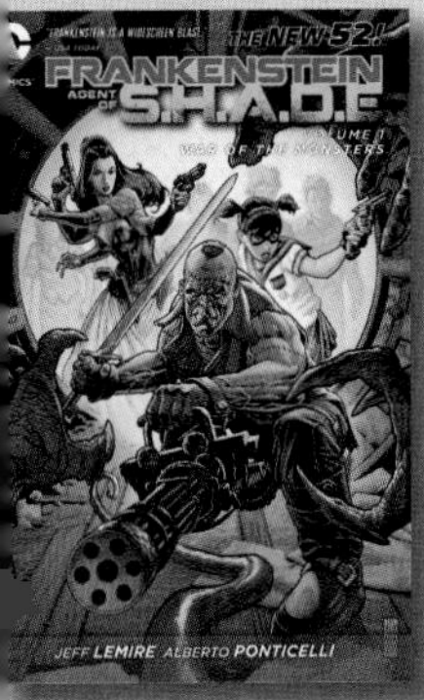
THE NEW 52!
FRANKENSTEIN AGENT OF S.H.A.D.E.
JEFF LEMIRE ALBERTO PONTICELLI

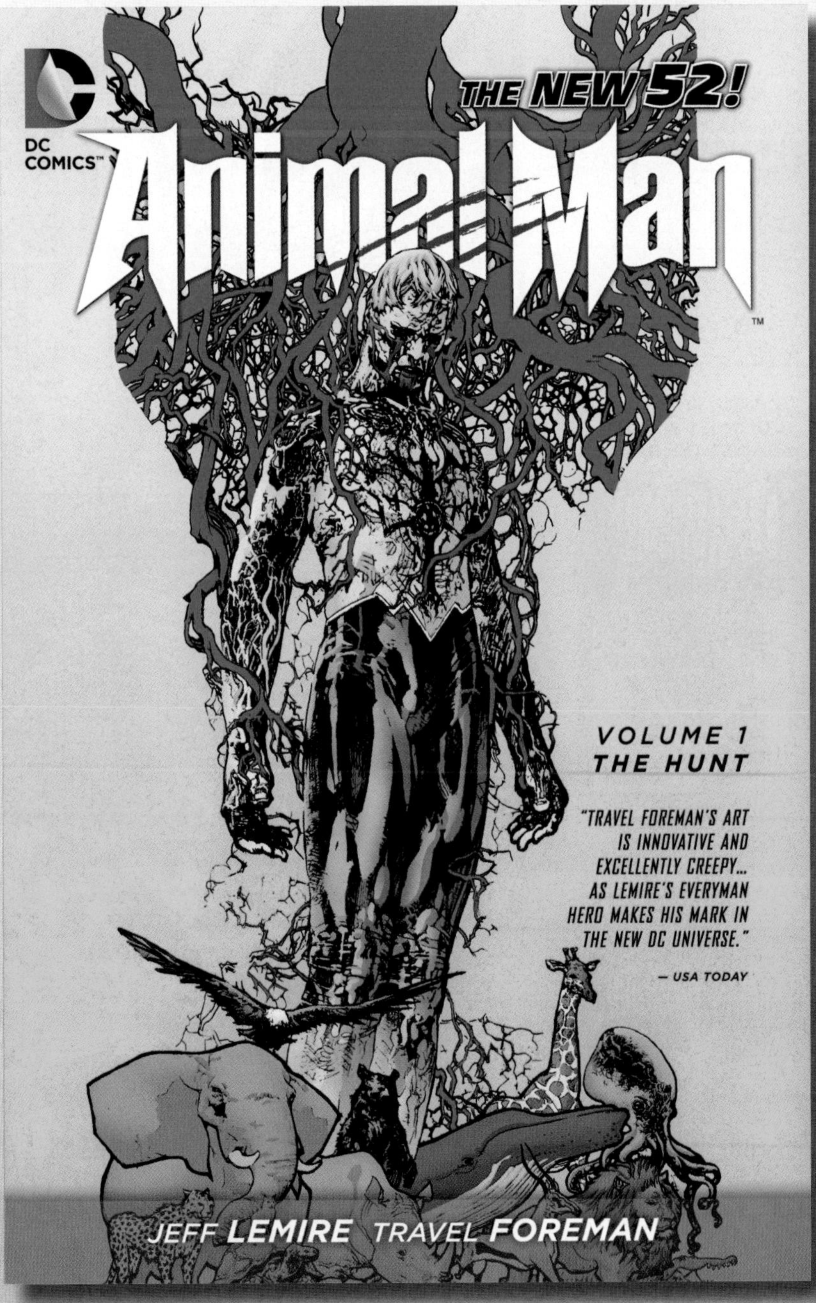
DC COMICS
THE NEW 52!
Animal Man
VOLUME 1
THE HUNT
"TRAVEL FOREMAN'S ART IS INNOVATIVE AND EXCELLENTLY CREEPY... AS LEMIRE'S EVERYMAN HERO MAKES HIS MARK IN THE NEW DC UNIVERSE."
— USA TODAY
JEFF LEMIRE TRAVEL FOREMAN

DC COMICS™

START AT THE BEGINNING

SWAMP THING VOLUME 1: RAISE THEM BONES

THE NEW 52!

DC COMICS™

SWAMP THING

"ANOTHER DISTURBINGLY BEAUTIFUL PIECE OF WORK."
—IGN

VOLUME 1
RAISE THEM BONES

SCOTT **SNYDER**   YANICK **PAQUETTE**   MARCO **RUDY**

START AT THE BEGINNING!

BATMAN VOLUME 1: THE COURT OF OWLS

BATMAN & ROBIN VOLUME 1: BORN TO KILL

Peter J. TOMASI Patrick GLEASON Mick GRAY

BATMAN: DETECTIVE COMICS VOLUME 1: FACES OF DEATH

TONY S. DANIEL

BATMAN: THE DARK KNIGHT VOLUME 1: KNIGHT TERRORS

DAVID FINCH PAUL JENKINS RICHARD FRIEND

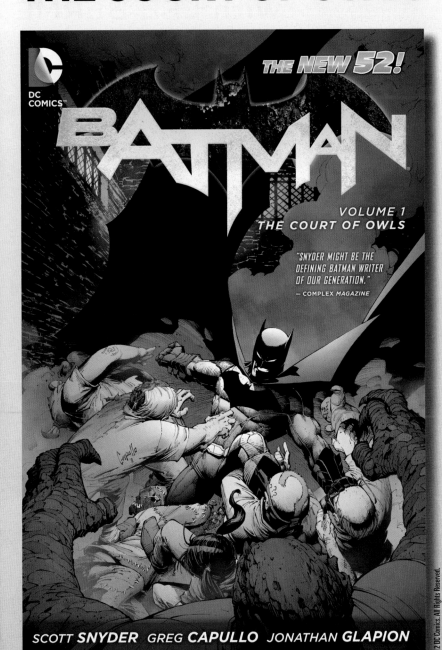

SCOTT SNYDER GREG CAPULLO JONATHAN GLAPION

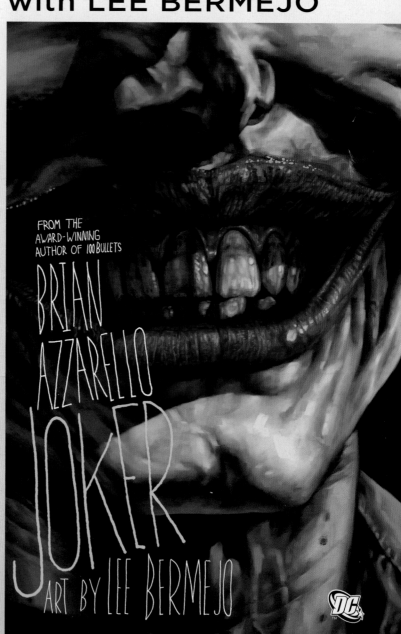